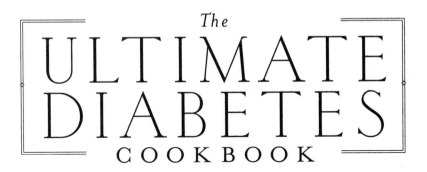

The

ULTIMATE DIABETES

COOKBOOK

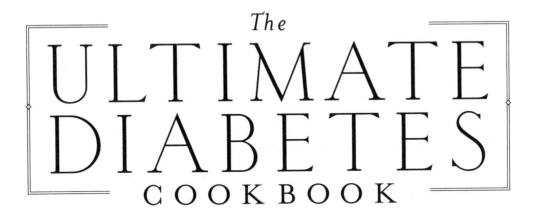

The
ULTIMATE DIABETES
COOKBOOK

CAROL GELLES

With a Foreword by
STANLEY MIRSKY, M.D.

BROADWAY BOOKS
NEW YORK

Broadway Books titles may be purchased for business or promotional use or for special sales. For information, please write to: Special Markets Department, Random House, Inc., 1745 Broadway, New York, New York 10019.

PRINTED IN THE UNITED STATES OF AMERICA

BROADWAY BOOKS and its logo, a letter B bisected on the diagonal, are trademarks of Broadway Books, a division of Random House, Inc.

Visit our website at www.broadwaybooks.com

Book design by Joel Avirom and Jason Snyder
Design assistant: Meghan Day Healey

Library of Congress Cataloging-in-Publication Data

Gelles, Carol.
The ultimate diabetes cookbook / Carol Gelles.
    p. cm.
Includes index.
ISBN 0-7679-0739-6
   1. Diabetes—Diet therapy—Recipes. I. Title.

RC662 .G453 2003
641.5'6314—dc21

                            2003027679

10 9 8 7 6 5 4 3 2 1

Dedicated to the memory of my parents,
Charlotte and Ernest Gelles,

and of my rabbi and teacher,
Marshall T. Meyer

FOREWORD

My introduction to nutrition and diabetes began fifty years ago at Northwestern University Medical School. A fellow first-year student and I studied the difference between a high-fat diet and a high-carbohydrate diet and their effect on blood sugar in rats. The experiment concluded that a high-fat diet produced higher blood sugars. Fifty years later a report in *The Journal of Diabetes* showed a low-fat diet would delay the onset of diabetes.

Over this period of time I strived to give diabetics a diet that controls blood sugar as well as making eating a pleasure not a chore. My diet was based on the teachings of Dr. Elliot P. Joslin in Boston, who stressed diet and taught his students and patients well. In his clinic a wonderful colleague, Dr. Priscilla White, took care of the children and pregnancy group. Dr. White used to say, "You take away so much from the diabetic; don't take away pleasure." If she were alive today, Dr. White would praise Ms. Gelles for giving diabetics the ability to enjoy gourmet foods without destroying or interfering with good blood sugar control.

When I read Carol Gelles's book, I was deeply impressed. My book *Controlling Diabetes the Easy Way* has been in print for twenty years and has been updated three times. It sets general practical rules. Ms. Gelles gives us the graduate course and also addresses the problems associated with heart disease and renal failure by stressing the roles of potassium and sodium in the diet.

This book is a tour de force for any intelligent, willing diabetic. You can live to eat or eat to live. Sometimes you can have it both ways.

—Dr. Stanley Mirsky,
author of *Controlling Diabetes the Easy Way*

PREFACE

Whenever I'm asked by a diabetic, "What should I eat?," I feel unsure how to reply. This question is difficult enough when posed by someone who is either newly diagnosed with diabetes or, for one reason or another, is experiencing the acute complications of poorly controlled blood sugar. If the question comes from someone who has long-standing diabetes and is now faced with heart disease, high blood pressure, or renal insufficiency, the answer is even harder to formulate. This is because diet management is a complex, lifestyle-dependent issue, and lifestyles or habits are very hard to change. Most often the person has been handed a one-page printed diet and told to follow it. However, we all know that these limited instructions are grossly inadequate for managing a serious condition for the rest of one's life. The individual needs not only a meal plan but also recipes, meal preparation techniques, and knowledge of portion sizing. This information cannot be imparted in a single twenty- or thirty-minute session with a diabetes educator.

All of which is why *The Ultimate Diabetes Cookbook* by Carol Gelles will prove invaluable. This is not just another "diabetic cookbook." It is designed specifically for the management of diabetes with one or more of its chronic complications. If you have purchased or are considering the purchase of this cookbook for any of the above-mentioned reasons, I strongly recommend that you first meet with a registered dietitian with experience in diabetes management, such as a Certified Diabetes Educator. Together you can design a plan for meals and snacks that will help slow the progression of problems while still allowing you to enjoy dishes that are not just tolerable, but tasty and satisfying. Once you have a meal plan, you can put *The Ultimate Diabetes Cookbook* to use.

First read the initial instructions to get a basic understanding of how to use the book. You will find the recipes themselves easy to follow. One of the biggest barriers to using a cookbook is lengthy preparation times and hard-to-find ingredients. Most of the recipes in this book have no more than four or five steps. The portion sizes are easy to adapt to any meal plan and the ingredients are common to any kitchen cabinet or refrigerator. Vegetarians will find many suitable recipes if they follow the reduced protein variations that substitute tofu or beans for meats or fish.

Carol Gelles took on the monumental task of putting together a cookbook that is designed to assist anyone with complications of diabetes in preparing meals that are delicious, satisfying, and healthy. Not only will her book benefit people with diabetes; professionals who provide nutrition counseling will also find this book an invaluable tool. The volume's more than 250 recipes provide the best possible answer to the question "What should I eat?"

—Sheila Gittens, RD, CDE

ACKNOWLEDGMENTS

This book would never have been started and could never have been finished without the help of many people. I will name just a few here. The rest of you know who you are.

This book needed considerable outside help. I am grateful to Dr. Stanley Mirsky for his expertise and enthusiasm; Dr. Robert Feidler for his patience; Dr. Franklin Klion for his advice; Sheila Gittens, RD, CDE, for all her work on the copy; Susan Hagman, RN, CDE, for all of her great suggestions; Beth Minsky, RD, for her hard work and computer skills.

My agent, Judith Weber, once again brought me an exciting project to work on.

Thanks to Jennifer Josephy, the kind of editor authors dream of having.

And of course I thank my friends and family, whose love and support are there unfailingly during the good times and the hard times. Special mention to Jennifer Consilvio and Jesse Weissman, who took on the task of tasting endless recipes every week as well as my sister Sherry, whose great palate and proofreading are also appreciated. And to Lorraine Klein who believes "attendance counts," and was always there when the going got tough.

CONTENTS

INTRODUCTION

The thing I remember most clearly from my first Therapeutic Nutrition course was my professor, Dorothy King, saying, "Diabetics have the healthiest diets of anyone in the population." Little did I know I would one day be joining that particular population. If you are reading this book, it is probably because you, or someone you love, has been diagnosed with diabetes. Diabetes is a disease. There, I've said it. It is not just a condition or a problem—although it is both—it is a disease. It is not to be taken lightly.

That being said, it is easy to go into denial about diabetes, especially if you have just been diagnosed, because in many cases there are no "real" symptoms. You can feel perfectly "normal" with diabetes. You can have diabetes and not even know it (there are estimates of as many as 8 million people with undiagnosed diabetes). So, if you don't feel bad, why should you have to give up french fries, brownies, ice cream, and other desserts or foods that you really love?

THE DIET

Frequently dieters are told not to say that they're on a diet, but rather that they have changed their lifestyle. For the person with diabetes, especially one who is experiencing complications, diet is not an optional lifestyle. The quality of your life depends on what you eat.

Which food plan you should be following is a decision for you and your doctor and/or dietitian, not one you should be making on your own. Further, there is no one plan that is right for every person with diabetes. If you have heart disease or kidney disease or other complications in addition to your diabetes, you may find yourself trying to figure out how to coordinate two (or more) seemingly incompatible diets. Say, for example, your renal (kidney) doctor wants you to limit your protein and sodium, potassium, and/or phosphorus intakes; your cardiologist wants you to limit your fat intake; and your endocrinologist wants you to limit your carbohydrate intake. *What does that leave!?* It leaves you with a lot of stress. The best way to deal with the situation is to visit a dietitian or nutritionist who will help you coordinate your various diets and find foods that are acceptable to you.

It would be foolish and even dangerous for me to prescribe which diet is right for you in an introduction to a cookbook. The purpose of this book is to help you find and prepare flavorful foods that fit into the diet your health professionals have already prescribed. To this end I have provided nutritional information for each recipe (more about that later). It is your job to choose the recipes compatible with your needs. It is my deepest hope that these recipes will help you realize that there is still pleasure to be found in eating and that limitations do not need to mean liabilities or deficits. You are now a member of that group of people who are eating healthfully, and, as you will see from these recipes, it can be a joyful experience if you allow it to be.

WHAT IS DIABETES?

Diabetes is a disorder of carbohydrate metabolism characterized by elevated blood glucose and defective insulin secretion or utilization. Translated into English:

The blood sugar (glucose) level is the concentration of glucose in the blood. It is measured in milligrams per deciliter (a value of 70 to 110 is considered normal). While blood sugar in a healthy person does vary according to the time of day and especially after meals, insulin regulates the sugar and keeps it at a pretty even level. In a person with diabetes this mechanism does not function correctly and blood sugar levels can rise to dangerous highs of 600 or more in people who have not treated their diabetes.

WHAT DOES "ALL TYPES OF DIABETICS" MEAN?

There are three commonly acknowledged categories of diabetes: Juvenile Onset (Type I), Adult Onset (Type II), and Gestational (diabetes brought on by/during pregnancy). These categories are fairly self-explanatory, although in reality the borderlines are somewhat blurred. Adults can develop Juvenile Onset diabetes and, unfortunately, Adult Onset is being seen more and more commonly in obese, inactive children. Gestational diabetes is usually, but not always, a temporary condition that disappears after pregnancy. These three categories comprise a group I call "uncomplicated" diabetes.

I suggest a second group exists that to date has not been formally labeled. I call this "complex" diabetes. This is the group of people who have developed one or more complications as a result of their diabetes. One of the insidious aspects of diabetes is that it invades all of the organs of the body and leaves many people with diabetes faced with the conundrum of following multiple, and sometimes conflicting, diets.

People with diabetes are four times more likely to develop coronary heart disease than the general public. Diabetes is also one of the four leading causes of blindness and renal (kidney) insufficiencies. These and other problems present the patient with complicated dietary requirements. In the "real" world, many people with diabetes (of all types) will need diets that are far more complicated than a simple "uncomplicated" diabetic diet.

WHAT ARE SOME GENERAL PRINCIPLES FOR LIVING WITH DIABETES?

HOW IS DIABETES TREATED?

The primary difference between Types I and II involves insulin output. The Type I diabetic produces little or no insulin and is most commonly treated with insulin injections as well as diet. The Type II diabetic frequently, but not always, produces insulin, but the body does not utilize it well or at all. It can also be controlled by a variety of oral medications or, when those fail, insulin injections. This type of diabetes can sometimes be controlled by weight loss, diet, and exercise alone.

The first step to treating diabetes is to be under the care of a health professional.

The second step is to become knowledgeable about your diabetes and your body. Test your blood sugar regularly. Follow your food plan. Take your medications as prescribed. Regard your diabetes seriously, not as something to be dealt with later, and . . . *exercise!*

Exercise is a very important part of diabetes treatment. It will contribute to weight loss—which is an important aspect of controlling blood sugars. It also promotes formation of muscle tissue. This is important because the cells of muscle tissue are more active biologically than fat cells, and the muscle cells use insulin more effectively than fat cells. Exercise also makes you feel good in general and gives you a sense of control over at least one part of your life.

WHAT IS A DIABETIC DIET?

Before I start any discussion of diabetic diets, I want to be clear that this is a cookbook—not a medical reference. Your diet should come from your physician or dietitian. The discussion that follows is strictly informational.

There is no one diabetic diet. It is whatever your physician or nutritionist prescribes for you.

Here are a few of the plans that are most commonly prescribed:

EXCHANGE LISTS: It is not uncommon for a patient just diagnosed with diabetes to be handed a diet to follow by his or her physician. This will usually include a meal plan that will tell you how many "exchanges" you can have each day, according to the number of calories the physician suggests for you, and an "exchange list" devised by the American Diabetes Association (ADA). The exchange list groups foods of similar nutrient content into categories. For example: a bread/starch "exchange" will be any complex carbohydrate serving of approximately 15 grams of carbohydrate, 80 calories, 3 grams of protein, 2 grams of fiber, and a bit of fat. The foods in this group include breads, pasta, cereal, legumes, starchy vegetables (such as corn or potatoes), and similar foods. The patient then plans meals for the day choosing foods from each exchange group (bread/starch; other carbohydrates/sugar; very lean meat/protein; lean meat; fruit; vegetables; milk—skim; fat) that meet the totals recommended in the plan. The recipes in this book include the number of diabetic exchanges in each recipe or variation. Exchange lists can be obtained by calling the American Diabetes Association at 800-342-2383.

THE GLYCEMIC INDEX: A newer list—the glycemic index (GI)—has become available. The theory behind the glycemic index is that the body does not process all foods identically. Even foods listed in the same ADA exchange categories (foods with similar nutritional values) are not metabolized at the same rates. The GI indicates how fast a food is metabolized when compared to white bread. The GI value for white bread is 100 and other foods are assigned values depending on whether they are metabolized slower (values less than 100) or faster (values more than 100) than white bread. The general theory being the slower you metabolize a food the less drastic the increase of blood glucose levels and the more even you can keep your blood sugar levels. This is the system on which the diet *Sugar Busters* by H. Leighton Steward, Dr. Morrison C. Bethea, Dr. Samuel S. Andrews, Ralph O. Brennan, and Dr. Luis A. Balart (Ballantine Books, 1998) is based. However, since foods are usually eaten in combination, many physicians are not sure how the glycemic index actually works.

CARBOHYDRATE COUNTING: A physician or nutritionist will prescribe a specific number of carbohydrates that s/he feels is appropriate to be consumed each day or will suggest how many carbohydrates to consume at each meal. The patient will keep track of how many carbohydrates are included in the foods s/he is consuming during the course of the day by consulting a nutrition counter or using the diabetic exchanges lists. The rest of the meal is filled in with protein and fat choices. This is the system on which *Controlling Diabetes the Easy Way* by Dr. Stanley Mirsky and Joan Rattner Heilman (Random House, 1998, updated 5th printing, 3rd edition, 2002) is based.

WHAT CAN I EAT?

Not to be too redundant, but this is a question for your physician or dietitian to answer. For many people with diabetes the answer is: Everything in moderation. The typical diabetic meal will be well balanced with some carbohydrates, protein, and fat. This book offers menu suggestions at the bottom of each entrée recipe to give you help planning a balanced meal. You will have to look at the meal as a whole—not just what's in the entrée—to stay within your prescribed guidelines. You don't have to have the entire meal suggested; use it as a guideline.

WHAT IS THE DIFFERENCE BETWEEN A DIABETIC RECIPE AND A "REGULAR" RECIPE?

Once upon a time physicians and the ADA (American Diabetic Association) recommended that people with diabetes avoid all sugar and follow lower carbohydrate diets (in fact, some physicians still make these recommendations). The current common position is that any food is acceptable in a diabetic program as long as it has been calculated into the allotted daily totals. Therefore, recipes for people with diabetes look largely like any other healthy, moderate- to low-fat recipe. The one noticeable difference will be portion size. Most of the portions in this book are very modest. An acceptable hamburger for a person with diabetes would be 3 ounces, cooked, as opposed to the 8-ounce burgers that many restaurants are so proud to serve—and forget the cheese and bacon!

You will find recipes in this book that use fruits and/or fruit juices, wine, and even sugar, molasses, or honey—all in modest amounts. Most frequently the amount of fruit or juice in a recipe serving four is less than one serving of fruit. My goal with these recipes is to bring a broad range of full-flavored foods into the guidelines for a diabetic meal.

HOW ARE THE NUTRITIONAL VALUES CALCULATED?

The values for each recipe are calculated on the nutritional software "The Food Processor" by ESHA Research. First the ingredients in each recipe are entered, then the number of servings is entered, and then the program provides the figures. I have chosen to report Diabetic Exchanges by ¼ exchanges; nutrients measured by grams are rounded up or down to the nearest gram.

The definition of terms is the same as that used for nutritional labeling. Since the definition of High and Low is based on the percentage of the amount of calories, there needs to be a specific number to measure against. I've chosen the value of 2000 calories per day—which is the figure used by the government for nutritional labeling. The suggested daily intake for a female 11 to 50 years old is 2200 calories. The suggested calorie intake for females over 50 is 1900 calories. For males 19 to 50 years old the suggested intake is 2900 calories. Over 50, the suggested intake is reduced to 2300 calories (close to the figures we are using). Males 11 to 14 require 2500 calories and males 15 to 18 require 3000 calories.

Introduction

HOW ACCURATE ARE THE FIGURES FOR NUTRITIONAL VALUES?

These figures are only as good as the information in the nutritional software program. I've entered figures for variations of recipes and sometimes the differences surprise me. For example, you would think that there is less protein in vegetable broth than in chicken broth, right?

Well, according to "The Food Processor," that depends on what brands you use. It seems that College Inn chicken broth has less protein than Swanson vegetable broth. However, generic chicken broth has more protein than Swanson vegetable broth, and College Inn chicken broth has less protein than College Inn low-sodium broth.

The moral of the story is to take these figures as approximations. I doubt that any software is totally accurate, especially since any food, even something as quantifiable as 4 ounces of carrot, will vary in nutritional value depending on soil, length of time in storage, conditions of the storage area, and weather conditions in the growing region.

WHY ARE THERE HIGH AND LOW BOXES?

I have provided extensive nutritional information for each recipe but felt that putting all those figures alongside each recipe would make the page look messy and confusing. To compare figures from different recipes you would have to flip from one page to the next. To simplify the process I put all the nutritional information into a chart at the back of the book. You need only to scan a column instead of flipping pages. On the other hand, I didn't want you to have to turn to the chart every time you were contemplating a recipe. So I created these boxes to give you the approximate nutrition at a glance. Many of the nutrients I've provided information on are not of interest to everyone. Some will just be counting carbohydrates or fat. Others will be concerned about protein or sodium. If the nutrient you are concerned about does not show up in either box, then you know that that recipe has a moderate amount in it. Not too much (or it would appear in the high box) and not too little (ditto the low box). If you need a specific amount of a nutrient, you will probably have to look in the table in the back for exact amounts. But if you are looking for a ballpark figure, the absence or presence of the nutrient in a box should be all you need. If there were no nutrients that were either high or low, we eliminated that category. So you will find many recipes with only a high or only a low box.

WHAT DO THE HIGH AND LOW BOXES INDICATE?

If the nutritional calculations for a recipe are higher than the "high" figure or lower than the "low" figure in the chart on page 8 then that nutrient will be listed in the box. Although the chart at the back of the book gives nutritional information for fourteen different nutrients, the boxes are for only the most commonly sought-after figures—calories, fat, saturated fat, protein, carbohydrates, fiber, cholesterol, calcium, iron, magnesium, phosphorus, potassium, and sodium.

These boxes take into consideration the recipe variations. For example, Vegetable Tomato Soup (page 44) has 382 milligrams of sodium per serving—which exceeds the 350 milligram definition of high-sodium content. However, following the recipe there is a Reduced Sodium variation whose sodium content is only 55 milligrams per serving. Therefore, sodium will appear in the high box, but will also appear in *italics* in the low box, indicating there is a variation that allows the recipe to be prepared with less than 140 milligrams of sodium.

ABOUT SPECIFIC INGREDIENTS

BEANS: Most of the beans used in this book are available canned, but they can also be prepared from dried beans. If you are watching your sodium carefully, you must use dried beans prepared without salt. If you are watching your sodium intake somewhat, you may use canned beans, after rinsing them under cold water. Rinsing will not remove all the sodium, but it will reduce it. In fact, this is a good practice even if you are not on a low-sodium diet. As for nutritional information, the values used in this book are for canned and drained (not rinsed) beans. Low-sodium variations are calculated for home-cooked without sodium. It may be possible to find low-sodium canned beans in health-food stores.

BROTH: When a recipe calls for broth, I have listed nutritional values in the order of broth called for in the ingredient list. That is, if the recipe calls for chicken or vegetable broth, the first nutritional value in the table at the end of the book will be for the recipe cooked with chicken broth, and the second will be for the recipe prepared with vegetable broth. I have used the nutritional values for College Inn chicken and beef broths, a generic low-sodium chicken broth, and Swanson vegetable broth, since I believe all these broths to be universally available. I am not assuming that the reader will prepare homemade versions of these broths. If you are using the homemade broth recipes in this book, I have provided the values for those below and you can figure out the substitutions by doing a little math.

Introduction

TABLE A: DEFINITIONS OF HIGH AND LOW NUTRIENT VALUES

HIGH CALORIE	400 calories (20% of daily intake of 2000 calories) or more
LOW CALORIE	40 calories (~2% of daily intake of 2000 calories) or less
HIGH FAT	13g or more
LOW FAT	3g or less
HIGH SATURATED FAT	4g or more
LOW SATURATED FAT	1g or less (FDA)
HIGH PROTEIN	10g (20% of adult women's recommended daily requirement) or more
LOW PROTEIN	2.5g (5% of adult women's recommended daily requirement) or less
HIGH CARBOHYDRATE	25g (20% of recommended daily carbohydrate intake for healthy person) or more
LOW CARBOHYDRATE	3g (~2% of recommended daily carbohydrate intake for healthy person) or less
HIGH FIBER	5g or more (FDA)
LOW FIBER	2g or less
HIGH CHOLESTEROL	60mg (20% of maximum daily recommendation of 300mg) or more
LOW CHOLESTEROL	20mg or less (FDA)
HIGH CALCIUM	160mg (20% of recommended daily requirement) or more
LOW CALCIUM	40mg (5% or less of recommended daily requirement) or less
HIGH IRON	3mg (20% of adult women's recommended daily requirement) or more
LOW IRON	.75mg (5% of adult women's recommended daily requirement) or less
HIGH MAGNESIUM	36mg (20% of recommended daily requirement) or more
LOW MAGNESIUM	14mg (5% or less of recommended daily requirement for women) or less
HIGH PHOSPHORUS	160mg (20% of recommended daily requirement) or more
LOW PHOSPHORUS	80mg (5% of recommended daily requirement) or less
HIGH POTASSIUM	350mg (10% of recommended daily requirement) or more
LOW POTASSIUM	100mg (~5% of minimum daily requirement) or less
HIGH SODIUM	400mg or more (FDA)
LOW SODIUM	140mg or less (FDA)

A= College Inn Chicken Broth
B= Campbell's Chicken Soup Broth
C= Dry cube + water
D= Low-sodium chicken broth

E= Swanson Vegetable Broth
F= College Inn Beef Broth
G= homemade Chicken Broth (page 44)
H= homemade Vegetable Broth (page 45)

TABLE B: COMPARISON OF NUTRIENT VALUES FOR DIFFERENT BROTHS

Values for 1 cup	A	B	C	D	E	F	G	H
Calories	40	60	12	31	20	20	35	31
Carbohydrates	—	4g	1.5g	1.5g	3g	—	0	7g
Protein	1g	4g	1g	3g	2g	4g	8g	0
Fiber	—	—	—	—	—	—	—	—
Fat	4g	4g	.3g	1.5g	1g	—	.6	.2g
Saturated Fat	1g	1g	.7g	.8g	—	—	.2g	0
Cholesterol	5mg	10mg	—	3.8mg	—	—	0	0
Calcium	—	—	12mg	15mg	—	—	22g	26.4g
Iron	—	—	.1mg	—	—	—	—	—
Magnesium	—	—	2.4mg	—	—	—	19.4mg	13.2mg
Phosphorus	—	—	12.5mg	—	—	—	.2mg	.2mg
Potassium	30mg	—	24.3mg	—	—	30mg	409mg	325mg
Sodium	999mg	540mg	792.2mg	106.7mg	1000mg	999mg	101mg	35mg

DAIRY PRODUCTS: When calling for dairy products such as milk or cheese, I have not specified percentage of fat. That is up to you. If you choose to use whole milk products the recipe will taste smoother and richer, but all recipes will also be successful if you choose to use fat-free products. Nutritional information is given for both whole milk and fat-free products. If you are using 1 or 2 percent milk products, you will have to "guesstimate" the exact figures for fat content. Two percent will be halfway between whole (4 percent fat content) and skim (fat-free) milk products.

GARLIC: These recipes are mostly prepared with fresh garlic. It's simply better than any of the prepared garlic alternatives. When a recipe calls for 1 clove of garlic, I am assuming that you are using a "normal"-size clove. I know that cloves can range from tiny to very large. If you have a very large clove of garlic, cut it into quarters; if each piece is the size of a peanut, then count the large clove as four cloves of garlic. A clove the size of an average-size almond I would count as 2 or 3 cloves of garlic (depending on how much you love garlic). If you prefer to measure, 1 clove of garlic equals ¼ teaspoon minced garlic.

Introduction

GRAINS: These are a great source of carbohydrates, fiber, and vitamins. In addition to being good for you, they are easy to keep in the pantry and available year round. Try to select whole grains such as brown rice, whole-grain wheat (wheat berries), wild rice, quinoa, or bulgur. These grains still have their bran and are higher in fiber and nutrients than their processed counterparts, such as pasta, polenta, couscous, white rice, or pearled barley. Although grains have a long shelf life, they do eventually become rancid. If you have had an open package around a long time, give it a little sniff before using. If you sense a strong odor, your grain has become rancid.

OIL: Whenever a recipe calls for vegetable oil, I use canola oil, as in current scientific thought it is generally considered to be the healthiest vegetable oil (with the possible exception of olive oil—and I call for that specifically when I intend you to use it). Therefore, the values in these recipes are for canola oil. In the grand scheme of things, there is no significant difference in the values of the nutrients given in this book between canola oil and vegetable oil. Oil that has been sitting around too long can become rancid. It is best to store open oils in the refrigerator. Fats that are saturated will remain solid at room temperature; unsaturated fats are liquid at room temperature, but in the refrigerator will become cloudy or solidify. Let the oil warm up a little and it will become liquid again. (If your oil smells a little like turpentine, it is rancid.)

TABLE C: COMPARISON OF NUTRIENTS OF DIFFERENT TYPES OF FATS

1 TEASPOON	CALORIES	FAT	SATURATED FAT	CHOLESTEROL
Olive oil	40	4.5g	.6g	0
Canola oil	40	4.5g	.3g	0
Soybean oil	40	4.5g	.6g	0
Corn oil	40	4.5g	.6g	0
Safflower oil	40	4.7g	.4g	0
Butter	33	3.8g	2.7g	10mg
Lard	38	4.3g	1.7g	4mg
Shortening	37	4.2g	1.1g	0

SALT/SODIUM: The calculation of the sodium count for these recipes assumes that you are not adding any salt to a recipe when it states "Salt to taste." For most of us this is a fantasy. In fact, you may find yourself adding a lot of salt until a recipe is to your taste. So here are the values for salt. Calculate the amount of salt you've added, then add the proper figure for the amount you've used, and don't forget to divide by the number of servings. If you are using sea salt instead of table salt, subtract 25 milligrams of sodium per teaspoon.

TABLE D: AMOUNT OF SODIUM IN MEASURING SPOONS OF SALT

	SERVINGS	SODIUM
1 teaspoon salt	1	2325mg
1 teaspoon salt	4	580mg
1 teaspoon salt	6	388mg
½ teaspoon salt	1	1263mg
½ teaspoon salt	4	318mg
½ teaspoon salt	6	210mg
¼ teaspoon salt	1	632mg
¼ teaspoon salt	4	158mg
¼ teaspoon salt	6	105mg

WHAT GUIDELINES WERE FOLLOWED TO CREATE THESE RECIPES?

The American Diabetic Association's current guidelines suggest that a person with diabetes can eat anything, including sugar and fruit and other items previously forbidden, as long as they are within the limits of a daily overall count. Hence you will find recipes that include fruits or fruit juices, wine, and sugar. On the other hand, except in some desserts, the amounts of these ingredients are small. Count these recipes as you would any other. I have provided the diabetic exchanges for each recipe directly following the serving size so that you can figure how to count the exchanges and use recipes that fit into the eating plan suggested by your health professional. More extensive nutritional information is found at the end of the book, starting on page 340.

WHY A DESSERT CHAPTER?

In reality most people with diabetes live with people who are not diabetic, for whom dessert is a common way to end a meal. According to the new ADA guidelines, desserts are not off limits to a person with diabetes as long as they are allotted for in the day's calculations. The desserts in this book are all "real"—that is, they are not made with artificial sweeteners, although occasionally I offer suggestions for using them. I do not encourage frequent consumption of dessert, but if you are going to eat something sweet, it should be something delicious. My own feeling is that artificial sweeteners are not good for anyone, and that eating a lot of artificially flavored foods only arouses a sweet tooth. If you feel that you must eat "sugar-free" foods, there are many available in packages in the supermarket and there are cookbooks dedicated to this subject. The recipes I have selected for the dessert chapter tend toward custards, puddings, and fruit desserts—which all have some redeeming nutritional values. Please, use desserts only occasionally and in small quantities. Eating "sweets" will not help you achieve your desired blood sugars, even if they are "allowed."

SPECIAL DIETS

A BRIEF PRIMER OF HOW TO FIND THE RIGHT RECIPES FOR YOUR NEEDS

I have tried to help you tailor recipes to your special needs by creating variations and providing the nutritional information for those variations. But you don't have to limit yourself to the variations I suggest. For example, if you are on a low-protein program and a recipe that appeals to you does not have a low-protein variation, you can adjust the portion size so that the item fits in with your needs, and then add rice or pasta as a side dish to bulk up the meal.

    If you are following a plan that restricts one nutrient or another, you may want to use the nutrition tables at the back of the book to help you select the right recipes for you. If, for example, you need a recipe very low in phosphorus, just look down the column for phosphorus content and check out only the recipes that meet your needs.

WHY DO ONLY SOME RECIPES HAVE VARIATIONS FOR SPECIAL DIETS?

The good news is that all of these recipes were written to be as "healthy" as possible. Many recipes do not need variations because they are acceptable to all diets as written.

    Although this might seem obvious, there are no variations for recipes that have only small amounts of "offending" nutrients. For example, Yellow Squash with Stewed Tomatoes uses 1 teaspoon of olive oil and serves four people. This is ¼ fat exchange per person. I felt the recipe would suffer if the oil were left out, so there is no Reduced Fat variation for this recipe. But there is a Reduced Sodium variation since you can significantly reduce the sodium count by using low-sodium canned tomatoes.

LOW-PROTEIN DIET

Usually protein-restricted diets come with other restrictions as well, such as sodium, potassium, and/or phosphorus. The best way to manage this is to check the exact values at the back of the book for all nutrients in the recipe to be sure they fit into your daily allowances.

    The most generalized advice for using any recipe is to serve only half portions and bulk up the rest of the meal with pasta or rice. I have also provided variations on recipes that reduce the protein levels. Whenever possible I have substituted tofu, beans, or additional vegetables for the meat and where necessary increased some of the seasonings to compensate for the loss of the "meaty" flavors.

LOW-SODIUM DIET

The recipes in this book are written without specific salt suggestions. If you are on a low-sodium diet, just don't add any salt. That should be adequate for most "no salt added" diets. If you are on a restricted sodium diet, look for the low-sodium variations of the recipes. Wherever canned products are called for, use salt-free products or homemade products prepared without salt. Check the sodium content of each recipe in the back of the book to be sure you are staying within your prescribed guidelines.

LOW CHOLESTEROL

Cholesterol and fat are two separate issues but they are frequently both of concern to the diabetic. Cholesterol is an issue for anyone at risk for heart disease, and as a diabetic your risk is greater than the general population. Therefore, many people with diabetes try to keep their cholesterol intake to less than 300 milligrams per day. Most of these recipes are moderate to low in fat and cholesterol. Whenever a recipe seems higher in cholesterol, I try to present a lower-cholesterol variation. The only fats that contain cholesterol are those that come from animal products, such as butter or ghee (clarified butter), lard, chicken fat, and suet. Of course there are also "invisible" fats such as the marble in meats or skin of poultry—or the not-so-invisible layer of fat outside a roast or ham. Oils from plants do not contain cholesterol. As a rule, any dish that is vegan (no meat/no dairy) is cholesterol-free. Look for reduced-protein variations to find vegetarian versions of meat/chicken/fish dishes that are also lower in cholesterol. Check for actual figures in the back of the book to see if the recipes fit in with your needs.

LOW SATURATED FAT

Although some physicians, such as Dean Ornish, prescribe very very low fat diets, not all sources agree with him. Many physicians feel that some fat is essential in the diet. Current findings indicate that eating monosaturates (molecules that have one double bond—consult your high school chemistry texts for further explanation), such as olive oil or canola oil, actually protects your heart. Polyunsaturates (molecules that have more than one double bond) are also considered healthy oil. They are safflower, sunflower, corn, cottonseed, and peanut oils. However, saturated fats (molecules with no double bonds), which come primarily from animal fats, as well as tropical oils are extremely unhealthy and should be limited to less than 10 percent of the daily total fat intake.

TABLE D: COMPARISON OF DIFFERENT PROTEINS AND THEIR RELATIVE NUTRITIONAL VALUES

	CALORIES	FAT	PROTEIN	CARBOHYDRATES	CHOLESTEROL
4 OUNCES RAW					
Chicken (white)	100	1.5g	26g	0	66mg
Beef shoulder	284	22g	21g	0	53mg
Pork loin	139	4g	24g	0	67mg
Lamb shoulder	170	5g	23g	0	54mg
Turkey breast	153	8g	20g	0	74mg
Veal loin	200	8g	28g	0	221mg
Beef liver	162	4g	23g	0	404mg
Salmon	207	12g	23g	0	67mg
Tuna	116	1.2g	25g	0	53mg
Tofu (firm)	87	5.1g	9g	3g	0
Soy burger	227	10.1g	24g	9g	0
Seitan	160	2g	24g	12g	0
1 CUP COOKED					
Potato	113	0	2g	26g	0
Rice	161	.3g	3g	35g	0
Pasta	188	.2g	10g	36g	0
Kidney beans	225	.9g	15g	40g	0
Lentils	230	.8g	18g	40g	0

LOW FAT

Although weight control and heart disease are probably the leading reasons for people to watch their fat intake, there are other conditions such as gallbladder and liver disease that also require fat counting. Most recipes have less than ½ teaspoon of fat content per serving. Whenever possible I have variations for even lower-fat methods to prepare recipes.

CARBOHYDRATES

When you say carbohydrates many people think bread, pasta/grain/cereal, beans, and potatoes. These carbohydrates are also known as starches. Although they are carbohydrates, they are just a small part of the carbohydrate universe. There are other foods that are also sources of carbohydrates: fruits, vegetables, dairy products, and sugars (including sugar, honey, molasses, syrups, and all the other sugars that can be hidden in prepared foods).

CALCIUM	IRON	MAGNESIUM	PHOSPHORUS	POTASSIUM	SODIUM
12mg	.8g	32mg	222mg	289mg	74mg
6mg	2.4g	22mg	198mg	346mg	67mg
5mg	.3g	24mg	220mg	372mg	48mg
14mg	2.0g	25mg	186mg	289mg	65mg
15mg	1.4g	27mg	211mg	312mg	67mg
28mg	1.0g	24mg	210mg	263mg	74mg
7mg	7.7g	22mg	360mg	366mg	83mg
13mg	.4g	32mg	264mg	410mg	66mg
33mg	1.2g	39mg	251mg	461mg	42mg
134mg	1.6g	52mg	167mg	198mg	9mg
34mg	2.5g	20mg	390mg	204mg	623mg
20mg	3.6g	—	—	—	361mg
6mg	.4g	31mg	61mg	477mg	6mg
13mg	1.0g	8mg	23mg	7mg	5mg
12mg	.8g	35mg	58mg	48mg	6mg
59mg	5.2g	80mg	251mg	713mg	4mg
38mg	6.6g	71mg	256mg	731mg	4mg

Sugars are known as simple carbohydrates. They consist of one or two molecules and not much else. These are foods that enter your bloodstream quickly. They are frequently referred to as "empty" calories because nutritionally they contribute very little to your daily requirements. Simple carbohydrates should be used sparingly, if at all. Besides sugar, other "empty" calories are found in candies, sodas (diet soda is okay), sweet wines, and chewing gum (sugar-free is okay). In addition to empty calories, there are foods that are not good carbohydrate choices: jellies, jams, candy, cakes and cookies, puddings and pies, fruit juices, and sweetened condensed milk or sweetened coconut milk. Although the current ADA guidelines suggest that you can find a place for sugars in your diet, it is still not advisable to do so often.

Complex carbohydrates are longer chains of molecules and provide other nutrients such as fiber, minerals, and vitamins as well as possibly some fat and/or protein. Even within the complex carbohydrate group there are some that impact your blood sugar more than others. The starches are higher in carbohydrates (that is, they have more grams of carbohydrate per 100 grams of weight) than vegetables. And there are some vegetables that are higher in carbohydrates than others. The starchy vegetables are artichokes, brussels sprouts, carrots, corn, kale, okra, onions (including onion family members such as leeks, scallions, chives), peas, red peppers, tomatoes, turnips, and winter squash. These vegetables should be counted and portions should be controlled more closely than the "watery" vegetables.

Vegetables with a lower ratio of grams of carbohydrate to weight, such as asparagus, broccoli, cabbage, cucumbers, lettuce, mushrooms, summer squash—you know, "vegetables"—can be eaten with much less regard to portion size, unless of course your physician or nutritionist has you on a very low carbohydrate diet.

MINERALS

Patients with renal complications may have specific limitations on some minerals—such as sodium, phosphorus, potassium, and others. This is something that you must keep track of carefully. For you, it is best to pick recipes by looking at the tables in the back and finding recipes with the amounts of minerals that fit in your daily food plan.

VEGETARIAN DIET

Diabetes is not picky—it strikes all populations, including vegetarians. Maintaining a healthy diabetic diet as a vegetarian can be a little trickier than for the meat eater. As usual, my advice is to consult your nutritionist. If you get the go-ahead, the best way to use this book is to look at the low-protein variations of the recipes. Many of them substitute tofu or beans for meat. When recipes call for broth, use vegetable broth instead of chicken or beef.

MEAL PATTERNS

Different physicians and nutritionists have different theories on the best way to manage diabetes. Some recommend three meals plus a snack. Others recommend smaller, more frequent meals. The portions in this book are suitable for the three-meal-a-day plan. If you are on a many-small-meals plan you can use any recipe in this book, but eat half of the serving suggestion. Other good small meals are soup-and-salad, if it is a hearty soup. If it is a vegetable soup, you might want soup plus a piece of bread or other starch. Appetizers are by definition small portions. Many of the appetizers would make a suitable small meals, as would salads.

MENU PLANNING

When considering a menu, it's best to decide what the entrée will be, and then build the meal around it. If you have chosen a dish that is primarily protein, such as a grilled or sautéed chicken breast, or a fish fillet, then try to include a starch such as a grain, pasta, or starchy vegetable plus at least one nonstarchy vegetable. After you've chosen your side dishes, consider adding a soup and/or salad and/or appetizer, and after that, see if you feel there's room in your allowances for a dessert. I have included menu suggestions after each entrée recipe. You do not have to make the entire meal. You certainly can skip the soup, appetizer, or dessert and still have an adequate meal.

SOME COOKING POINTERS AND KITCHEN TIPS

A NOTE TO EXPERIENCED COOKS Although it is tempting to alter recipes you find in a cookbook, remember that if you are using the nutritional information provided for these recipes—that information is valid only if you have followed the recipes exactly and measured out the ingredients.

I try to make my recipes as specific as possible so you, the reader, will not have to speculate about what I intended. For example, I call for 1 cup chopped onion, not 1 medium onion, chopped. This way you don't have to look at an onion and wonder if it is medium or large, or medium large or medium small. Too many decisions. A cup is a cup. The question is how much do you have to buy to equal 1 cup chopped? To help, I have included a shopping guide on page 18 that will tell you how many or how much you must buy of a fruit or vegetable to equal 1 cup chopped.

To have good results you should be using the proper tools for the job. For diabetic cooking, measurements are critical! The nutritional values are calculated assuming that you are measuring the ingredients properly. Although a cup is a cup is a cup, just to confuse the issue there are two types of measuring cups. One (usually glass or clear plastic) has a handle and spout, while the other comes in a set of nested cups (technically known as marianne cups). The glass measuring cup is used for liquids—if the ingredient that you are using pours, use the liquid cup, and measure the liquid at eye level. If it is solid or powdery (like flour), use the nested cups, making sure that the ingredients are level with the top of the cup. If it plops (like ketchup or mayonnaise), use the nested cups as well. The table below will help you figure out what size or weight of a vegetable to buy to equal a cup of chopped or sliced ingredients.

"Tablespoons" and "teaspoons" refer to that set of spoons held together by a ring, sold in kitchenware stores or departments. They do not refer to the soup spoons and teaspoons that come with your flatware (or silverware if you are fancier). These spoons are used to measure liquids and solids and ploppy stuff. Be sure to use level amounts; do not use rounded (or mounded) amounts of ingredients unless the recipe so specifies (as in Oatmeal Currant Crispies, where you are asked to drop the batter by rounded teaspoonful).

Use the pot sizes specified because in addition to being the proper size to hold the amount of ingredients, rates of evaporation will vary in different-size pots (assuming that the item is cooked uncovered—an item cooked covered will be less dependent on pot size). For example, if you are cooking a soup in a 5-quart pot when the recipe called for a 4-quart pot, don't be surprised if the yield will be smaller than that given in the recipe and if the soup is thicker than described in the headnote. The larger pot had more surface area and therefore allowed for quicker evaporation than the smaller pot.

SHOPPING GUIDE

ITEM	SIZE	WEIGHT	CUT-UP MEASUREMENT
Apple	1 medium	4 ounces	1 cup chopped or diced
	1 large	5⅓ ounces	1 cup shredded
Asparagus	5 medium	3½ ounces	1 cup pieces
Broccoli	2 medium stalks	9 ounces	1 cup florets
Cabbage	1 medium wedge	3 ounces	1 cup chopped
	1 small wedge	2 ounces	1 cup shredded
Carrot	1 large	6 ounces	1 cup sliced, chopped, or shredded
Cauliflower	¼ small head	4 ounces	1 cup florets
Celery	2 medium stalks	4 ounces	1 cup sliced
	2 small stalks	6 ounces	1 cup chopped
Cucumber	¾ medium	6 ounces	1 cup sliced or chopped
Eggplant	¼ small	3½ ounces	1 cup cubed
Green beans	24 medium	3½ ounces	1 cup cut into pieces
Mushrooms	4 medium	3 ounces	1 cup sliced or chopped
Onion	1 medium	4 ounces	1 cup chopped
	1 large	7 ounces	1 cup finely chopped
Pepper (bell)	1 small	4½ ounces	1 cup chopped or diced
Potato	1 medium	5½ ounces	1 cup cubed
	1 small	4¾ ounces	1 cup shredded
Tomato	1 medium	6 ounces	1 cup diced or chopped
Zucchini	1 small	3½ ounces	1 cup sliced

THE ULTIMATE DIABETES COOKBOOK

Oven thermostats are notoriously inaccurate. I recommend buying a good oven thermometer. Even a 25-degree error will make a difference in the final result of your baked product.

Have a salad spinner on hand. Next to my knives and measuring cups (and pots and pans) it's the one piece of equipment I use on a daily basis. You will be amazed at how much dirt comes out of anything leafy—mere rinsing will rarely be sufficient. I usually put my greens into the inner basket uncut, then place that into the outer bowl. Fill the bowl with cool water and swish the greens around. Lift out the inner basket and discard the water from the outer basket. Repeat this as many times as necessary until there is no dirt or grit in the bowl after you empty the water (I sometimes have to do this as many as four or five times). Then spin the greens. Don't assume that your fresh parsley or other fresh herbs are clean—they may not be.

A juice extractor is a nice piece of equipment to have, especially if you are on a low-sodium diet. Many recipes start with broth as the flavor base; by using a juice extractor you can make a quick and flavorful vegetable broth. Here's how: juice a few carrots, celery stalks, a small parsnip, some cabbage and fresh parsley, and a tomato. Pour into a pot with an equal amount of water. Throw in any pulp that may have accumulated in the juicer along with a small onion or some leek. Bring to a boil. Reduce heat and simmer, uncovered, 30 minutes. Strain off the pulp. If you are not watching your sodium intake, add salt to taste.

ATTITUDE IS ALL You can approach diabetes as a fate worse than death or as a challenge you embrace.

The first attitude will leave you depressed and possibly in denial. It will not change the fact that you have this disease. It will not help you take care of yourself. It will not make you pleasant to be around.

If you embrace the challenge, exercise daily, eat properly, and take your medications (if applicable), you will soon find that your blood sugars will be in the normal range. You will be helping yourself in the long term. Furthermore, you will find that life still is worthwhile and so are you!

Just in case I haven't said this enough: **This is strictly a cookbook. It is not intended to tell you how to manage your diabetes. That is a job for you and your physician or diabetes educator. This book is designed to help you follow the food plan that was already prescribed specifically for you.**

To that end, I provided as much nutritional information as I felt would be helpful to you; I developed recipes that fit in with the most commonly prescribed food plans; and most importantly, I tried to create foods that you and your family will enjoy together. It is my thought that if you have foods you love, you will not feel deprived and will be more willing to follow the food plan that will help you achieve a long and healthy life.

Introduction

Appetizers

Appetizers do not have to be throw-away recipes you use to set the mood for a meal. They can be perfect little meals, especially valuable for people who are on a several-small-meals-a-day plan from their doctor or nutritionist. Many of the recipes in this chapter can also be doubled to become entrées, for example: Orange Teriyaki Salmon, Tuna with Black Olive Vinaigrette, or Ginger Lamb with (or without) Watercress Salad. Some of the appetizer salads and spreads make nice luncheon fare.

When using the appetizers as appetizers, be sure to calculate them into your daily nutritional allotments. If you've planned a meal that is high in carbohydrates, you may want to choose an appetizer salad or a dip with crudités. If your meal is low in carbohydrates, then an appetizer that includes bread or beans may be just the right touch.

BLACK BEAN DIP

This is a real hit whenever I serve it. A nice change from hummos or other Middle Eastern spreads. It's a little thick to use as a dip with chips so I use it with pita bread. If you would prefer a lighter dip, loosen the consistency with some yogurt or a little lime juice, or extra salsa—but if you're using more salsa, omit the ground red pepper from the recipe.

> **1 cup black beans, rinsed and drained**
> **⅓ cup sliced scallion (white and green parts)**
> **¼ cup cilantro leaves (fresh coriander)**
> **1 tablespoon olive oil**
> **½ teaspoon ground cumin**
> **2 cloves garlic, minced**
> **⅛ teaspoon ground red pepper**
> **Salt to taste**
> **⅓ cup salsa**

1   Place the beans, scallion, cilantro, oil, cumin, garlic, red pepper, and salt into a food processor container fitted with a steel blade. Cover and process until smooth.

2   Add the salsa and pulse until combined.

SERVES: 6
Diabetic Exchanges: ½ bread; ¼ very lean meat; ¼ vegetable; ½ fat

REDUCED FAT: Omit the olive oil and use 1 tablespoon water.
Diabetic Exchanges: ½ bread; ¼ very lean meat; ¼ vegetable

REDUCED SODIUM: Use home-cooked black beans without any salt (not canned); use home-made salsa.
Diabetic Exchanges: ½ bread; ¼ vegetable; ½ fat

BABA GHANOUJ

Serve this as a spread with pita bread, or as a dip with crudités. For a very nice lunch, serve a Middle Eastern "combo" plate with this baba ghanouj, Tabouli (page 299), and Cucumber Feta Dip (page 23), if that fits in with your food plan.

> **1 medium eggplant (1 pound)**
> **¼ cup tahini**
> **2 tablespoons fresh lemon juice**
> **2 cloves garlic, minced**
> **¼ teaspoon ground cumin**
> **⅛ teaspoon ground red pepper**
> **Salt to taste**

1   Preheat oven to 400°F.

2   Pierce the eggplant with a fork and bake on an oven rack 40 minutes or until soft (you may want to put some foil on the floor of the oven to catch any drips). Peel the eggplant and scrape off any flesh clinging to it; discard the skin.

3   Place the eggplant, tahini, lemon juice, garlic, cumin, pepper, and salt in a food processor container fitted with a steel blade. Cover and process until smooth.

SERVES: 8
Diabetic Exchanges: ¾ vegetable; ¾ fat

REDUCED FAT: Reduce the tahini to 2 tablespoons; add 1 extra clove garlic and 1 tablespoon more lemon juice.
Diabetic Exchanges: ¾ vegetable; ½ fat

Cucumber Feta Dip

Use this dip as a sauce for cold poached or grilled chicken or salmon. As a dip, serve it with either crudités or pita wedges.

> ⅓ **cup packed feta cheese**
> ½ **cup plain yogurt, divided**
> ½ **cup coarsely shredded cucumber**
> **1 tablespoon snipped fresh dill**
> **1 small clove garlic, minced**
> ⅛ **teaspoon ground black pepper**

In a medium bowl, mash the feta cheese with a fork. Add 2 tablespoons yogurt and continue to mash until fairly smooth. Gently stir in the rest of the yogurt. Stir in the cucumber, dill, garlic, and pepper. Let stand at least 20 minutes in the refrigerator.

SERVES: 6
Diabetic Exchanges: ¼ lean meat; ½ fat

REDUCED CHOLESTEROL/FAT: Use low-fat feta cheese and fat-free yogurt.
Diabetic Exchanges: ¼ lean meat; ¼ milk

REDUCED SATURATED FAT/PROTEIN/CHOLESTEROL/SODIUM: Omit feta cheese; increase garlic to 2 cloves and dill to 2 tablespoons.
Diabetic Exchanges: ¼ milk

Tomato Salsa

I was originally going to give you a recipe for homemade baked tortilla chips to go with the salsa, but they came out hard instead of crisp. I thought about where I'd gone wrong, and then I had a bright idea—just buy the chips! Use the baked chips, not the fried ones. If you have really flavorful tomatoes, you may be able to get away without using the tomato juice. Use only mild chilies (not jalapeño peppers).

> **1 cup chopped tomato**
> **¼ cup chopped onion**
> **¼ cup chopped canned green chilies (roasted peeled peppers), or more to taste**
> **2 tablespoons tomato sauce**
> **1 teaspoon lemon juice**
> **6 sprigs cilantro (fresh coriander)**
> **Salt to taste**

Place the tomato, onion, chilies, tomato sauce, lemon juice, and cilantro in a food processor container. Cover and process until finely chopped. Season with salt, if using.

SERVES: 6
Diabetic Exchanges: ½ vegetable

REDUCED SODIUM: Use minced fresh jalapeño pepper to taste instead of the canned chilies.
Diabetic Exchanges: ½ vegetable

THYME STUFFED MUSHROOMS

Use medium-size mushrooms. There should be about fifteen mushrooms in an 8-ounce container. Pick out the twelve nicest, then chop any that remain. My sister thought these were a little heavy on the thyme, but I liked it and so did the other tasters.

One 8-ounce package medium white mushrooms

2 teaspoons olive oil, divided

1 tablespoon minced shallot

1 clove garlic, minced

1½ tablespoons plain bread crumbs

1 teaspoon chopped fresh parsley

⅛ teaspoon dried thyme

⅛ teaspoon ground black pepper

Salt to taste

1   Preheat oven to 375°F.

2   Rinse the mushrooms until clean. Set aside 12 mushrooms, removing the stems. Chop the remaining mushrooms along with the 12 stems. Pour 1 teaspoon of the olive oil into an 8-inch-square baking pan. Toss the 12 mushroom caps in the oil; arrange well side up.

3   In a small nonstick skillet, heat the remaining 1 teaspoon oil over medium-high heat. Add the shallot, garlic, and chopped mushrooms. Cook, stirring, until softened, about 2 minutes. Stir in bread crumbs, parsley, thyme, pepper, and salt.

4   Fill the wells of the mushrooms with the bread-crumb mixture. Bake 12 minutes, or until mushrooms are cooked through.

SERVES: 4

Diabetic Exchanges: ¾ vegetable; ½ fat

LOW: saturated fat, protein, fiber, cholesterol, calcium, iron, magnesium, phosphorus, sodium, *fat*

ROASTED RED PEPPERS *with* FENNEL SALAD *and* PIGNOLI

There is not a huge amount of salad here, so I serve this on bread plates instead of salad plates. I originally prepared this salad using 1 tablespoon of lemon juice, but thought it was a bit too tart so I cut back to 2 teaspoons. But then I couldn't decide which one I really preferred. So try this one as written, but feel free to add a little extra lemon juice if you like.

> **2 small red bell peppers**
> **1 tablespoon pignoli (pine nuts)**
> **1½ cups very thinly sliced fennel**
> **1 tablespoon olive oil**
> **2 teaspoons fresh lemon juice**
> **1 teaspoon chopped fennel fronds**
> **Salt to taste**

1   Preheat broiler.

2   Cut the peppers in half lengthwise. Discard seeds and pith. Place on a baking pan. Broil, 4 inches from the heat, 5 minutes or until quite charred. Turn and cook until second side is charred, about 5 minutes. Place in paper bag and cool. Peel and discard skin.

3   In a dry small skillet, cook the pignoli, stirring constantly, for about 3 minutes, or until the pignoli start to brown a little. Remove from skillet and set aside.

4   In a medium bowl combine the sliced fennel, oil, lemon juice, fennel fronds, and salt.

5   Place a roasted pepper half on each plate, top with ¼ of the salad mixture, then top each with some of the toasted pignoli.

SERVES: 4
Diabetic Exchanges: 1 vegetable; ¾ fat

REDUCED FAT: Omit pignoli; reduce oil to 2 teaspoons.
Diabetic Exchanges: 1 vegetable; ½ fat

LEMON ZUCCHINI RIBBONS *with* ROASTED RED PEPPER SAUCE

If you don't want to make the sauce, just serve the ribbons as a side dish or serve them with a prepared marinara sauce. You have to press down with the peeler to get nice even zucchini ribbons.

1 medium zucchini

2 teaspoons olive oil

¼ teaspoon dried rosemary, crumbled

1 teaspoon fresh lemon juice

1 small roasted red bell pepper (page 26 or jarred)

2 tablespoons water

1 tablespoon tomato paste

½ clove garlic

¼ teaspoon sugar

⅛ teaspoon ground red pepper

Salt to taste

1   Slice off the ends of the zucchini; cut the zucchini in half lengthwise. Using a vegetable peeler, going perpendicular to the cut side, peel the zucchini into long, thin ribbons (you should have 3 cups).

2   In a large skillet, heat the oil over medium-high heat. Add the zucchini and rosemary; cook, stirring, until slightly softened, about 2 minutes. Stir in the lemon juice.

3   Place the roasted red pepper, water, tomato paste, garlic, sugar, ground red pepper, and salt in a blender container. Cover and process until smooth.

4   Divide the zucchini into 4 portions and place each portion on a small dish. Place a dollop of red pepper sauce in the center of each.

SERVES: 4
Diabetic Exchanges: ½ vegetable; ½ fat

REDUCED SODIUM: Use low-sodium tomato paste and homemade roasted red peppers.
Diabetic Exchanges: ½ vegetable; ½ fat

TOMATO *and* MOZZARELLA *with* BASIL CHIFFONADE

Chiffonade simply means thinly sliced or shredded. I find it easiest to make a chiffonade by stacking the basil leaves one on top of the other, then rolling them into a "log" lengthwise and just cutting the "log" into thin slices. For this recipe to be fabulous you must use only top-notch ingredients: extra-virgin olive oil, ripe tomatoes, fresh (or if you must use packaged, use the kind packed in water) mozzarella, and basil. The sodium count will vary widely depending on the mozzarella you use.

> **1 tablespoon olive oil**
>
> **1 clove garlic, minced**
>
> **2 ripe medium tomatoes**
>
> **8 ounces fresh mozzarella**
>
> **Salt and freshly ground pepper to taste**
>
> **⅓ cup shredded fresh basil**

1   In a small bowl, stir together the oil and garlic; let stand 10 minutes.

2   Cut the tomatoes and mozzarella into ¼ inch slices. Arrange the mozzarella on top of the tomato slices. Drizzle the oil over the cheese; top with salt and pepper if using.

3   Sprinkle with the basil.

SERVES: 4
Diabetic Exchanges: 1½ lean meat; ½ vegetable; 2½ fat

REDUCED SATURATED FAT/PROTEIN/CHOLESTEROL: Use only 2 ounces low-fat shredded mozzarella sprinkled over tomatoes.
Diabetic Exchanges: ½ very lean meat; ½ vegetable; ¾ fat

REDUCED FAT/SATURATED FAT/PROTEIN/CHOLESTEROL: Use only 2 ounces low-fat shredded mozzarella, sprinkled over tomatoes; omit oil.
Diabetic Exchanges: ½ very lean meat; ½ vegetable

REDUCED SODIUM: Use unsalted mozzarella.
Diabetic Exchanges: 2¼ lean meat; ½ vegetable; 1½ fat

ROASTED ASPARAGUS *with* STILTON

You can substitute another blue cheese such as Danish blue or Saga blue for the Stilton, and if you don't like blue cheese at all use something mild like Muenster or Jarlsberg.

> **24 medium stalks asparagus (about ¾ pound)**
> **1 tablespoon olive oil**
> **2 cloves garlic, slivered**
> **Freshly ground pepper to taste**
> **Salt to taste**
> **⅓ cup crumbled Stilton**

1   Preheat oven to 400°F.

2   Hold the asparagus stalk with one hand on the bottom of the stalk and one hand in the middle. Bend the asparagus until the bottom breaks off. Discard bottom.

3   Pour the olive oil into a 9-inch square baking pan and shake the pan to spread the oil. Place the asparagus in the pan and turn to coat with the oil. Sprinkle with the garlic, pepper, and salt. Bake 30 minutes or until the asparagus are roasted.

4   Sprinkle the Stilton over the asparagus and bake 3 minutes longer or until Stilton is warmed through.

SERVES: 4
Diabetic Exchanges: ¼ lean meat; 1 vegetable; 1 fat

REDUCED SATURATED FAT/PROTEIN/CHOLESTEROL/SODIUM: Omit the cheese and sprinkle with 2 teaspoons fresh lemon juice before serving.
Diabetic Exchanges: 1 vegetable; ¾ fat

White Beans *with* Beets

The beets are a lovely visual and taste contrast to the marinated beans. The mint adds a subtle taste. Be sure to use mild onions for this dish.

1 cup cooked cannellini beans or great northern beans (to cook from dried, see page 61; or use canned, drained)

⅓ cup finely chopped fennel

3 tablespoons chopped mild onion (such as Vidalia or Wala Wala)

1 tablespoon chopped fresh parsley

1 teaspoon finely chopped fresh mint, or ¼ teaspoon dry mint, crumbled

2 cloves garlic, finely chopped

1 tablespoon olive oil

1½ teaspoons red wine vinegar

1½ teaspoons fresh lemon juice

⅛ teaspoon ground black pepper

Salt to taste

4 small whole cooked beets, quartered (fresh-cooked or canned, drained)

In a medium bowl, combine the beans, fennel, onion, parsley, mint, and garlic. In a small bowl, combine the oil, vinegar, lemon juice, pepper, and salt. Pour dressing over beans and toss to combine. Divide among 4 serving plates. Garnish with beet wedges.

SERVES: 4

Diabetic Exchanges: ½ bread; 1 vegetable; ¾ fat

REDUCED SODIUM: Use home-cooked dried beans and beets prepared without salt.

Diabetic Exchanges: ½ bread; 1 vegetable; ¾ fat

SALMON *and* SMOKED SALMON PÂTÉ

I like to serve this with a dense whole-grain bread, but it's also very good on crackers or stuffed in celery or mushroom caps. It's also a good lunch spread.

1 cup cooked skinless and boneless salmon (fresh or canned)

¼ cup cottage cheese

1½ tablespoons snipped fresh dill or ½ teaspoon dried dill weed

1 tablespoon thinly sliced scallion (white and green parts)

1 tablespoon plain yogurt

1 tablespoon olive oil

2 teaspoons Dijon mustard

¼ teaspoon Worcestershire sauce

⅛ teaspoon Tabasco

½ cup smoked salmon (3 ounces)

1 Place the cooked salmon, cottage cheese, dill, scallion, yogurt, olive oil, mustard, Worcestershire sauce, and Tabasco in a food processor container fitted with a steel blade. Cover and process until smooth. Add the smoked salmon; cover and process until the smoked salmon is finely chopped.

2 Place in crock or serving bowl and chill at least 1 hour.

SERVES: 8

Diabetic Exchanges: ½ very lean meat; ¼ lean meat; ½ fat

REDUCED SODIUM: Omit smoked salmon; use unsalted cooked or canned salmon; use low-sodium cottage cheese.

Diabetic Exchanges: ¾ lean meat; ½ fat

SHRIMP *with* RÉMOULADE SAUCE

Cornichon are tiny pickles. You can usually find them in the supermarket section that has capers, roasted red peppers, and marinated artichokes. If you can't find them, you can just chop any sour pickle.

½ pound small shrimp, peeled and deveined

1 tablespoon mayonnaise

1 tablespoon finely chopped fresh parsley

1 tablespoon finely chopped cornichon

1 teaspoon Dijon mustard

½ teaspoon capers

½ clove garlic, minced

¼ teaspoon dried tarragon

3 drops Tabasco

¼ cup plain yogurt

2 cups chiffonade of arugula (see page 28)

1   In a 1½-quart saucepan, cook the shrimp in boiling water for 1 to 2 minutes or until no longer translucent. Drain and run under cold water to chill; drain.

2   In a medium bowl combine the mayonnaise, parsley, cornichon, mustard, capers, garlic, tarragon, and Tabasco. Gently fold in the yogurt until completely combined. Fold in the shrimp.

3   Divide arugula among 4 plates and top with shrimp.

SERVES: 4 as appetizer
Diabetic Exchanges: 1 very lean meat; ¾ fat

REDUCED FAT/SATURATED FAT/CHOLESTEROL: Omit the mayonnaise or substitute fat-free mayonnaise; use fat-free yogurt.
Diabetic Exchanges: 1 very lean meat

REDUCED SODIUM: Omit the capers and use low-sodium pickles and mayonnaise; add 1 tablespoon snipped fresh dill; increase garlic to 1 clove.
Diabetic Exchanges: 1 very lean meat; ¾ fat

CURRIED SHRIMP

These shrimp are irresistible; serve them as an hors d'oeuvre in a bowl with toothpicks so guests can help themselves. Or as an appetizer or luncheon entrée, serve on a lettuce leaf and garnish with lemon slices. Feel free to use frozen peeled shrimp (cooked according to package directions) instead of fresh shrimp for this recipe.

½ pound medium shrimp, peeled and deveined

1 tablespoon mayonnaise

2 teaspoons chopped mango chutney

2 teaspoons thinly sliced scallion

1 teaspoon curry powder

½ clove garlic, minced

Pinch cinnamon

Pinch ground red pepper

Salt to taste

2 tablespoons yogurt

1   In a 1½-quart saucepan, cook the shrimp in boiling water for 1 to 2 minutes or until no longer translucent. Drain and run under cold water to chill; drain.

2   In a medium bowl, combine the mayonnaise, chutney, scallion, curry powder, garlic, cinnamon, red pepper, and salt. Gently fold in the yogurt until completely combined. Fold in the shrimp.

SERVES: 6 as hors d'oeuvre; 4 as appetizer
Diabetic Exchanges: 1 very lean meat; ½ fat

REDUCED FAT/SATURATED FAT/CHOLESTEROL: Omit the mayonnaise or use fat-free mayonnaise; use fat-free yogurt.
Diabetic Exchanges: 1 very lean meat

SCALLOPS *with* ESSENCES *of* ORANGE *and* ROSEMARY

I first tested this without the ginger, and thought the flavor needed a little something, so I stirred a little ginger into half of the recipe and Dijon mustard into the other half. Both tasted really good, but I opted for the ginger.

> ¼ **cup orange juice**
> **1 teaspoon minced ginger**
> ½ **teaspoon grated orange rind**
> ¼ **teaspoon dried rosemary, crumbled**
> **Salt to taste**
> **2 teaspoons butter**
> ½ **pound scallops**

1   In a small bowl, stir together the orange juice, ginger, orange rind, rosemary, and salt.

2   In a medium nonstick skillet, melt butter over medium-high heat. Add the scallops and cook until lightly browned, about 3 minutes. Remove scallops from skillet. Pour the orange mixture into the skillet and cook until slightly thickened, about 1 to 2 minutes. Return scallops to skillet and toss, coating in the sauce.

SERVES: 4

Diabetic Exchanges: 1½ very lean meat; ½ fat

REDUCED SATURATED FAT/CHOLESTEROL/SODIUM: Use olive oil instead of butter.
Diabetic Exchanges: 1½ very lean meat; ½ fat

SEARED TUNA *with* THYME *and* BUTTER BEANS

I tasted this dish at a restaurant and thought it was so delicious I re-created it for this book. Hand-chop the garlic for this recipe (don't use a garlic press), and leave the pieces slightly larger than minced. Try to get fresh thyme as it is an important flavor in the dish. If you can't find butter beans, fava or giant lima beans would be good substitutes.

> **¾ pound tuna steak (cut 1 inch thick)**
> **Ground pepper to taste**
> **Salt to taste**
> **1 tablespoon olive oil, divided**
> **2 cloves garlic, finely chopped**
> **1 teaspoon chopped fresh thyme or ¼ teaspoon dried thyme**
> **¾ cup cooked butter beans (from dried or canned, drained)**

1   Slice the tuna steak into ¼-inch-thick slices (or for rare tuna, cook it to desired doneness before slicing). Season with pepper and salt; let stand 20 minutes or longer in the refrigerator.

2   In a medium nonstick skillet, heat 1 teaspoon of the oil over high heat. Add the garlic and thyme to the skillet, then the tuna. Cook the tuna about 1 minute per side or until desired doneness. Remove the tuna from the skillet.

3   Add the remaining 2 teaspoons oil to the skillet. Add the butter beans and cook, stirring, about 3 minutes or until heated through.

4   Divide the beans among 4 small plates; top with slices of tuna.

SERVES: 4
Diabetic Exchanges: ¼ bread; 2 very lean meat; ¾ fat

REDUCED SODIUM: Use home-cooked beans without any salt, or low-sodium canned. (Reduced-sodium canned lima beans were used for analysis.)
Diabetic Exchanges: ½ bread; 2 very lean meat; ¾ fat

TUNA *with* BLACK OLIVE VINAIGRETTE

I served this as part of a meal of many courses to Liz and Richard Forgang (Liz is food editor at the New York *Daily News*), and we all agreed this dish was superb!

¾ pound tuna steak (½ inch thick)

Salt to taste

Ground black pepper to taste

1 tablespoon olive oil, divided

¼ cup finely chopped black olives

3 tablespoons chopped fresh parsley

2 teaspoons balsamic vinegar

1 teaspoon fresh lemon juice

1 clove garlic, minced

1   Season the tuna with salt and pepper; let stand 20 minutes or longer in the refrigerator.

2   In a small bowl, combine 1 teaspoon of the olive oil, the black olives, parsley, vinegar, lemon juice, and garlic.

3   In a medium nonstick skillet, heat the remaining 2 teaspoons oil over high heat. Add the tuna; cook the tuna about 1 to 2 minutes per side or until desired doneness. Remove the tuna from the skillet. Cut the tuna into slices. Arrange on 4 salad plates. Top each with a quarter of the olive mixture.

SERVES: 4

Diabetic Exchanges: 2 lean meat; ¼ vegetable; 1 fat

REDUCED SODIUM: Substitute finely chopped peeled and seeded tomatoes for the olives.
Diabetic Exchanges: 2 lean meat; ¾ fat

ORANGE TERIYAKI SALMON

I serve this with molded cooked brown rice. Grease a metal ¼ cup measuring cup and then pack the rice into the cup. Turn it over onto the plate to unmold. Top with slices of scallion. Place two skewers on each plate. This makes enough to serve two people as an entrée. The nutritional information does not include the rice.

> **½ pound skinless salmon fillet**
> **1 tablespoon soy sauce**
> **1 tablespoon orange juice**
> **1 teaspoon mirin or sherry**
> **½ teaspoon grated orange rind**
> **½ teaspoon sugar**
> **1 clove garlic, minced**

1   Cut the salmon into ¾-inch cubes.

2   In a medium bowl, combine the soy sauce, orange juice, mirin, orange rind, sugar, and garlic. Add the salmon and toss. Let stand 10 minutes.

3   Preheat broiler.

4   String the salmon onto 8 small skewers. Broil 1 to 2 minutes per side or until desired doneness.

SERVES: 4
Diabetic Exchanges: 1¾ lean meat; ½ fat

REDUCED SODIUM: Use reduced-sodium soy sauce.
Diabetic Exchanges: 1¾ lean meat; ½ fat

GINGER LAMB
with WATERCRESS SALAD

You can use a multiple of this garlic-ginger mixture on leg or rack of lamb for a smashing main dish. I use meat from the leg or shoulder of the lamb for this recipe. Instead of daikon radish (which is very mild), you can substitute shredded jicama or slightly underripe pear or Asian pear.

> **1 tablespoon minced ginger**
>
> **2 cloves garlic, minced**
>
> **½ pound boneless lamb**
>
> **Salt to taste**
>
> **2 cups lightly packed watercress leaves**
>
> **½ cup sliced cucumber**
>
> **¼ cup sliced and quartered daikon radish**
>
> **1 tablespoon balsamic vinegar**
>
> **1 teaspoon olive oil**
>
> **Ground black pepper to taste**

1   Combine the ginger and garlic. Press onto all sides of the lamb; let stand 15 minutes or longer in the refrigerator.

2   Preheat broiler.

3   Place the lamb on a broiler pan; season with salt. Cook 2 to 3 minutes per side for medium-rare; slice.

4   In a medium bowl combine the watercress, cucumber, radish, vinegar, oil, and pepper. Toss to combine.

5   Place a quarter of the watercress mixture on each of 4 plates. Top with slices of the lamb.

SERVES: 4

Diabetic Exchanges: 1¾ very lean meat; ¼ vegetable; ¾ fat

REDUCED FAT/CHOLESTEROL/SATURATED FAT: Substitute chicken cutlets for the lamb.
Diabetic Exchanges: 2 very lean meat; ¼ vegetable; ¼ fat

THAI BEEF SALAD

My sister thought this dressing needed a little extra sweetness; my friend Jeff thought it needed to be a little more tart; Ricki and I thought it was just right! I like to use red leaf lettuce but Boston or any soft lettuce would also be nice. Double the recipe for an entrée salad.

½ pound London broil (½ inch thick)

Salt to taste

Ground black pepper to taste

4 cups bite-size lettuce pieces

2 cups tomato wedges

1 cup sliced cucumber

½ cup sliced red onion

3 tablespoons fresh lime juice

4 teaspoons soy sauce

1 tablespoon chopped cilantro leaves (fresh coriander)

2 teaspoons sugar

2 teaspoons water

1 clove garlic, minced

Pinch crushed red pepper

1   Preheat broiler or grill.

2   Sprinkle steak with salt and pepper to taste. Place on grill or broiler pan and cook, 5 to 6 inches from the heat, for 2 minutes per side for medium-rare. Let cool; cut across the grain into ¼-inch-thick slices.

3   In a large bowl, combine the lettuce, tomatoes, cucumber, and onion.

4   In a small bowl, combine the lime juice, soy sauce, cilantro, sugar, water, garlic, and crushed pepper, stirring until the sugar dissolves. Pour over the salad and toss.

5   Divide the salad among 4 plates; top with sliced beef.

(continued)

SERVES: 4

Diabetic Exchanges: 1¾ very lean meat; 1½ vegetable; ¾ fat

REDUCED SATURATED FAT/PROTEIN/CHOLESTEROL: Substitute 8 ounces pressed or baked tofu for the beef. Skip steps 1 and 2.

Diabetic Exchanges: 1 lean meat; 1½ vegetable; ¼ fat

REDUCED SODIUM: Use low-sodium soy sauce.

Diabetic Exchanges: 1¾ very lean meat; 1½ vegetable; ¾ fat

Soups

When people ask me if I specialize in any one type of cooking I generally answer "no." But to be truthful, of everything I cook I think I'm best at soup making, and I enjoy it most. Soups can be a very important part of the diabetic diet. They make excellent snacks. As main dishes for small meals (especially a hearty bean soup) just pair them with a salad, perhaps a slice of bread, and a piece of fruit. You can also carry them to work or school—all you need is a good thermos and you're prepared. Since soups freeze well (except cold soups) you can always have them on hand for a quick meal. Many of the broths and vegetable soups are low in calories, fat, and protein and so make a great filler-upper when you are hungry. Also, since most of them contain lots of vegetables and at least some fiber, they are good for you in that way too. Just watch out for the sodium content of any prepared broth or bouillon you may be using.

Hot Soups

Many of my hot soups start with broth as the base. That's because the broth gives depth to the rest of the flavors in the soup. You'll notice that I use fresh lemon juice in many of my brothy soups. That's because I frequently rely on canned broth or bouillon cubes. The lemon makes these prepared broths taste fresher. Soups that have more body don't need the lemon juice, even if they contain some broth.

Wherever possible I suggest using either chicken or vegetable broth, making vegetarian soups an option. I tend to use chicken broth because I prefer to use canned broth over bouillon cubes and find canned chicken broth better than canned vegetable broth. But, of course, homemade broth, be it vegetarian, chicken, turkey, or beef, is always better than canned. You can prepare homemade broth and then freeze it in 1-cup servings so they just have to be defrosted whenever you start a recipe calling for broth.

CHICKEN BROTH

This broth is intended to be used in recipes to increase the depth of flavors. For "eating" soup I would add parsnip and fresh dill. When I use leeks in a recipe—usually using only the white or light green parts—I clean and freeze the dark green parts for use in broth. If you don't have leeks on hand, just use onion.

> **2 pounds chicken pieces**
>
> **10 cups water**
>
> **4 carrots**
>
> **4 large stalks celery**
>
> **1 medium leek, including dark green part**
>
> **1 bunch parsley**
>
> **½ cup lightly packed celery leaves**
>
> **2 cloves garlic**

1   In a 6-quart pot, bring the chicken and water to a boil over high heat. Cook 10 minutes until scum rises to the top. Skim off the scum.

2   Add the carrots, celery, leek, parsley, celery, and garlic. Return to the boil. Reduce heat and simmer uncovered 50 minutes.

3   Remove the chicken pieces, carrots, and celery to a bowl (the vegetables are good as a side dish and I use the chicken in salads).

4   Pour the soup and "greens" through a strainer. Press the greens with the back of a glass to release the juices into the broth. Discard the pressed greens. Chill the broth and remove the fat from the top before using.

SERVES: 7 (makes 7 cups)
Diabetic Exchanges: ½ very lean meat

VEGETABLE BROTH

Homemade broth is definitely better than store-bought, since most brands are very salty, whether canned or in cube form. I use a food processor to chop the vegetables because I want them to be very finely chopped (almost minced). The more surface area of vegetable, the more flavor you can get. If I'm using only ¼ of my turnip and cabbage—what should I do with the rest? One solution is to chop everything up, put the extras into plastic freezer bags, and freeze them, for the next time you want to make broth. I like to keep 1 cup of the broth in a container in the refrigerator, where it lasts about a week, and freeze the rest in 1-cup amounts, so I can just pull out a cup when I need it.

5 carrots (¾ pound) (2 cups very finely chopped)
5 large stalks celery (¾ pound) (2 cups very finely chopped)
3 parsnips (¾ pound) (2½ cups very finely chopped)
¼ large head cabbage (¾ pound) (3 cups very finely chopped)
¼ rutabaga (wax or yellow turnip) (6 ounces) (1½ cups very finely chopped)
1 medium tomato (8 ounces) (1 cup very finely chopped)
12 cups water
1 medium onion (5 ounces), quartered
1 small bunch parsley (1½ ounces)
½ cup lightly packed celery leaves
3 cloves garlic
Salt to taste

1   Cut the carrots, celery, parsnips, cabbage, rutabaga, and tomato into 1-inch cubes. Process each vegetable separately in a food processor fitted with a steel blade until very finely chopped, transferring each batch to an 8-quart pot.

2   Place the water, onion, parsley, celery leaves, and garlic in the pot with the chopped vegetables. Bring to a boil. Reduce heat. Simmer, uncovered, 40 minutes, stirring occasionally.

3   Pour the soup through a fine strainer, gently pressing the liquid from the vegetables back into the broth; discard the pressed vegetables. Season with salt, if desired.

SERVES: 9 (makes 9 cups)
Diabetic Exchanges: ½ bread

VEGETABLE TOMATO SOUP

I cook this soup for a relatively short period of time so the vegetables don't become too soggy. If, on the other hand, you are a fan of canned soup you may want to cook the soup longer.

1 tablespoon olive oil

1 cup chopped onion

1 cup chopped green bell pepper

1 cup sliced mushrooms

2 cloves garlic, minced

3 cups vegetable broth

One 28-ounce can crushed tomatoes

2 cups water

1 tablespoon sugar

1 teaspoon dried oregano

½ teaspoon dried basil

1 bay leaf

¼ teaspoon ground black pepper

1½ cups coarsely chopped celery

1 cup sliced carrots

1½ cups coarsely chopped zucchini

1 cup green beans cut into 1½-inch pieces

⅓ cup chopped fresh parsley

Salt to taste

1   In a nonstick 5-quart pot, heat the oil over medium-high heat. Add the onion, green pepper, mushrooms, and garlic; cook, stirring, until vegetables are softened, about 4 minutes. Stir in the broth, crushed tomatoes, water, sugar, oregano, basil, bay leaf, and pepper. Bring to a boil.

2   Stir in the celery and carrots. Return to the boil. Reduce heat and simmer, uncovered, 10 minutes. Stir in the zucchini, green beans, and parsley. Return to the simmer, reduce heat, and simmer 10 minutes. Discard bay leaf; stir in salt, if using, before serving.

SERVES: 12

Diabetic Exchanges: 2 vegetable; ¼ fat

REDUCED SODIUM: Use low-sodium chicken broth and low-sodium whole peeled tomatoes, puréed in a blender or food processor.

Diabetic Exchanges: 1¾ vegetable; ¼ fat

HIGH: **potassium, sodium**

LOW: **saturated fat, protein, cholesterol, iron, phosphorus,** *sodium*

BOURBON STREET VEGETABLE SOUP

This is a really wonderful soup (of course I say that about a lot of soups—but that's because I am a wonderful soup maker!) that uses many of the flavors you would find in Creole cooking. It's so chock-full of stuff that it's almost a meal in itself. In fact, I think if you added some cooked chicken to it, you would have a great entrée.

1 tablespoon vegetable oil

3 cups shredded cabbage

1 cup chopped onion

½ cup chopped green bell pepper

2 cloves garlic, minced

1 teaspoon ground turmeric

2 cups water

1 cup chicken or vegetable broth

1½ cups chopped tomatoes

1 cup sliced okra

2 teaspoons Old Bay Seasoning

½ teaspoon sugar

¼ teaspoon dried thyme

1 bay leaf

⅛ teaspoon ground red pepper

Salt to taste

(continued)

1   In a 4-quart nonstick pot, heat the oil over medium-high heat. Add the cabbage, onion, green pepper, and garlic. Cook, stirring, until vegetables are softened, about 3 minutes. Stir in the turmeric until absorbed.

2   Add the water and broth and bring to a boil. Add the tomatoes, okra, Old Bay Seasoning, sugar, thyme, bay leaf, and pepper; return to the boil. Reduce heat and simmer, uncovered, 30 minutes. Stir in salt, if using, and discard the bay leaf before serving.

SERVES: 5
Diabetic Exchanges: 2 vegetable; ½ fat

REDUCED SODIUM: Omit the Old Bay Seasoning.
Diabetic Exchanges: 2 vegetable; ½ fat

ZUCCHINI ESCAROLE SOUP

This is a handy soup to have around all the time. It's low in everything you don't want. I eat this whenever I'm feeling really hungry. It fills me up so I don't overeat foods that are more calorie or carbohydrate or protein intensive.

> **2 teaspoons olive oil**
>
> **1 cup chopped onion**
>
> **2 cups chicken or vegetable broth**
>
> **1 cup water**
>
> **2 cups coarsely shredded zucchini**
>
> **¼ cup snipped fresh dill**
>
> **½ teaspoon poultry seasoning**
>
> **2 cups lightly packed, coarsely chopped escarole**
>
> **1 tablespoon fresh lemon juice**
>
> **1 teaspoon sugar**
>
> **¼ teaspoon ground black pepper**
>
> **Salt to taste**
>
> **1 tablespoon thinly sliced scallion (dark green part)**

1   In a 2-quart nonstick saucepan, heat the oil over medium-high heat. Add the onion and cook, stirring, until slightly softened, about 2 minutes. Add the broth and water; bring to a boil.

2   Add the zucchini, dill, and poultry seasoning; return to the boil. Reduce heat and simmer, uncovered, 5 minutes.

3   Add the escarole, lemon juice, sugar, pepper, and salt; simmer, uncovered, 5 minutes longer. Sprinkle with the scallion.

SERVES: 4

Diabetic Exchanges: ¼ bread; 1 vegetable; 1 fat

REDUCED SODIUM: Use low-sodium broth.

Diabetic Exchanges: ¼ bread; ¼ lean meat; 1 vegetable; ½ fat

HIGH: **potassium, sodium**

LOW: **fat, saturated fat, cholesterol, phosphorus,** *sodium*

BROCCOLI FENNEL VELVET SOUP

The texture of this soup should be as smooth and luxurious as velvet. I sampled a version of this at L'Ecole, a restaurant staffed by the students of The French Culinary Institute in New York City. They served this together with a cauliflower soup ladled into the bowl side by side. You can make a similarly dramatic presentation using the Red Pepper Bisque on page 55.

> **2½ cups chicken or vegetable broth**
>
> **1 cup water**
>
> **3 cups broccoli florets**
>
> **2 cups chopped fennel**
>
> **½ cup sliced leek (white and light green parts)**
>
> **2 tablespoons lightly packed fennel fronds**
>
> **½ teaspoon dried tarragon**
>
> **¼ teaspoon ground black pepper**
>
> **Salt to taste**
>
> **¼ to ½ cup milk or additional broth (optional)**

1   In a 2-quart saucepan, bring the broth and water to a boil. Add the broccoli, fennel, leek, fennel fronds, tarragon, and pepper; return to the boil. Reduce heat and simmer, uncovered, 40 minutes or until vegetables are very soft.

2   Pour the soup into a blender or food processor container fitted with a steel blade. Cover and process until smooth. Season with salt, adding enough milk or additional broth to make a soup that is very thick but still pours easily into a bowl—or to desired consistency.

SERVES: 4

Diabetic Exchanges: 1½ vegetable; ¾ fat

REDUCED PROTEIN: Use broth instead of milk.
Diabetic Exchanges: 1½ vegetable; ½ fat

REDUCED SODIUM: Use low-sodium broth.
Diabetic Exchanges: ¼ lean meat; 1½ vegetable; ¼ fat

THE ULTIMATE DIABETES COOKBOOK

CREAMY PORTOBELLO MUSHROOM SOUP

I do not usually use expensive, hard-to-find ingredients, but here I call for a little white truffle oil (I paid about $10 for a very small bottle). The soup is very good without it, but the truffle oil enhances and rounds out the mushroom flavor, giving it that extra richness.

1 tablespoon butter

4 cups chopped portobello mushrooms

⅔ cup chopped onion

¼ cup all-purpose flour

2 cups chicken or vegetable broth

½ cup milk

⅛ teaspoon ground black pepper

⅛ teaspoon dried thyme

1 bay leaf

1 teaspoon white truffle oil

Salt to taste

1   In a 2-quart nonstick saucepan, melt the butter over medium-high heat. Add the mushrooms and onion; cook, stirring, until completely softened, about 6 minutes.

2   Remove from heat, stir in the flour until completely absorbed. Add the broth, milk, pepper, thyme, and bay leaf. Cook over medium heat, stirring, until mixture comes to a boil, about 6 minutes. Discard the bay leaf. Add the truffle oil and salt, briefly returning to the boil before serving.

SERVES: 4

Diabetic Exchanges: ½ bread; 2 vegetable; 1½ fat

REDUCED SATURATED FAT/CHOLESTEROL: Use olive oil instead of butter, and low-fat broth and skim milk.

Diabetic Exchanges: ½ bread; ¼ very lean meat; 2 vegetable; ¾ fat

(continued)

REDUCED FAT: Use 2 teaspoons olive oil instead of butter, omit truffle oil, and use low-fat broth and skim milk.

Diabetic Exchanges: ½ bread; ¼ lean meat, 2 vegetable; ½ fat

REDUCED SODIUM: Use low-sodium broth and unsalted butter.

Diabetic Exchanges: ½ bread; ¼ very lean meat; 2 vegetable; ¾ fat

---

HIGH: **sodium**

LOW: **cholesterol, iron, phosphorus,** *fat, saturated fat, sodium*

HUNGARIAN CAULIFLOWER *and* CABBAGE SOUP

Try to find genuine sweet (not hot) Hungarian paprika (sold in most supermarket spice sections in a red tin), which is more flavorful than any other type. I purée only part of the soup to give it a little extra body, but you can also purée the entire soup. The results are equally delicious, but the consistency is extremely different. Don't be dismayed that the yogurt looks slightly curdled in the soup. . .this doesn't affect the flavor at all. Top the soup with additional yogurt, if desired.

> **1 tablespoon vegetable oil**
> **3 cups coarsely chopped cabbage**
> **1 cup chopped onion**
> **1 clove garlic, minced**
> **1 tablespoon Hungarian sweet paprika**
> **1¾ cups chicken or vegetable broth**
> **1¼ cups water**
> **3 cups cauliflower florets**
> **Salt to taste**
> **¼ teaspoon ground black pepper**
> **¾ cup plain yogurt**

1   In a 4- or 5-quart nonstick saucepan, heat the oil over medium-high heat. Add the cabbage, onion, and garlic, and cook, stirring, until slightly softened, about 4 to 5 minutes. Stir in the paprika until absorbed.

2   Add the broth and water, and bring to a boil. Add the cauliflower and simmer, uncovered, 20 minutes or until the cauliflower is soft. Stir in salt and pepper.

3   Place 2 cups of the soup into a blender or food processor container fitted with a steel blade. Cover and process until smooth. Stir purée into soup. Stir in the yogurt; reheat if necessary, but do not boil.

4   Serve in bowls, topped with additional yogurt dollops, if you like.

SERVES: 5
Diabetic Exchanges: 1½ vegetable; 1 fat

REDUCED FAT/SATURATED FAT/CHOLESTEROL: Reduce the oil to 2 teaspoons, and use fat-free broth and fat-free yogurt.
Diabetic Exchanges: ¼ lean meat; 1½ vegetable; ¼ milk; ½ fat

REDUCED SODIUM: Use low-sodium broth.
Diabetic Exchanges: ¼ lean meat; 1½ vegetable; ¾ fat

REDUCED SATURATED FAT/PROTEIN/CHOLESTEROL: Omit the yogurt and use vegetable broth.
Diabetic Exchanges: 1¾ vegetable; ½ fat

CURRIED CAULIFLOWER SOUP *with* SCALLION RAITA

Definitely spicy! The yogurt helps with the burn, however, and you can cut back on the ground red pepper or eliminate it completely if you are not partial to hot foods. Speaking of hot, this is also lovely served chilled. This soup is a perfect filler-upper with not too many calories and carbohydrates.

>   **2 teaspoons vegetable oil**
>
>   **1 cup chopped onion**
>
>   **2 cloves garlic, minced**
>
>   **1 tablespoon curry powder**
>
>   **⅛ teaspoon ground cumin**
>
>   **⅛ teaspoon ground red pepper (or less), to taste**
>
>   **1¾ cups chicken or vegetable broth**
>
>   **1¾ cups water**
>
>   **4 cups cauliflower florets**
>
>   **¼ cup cilantro leaves (fresh coriander)**
>
>   **Salt to taste**

Scallion Raita

>   **½ cup plain yogurt**
>
>   **1 tablespoon thinly sliced scallion (green part)**
>
>   **1 teaspoon chopped cilantro leaves**
>
>   **½ small clove garlic, minced**

1   In a 2-quart nonstick saucepan, heat the oil over medium-high heat. Add the onion and garlic and cook, stirring, until slightly softened, about 2 to 3 minutes. Stir in the curry, cumin, and ground red pepper until absorbed.

2   Add the broth and water and bring to a boil. Add the cauliflower and simmer, uncovered, 20 minutes, or until the cauliflower is soft; stir in the cilantro.

3 Place half the soup in a blender or food processor container fitted with a steel blade. Cover and process until smooth; repeat with remaining soup. Season with salt.

4 For the Raita: in a small bowl, stir together the yogurt, scallion, cilantro, and garlic.

5 Serve soup topped with Scallion Raita.

SERVES: 4
Diabetic Exchanges: 1¾ vegetable; 1 fat

REDUCED SATURATED FAT/PROTEIN/CHOLESTEROL: Use vegetable broth instead of chicken and omit the Raita.
Diabetic Exchanges: 1¾ vegetable; ¾ fat

REDUCED FAT/SATURATED FAT/CHOLESTEROL/SODIUM: Use low-sodium/low-fat broth and omit the Raita.
Diabetic Exchanges: 1¾ vegetable; ½ fat

Soups

SNAP PEA SOUP *with* ROSEMARY

The rosemary flavor is very prominent in this delicious soup. As with so many of my puréed soups, this one is a little spicy and benefits from a dollop of yogurt. Be sure to remove all the stringy parts from the top and bottom of the snap peas (also called sugar snaps) before you cook them.

> **2 cups chicken or vegetable broth**
>
> **1½ cups water**
>
> **2 cups snap peas**
>
> **½ cup green peas (fresh or frozen, not canned)**
>
> **½ cup diced potato**
>
> **½ cup sliced leek (white and light green parts)**
>
> **½ teaspoon dried rosemary**
>
> **⅛ teaspoon ground red pepper**
>
> **¼ cup plain yogurt (optional)**

1   In a 2-quart saucepan, combine the broth, water, snap peas, green peas, potato, leek, rosemary, and pepper. Bring to a boil over high heat. Reduce heat and simmer, covered, 10 minutes; uncover and simmer 20 minutes longer or until the potato is soft.

2   Pour the soup into a blender or food processor container fitted with a steel blade. Cover and process until smooth.

3   Pour into individual bowls, adding a dollop of yogurt, if desired.

SERVES: 4

Diabetic Exchanges: ½ bread; 2½ vegetable; ¾ fat

REDUCED SODIUM: Use low-sodium broth.

Diabetic Exchanges: ½ bread; ¼ very lean meat; 2½ vegetable

RED PEPPER BISQUE

This is a pretty thick soup. For a thinner one, either cook the vegetables covered or add some extra broth to thin the puréed soup.

> **1 teaspoon vegetable oil**
>
> **¾ cup sliced leek (white part only)**
>
> **1 clove garlic, minced**
>
> **3 cups chicken or vegetable broth**
>
> **1 cup peeled, cubed potato**
>
> **1 tablespoon tomato paste**
>
> **2 medium red bell peppers, halved and roasted**
> **(See page 26 for instructions on roasting red peppers.)**
>
> **1 teaspoon sugar**
>
> **Pinch ground nutmeg**
>
> **⅛ teaspoon ground red pepper**
>
> **1 cup buttermilk**
>
> **Salt to taste**

1   In a 3-quart nonstick saucepan, heat the oil over medium-high heat. Add the leek and garlic; cook, stirring, until softened, about 2 minutes.

2   Add the broth, potato, and tomato paste, and bring to a boil. Reduce heat and simmer, uncovered, 30 minutes.

3   Place the soup, roasted peppers, sugar, nutmeg, and pepper in a blender or food processor container fitted with a steel blade. Cover and process until smooth. Add buttermilk and salt, and process until combined.

SERVES: 4

Diabetic Exchanges: ½ bread; 1½ vegetable; ¼ milk; 1¼ fat

REDUCED FAT/SATURATED FAT/CHOLESTEROL/SODIUM: Use low-sodium, low-fat broth and low-sodium tomato paste.

Diabetic Exchanges: ½ bread; ¼ very lean meat; 1½ vegetable; ¼ milk; ¾ fat

CREAMY KOHLRABI *and* POTATO SOUP

This is really a potato leek soup with kohlrabi substituted for some of the potatoes. In addition to reducing the starchiness, it adds a nice flavor.

> 2½ cups chicken or vegetable broth
>
> 1½ cups water
>
> 2 cups peeled, cubed kohlrabi
>
> 1½ cups peeled, cubed potatoes
>
> ¾ cup sliced leek
>
> 1 bay leaf
>
> ¼ teaspoon dried thyme
>
> ⅛ teaspoon ground black pepper
>
> Salt to taste
>
> ¼ cup plain yogurt (optional)

1   In a 2-quart nonstick saucepan, bring the broth and water to a boil. Add the kohlrabi, potatoes, leek, bay leaf, thyme, pepper, and salt.

2   Return to the boil. Reduce heat and simmer, covered, 25 minutes or until the potatoes are tender. Discard the bay leaf.

3   Transfer the soup, in 2 or 3 batches, into a blender or food processor container fitted with a steel blade and process until puréed.

4   Serve topped with yogurt, if desired.

SERVES: 4

Diabetic Exchanges: ½ bread; 1½ vegetable; ¼ milk; ½ fat

REDUCED FAT/SATURATED FAT/PROTEIN/CHOLESTEROL/SODIUM: Use low-sodium and -fat broth and don't dollop with yogurt.

Diabetic Exchanges: ½ bread; ¼ very lean meat; 1¼ vegetable

MANHATTAN CLAM CHOWDER

Omit the clams and you have a lovely vegetable soup—or substitute cod (or another firm-fleshed white fish) and you have a delicious fish chowder. If you are accustomed to potatoes in your chowder, add diced boiling potatoes to the soup when you add the tomatoes, but don't forget they will increase the carbohydrate and potassium counts.

> **2 teaspoons olive oil**
> **½ cup chopped onion**
> **½ cup sliced red bell pepper**
> **½ cup chopped green bell pepper**
> **½ cup chopped celery**
> **1 clove garlic, minced**
> **1 teaspoon Hungarian paprika**
> **1 cup clam juice or chicken or vegetable broth**
> **1 cup water**
> **1 cup chopped tomatoes**
> **One 6 ½-ounce can minced or chopped clams, undrained**
> **1 tablespoon tomato paste**
> **½ teaspoon sugar**
> **1 bay leaf**
> **⅛ teaspoon dried oregano**
> **⅛ teaspoon dried thyme**
> **⅛ teaspoon ground black pepper**
> **Salt to taste**

1   In a 2-quart nonstick pot, heat the oil over medium-high heat. Add the onion, red and green pepper, celery, and garlic. Cook, stirring, until vegetables are slightly softened, about 4 minutes. Stir in the paprika until absorbed.

2   Add the clam juice or broth and water; bring to a boil. Add the tomatoes, clams with their liquid, tomato paste, sugar, bay leaf, oregano, thyme, and pepper; return to the boil. Reduce heat and simmer, uncovered, 40 minutes. Discard bay leaf. Add salt if using.

(continued)

Soups

SERVES: 4

Diabetic Exchanges: 1½ very lean meat; 1½ vegetable; ½ fat

REDUCED PROTEIN: Omit clams and enjoy as vegetable soup.

Diabetic Exchanges: 1½ vegetable; ½ fat

REDUCED SODIUM: Omit canned clams and add 12 fresh clams to the soup. When clams have opened, remove from soup, discard shells, and chop the clam meat. Add chopped clams to soup. Use low-sodium broth and tomato paste.

Diabetic Exchanges: 1¼ very lean meat; 1¾ vegetable; ½ fat

SPLIT PEA *and* BARLEY SOUP

This is a lovely split pea soup, not too thick, not too thin. Sometimes I use yellow split peas, sometimes green, or sometimes some of each. It works well any which way. When I first prepared this recipe I included a tablespoon of sherry. I wasn't crazy about it but my guests were, so try it if you like.

4 cups chicken or vegetable broth

2 cups water

1½ cups chopped celery

1 cup chopped onion

¾ cup chopped carrot

⅔ cup green or yellow split peas

3 tablespoons pearl barley

3 tablespoons snipped fresh dill

½ teaspoon poultry seasoning

¼ teaspoon ground pepper

Salt to taste

1   In a 3-quart saucepan, bring the broth and water to a boil over high heat. Add the celery, onion, carrot, and peas; return to the boil. Reduce heat and simmer, covered, 1 hour.

2   Add the barley, dill, poultry seasoning, and pepper. Return to the boil; reduce heat and simmer, uncovered, 40 minutes longer or until the peas have dissolved. Season with salt.

SERVES: 5

Diabetic Exchanges: 1½ bread; 1¼ vegetable; ½ fat

REDUCED FAT/SATURATED FAT/CHOLESTEROL/SODIUM: Use low-sodium and fat-free broth.
Diabetic Exchanges: 1½ bread; ¼ lean meat; 1¼ vegetable

HIGH: protein, carbohydrate, fiber, iron, magnesium, phosphorus, potassium, sodium

LOW: fat, saturated fat, cholesterol, *sodium*

LENTIL KALE SOUP

Although not technically high-calorie by our definition of 20 percent of the daily intake of calories, this soup does have 225 calories per serving. But it makes a nice light meal—which more than justifies the calories.

> 3 cups water
>
> 2 cups chicken or vegetable broth
>
> 1 cup lentils
>
> ¾ cup chopped onion
>
> ¾ cup chopped celery
>
> ¾ cup chopped carrots
>
> 1 bay leaf
>
> 2 cups chopped kale
>
> 1½ tablespoons fresh lemon juice
>
> ½ teaspoon ground black pepper
>
> Salt to taste

1 In a 3-quart saucepan, bring the water and broth to a boil over medium-high heat. Add the lentils, onion, celery, carrots, and bay leaf. Return to the boil; reduce heat and simmer, uncovered, 35 minutes.

2 Add the kale, lemon juice, pepper, and salt. Simmer uncovered 15 minutes longer.

SERVES: 5

Diabetic Exchanges: 1¾ bread; ½ very lean meat; 1¾ vegetable; ½ fat

REDUCED SODIUM: Use low-sodium broth.

Diabetic Exchanges: 1¾ bread; ½ very lean meat; ¼ lean meat; 1¾ vegetable

CUBAN BLACK BEAN SOUP

Once upon a time I used to start this soup with a couple of slices of bacon. My conscience doesn't allow me to do that anymore—and I can't say that the soup suffers from lack of flavor in any way. I like to purée about two thirds of the beans and vegetables in the soup, leaving some beans whole. You may choose to purée the whole thing, for a smooth soup.

> **1 cup black beans**
> **7 cups water, plus additional water for soaking**
> **1 cup chopped onion**
> **¾ cup chopped green bell pepper**
> **¾ cup chopped celery**
> **4 cloves garlic, minced**
> **1 teaspoon dried oregano**
> **½ teaspoon ground cumin**
> **¼ teaspoon ground black pepper**
> **1 bay leaf**
> **¼ cup chopped cilantro leaves (fresh coriander)**
> **Salt to taste**

1   Let beans soak covered in water overnight, or bring beans covered with water to a boil over medium-high heat, then remove from heat and let stand, covered, 1 hour.

2   In a 3-quart saucepot, bring the 7 cups of water to a boil. Add the soaked (and drained) beans, onion, bell pepper, celery, garlic, oregano, cumin, pepper, and bay leaf. Return to the boil. Reduce heat and simmer, uncovered, 1¼ hours. Stir in the cilantro and salt and cook 15 minutes longer. Discard bay leaf before serving.

3   Place 3 cups (or all) of the soup into a blender or food processor container fitted with a steel blade; cover and process until smooth. Stir into remaining soup.

SERVES: 5
Diabetic Exchanges: 1½ bread; 1 vegetable

TUSCAN WHITE BEAN *and* VEGETABLE SOUP

In addition to being a delicious soup, this works beautifully as a sauce for spaghetti squash and also as a base for a chicken cacciatore–like dish: place 2 pounds of skinless chicken parts (with bones in) into a 6-quart pot, add about 3 cups of soup and 1 cup of water. Bring to a boil, then cover and simmer about 40 minutes or until the chicken is cooked. If you want a thicker sauce, you can uncover the pot for the last 20 minutes.

2 tablespoons olive oil

4 cups chopped eggplant

1 cup sliced leek

1 cup chopped red bell pepper

3 cloves garlic, minced

One 28-ounce can whole peeled tomatoes in thick purée, undrained

2 cups water

2 cups sliced zucchini

1 cup sliced yellow squash

1 cup cooked small white beans or cannellini

⅓ cup chopped fresh parsley

1 tablespoon sweet vermouth (optional)

1 tablespoon sugar

⅛ teaspoon ground black pepper

Salt to taste

1   In a 6-quart nonstick pot, heat the oil over medium-high heat. Add the eggplant, leek, red bell pepper, and garlic. Cook, stirring, until the vegetables are slightly softened, about 5 minutes.

2   Add the tomatoes with purée, breaking them up with the back of a spoon. Stir in the water. Bring to a boil. Reduce heat and cook, covered, 30 minutes, stirring occasionally.

3   Add the zucchini, yellow squash, beans, parsley, vermouth (if using), sugar, pepper, and salt. Return to the boil. Reduce heat and simmer, covered, 40 minutes longer.

SERVES: 8

Diabetic Exchanges: ½ bread; 1 sugar; 1½ vegetable; ¾ fat

REDUCED FAT: Reduce the oil to 2 teaspoons.

Diabetic Exchanges: ½ bread; 1 other carbohydrate; 1½ vegetable; ¼ fat

REDUCED PROTEIN: Omit the beans.

Diabetic Exchanges: 1 other carbohydrate, 1½ vegetable; ¾ fat

REDUCED SODIUM: Use low-sodium canned tomatoes for the canned tomatoes; use beans that have been cooked from dried without salt instead of the canned; increase the sugar if necessary.

Diabetic Exchanges: ½ bread; 1 other carbohydrate; 1½ vegetable; ¾ fat

Soups

Cold Soups

When I think of soup I usually envision a cold winter's night and the warming satisfaction of a bowl of hot soup. But cold soups should not be overlooked as an asset to a menu. The virtues of cold soups are many. They (at least the ones in this book) are low in calories, carbohydrates, protein, and fat. This makes them excellent snack foods and also an easy item to add to a dinner menu without adding too many diabetic exchanges.

THE ULTIMATE DIABETES COOKBOOK

MANGO GAZPACHO

The color of this soup is not the bright red that you would expect, but the flavor is lovely—slightly sweet, slightly hot, and cool. Be sure your mango is ripe and sweet, as the mango gives this gazpacho its distinct character. If you want to make plain gazpacho (4 cups), omit the mango and cumin from this recipe.

> **3 cups cubed tomatoes**
>
> **2 cups peeled, cubed cucumber**
>
> **1½ cups cubed green bell pepper**
>
> **½ cup cubed mango**
>
> **3 tablespoons sliced scallion (green and white parts)**
>
> **3 tablespoons fresh lime juice**
>
> **1 tablespoon firmly packed cilantro leaves (fresh coriander)**
>
> **1 teaspoon packed fresh mint leaves, or ¼ teaspoon dried mint**
>
> **1 teaspoon olive oil (optional)**
>
> **⅛ teaspoon ground cumin**
>
> **Dash ground red pepper, or to taste (optional)**
>
> **Salt to taste**
>
> **¾ cup diced mango**

Place all ingredients, except the ¾ cup diced mango, in a blender or food processor container fitted with a steel blade. Cover and process until finely chopped. Stir in the diced mango. Chill at least an hour to allow flavors to meld.

SERVES: 5
Diabetic Exchanges: 1¼ fruit; 2¼ vegetable; ¼ fat

REDUCED CARBOHYDRATE: Omit the mango.
Diabetic Exchanges: 1 fruit; 2 vegetable; ¼ fat

CHILLED YOGURT BASIL SOUP

This soup is superb especially during the summer when basil is at its peak and the cooling soup helps you forget the rising temperatures outside.

3 cups peeled, cubed cucumber

1 cup cubed zucchini

1 cup vegetable broth

½ cup cubed green bell pepper

½ cup cubed onion

½ cup lightly packed basil leaves

2 tablespoons lightly packed fresh parsley leaves

1 tablespoon lightly packed mint leaves

2 teaspoons red wine vinegar

1 teaspoon olive oil

1 clove garlic, minced

¼ teaspoon ground black pepper

1 cup plain yogurt

Salt to taste

1   In a blender or food processor container fitted with a steel blade, combine the cucumber, zucchini, broth, green pepper, onion, basil, parsley, mint, vinegar, oil, garlic, and pepper. Cover and process until smooth.

2   Add the yogurt and blend on low speed until mixed. Season with salt if desired.

SERVES: 4

Diabetic Exchanges: 1½ vegetable; ¼ milk; ½ fat

REDUCED FAT/SATURATED FAT/CHOLESTEROL: Omit the olive oil and use fat-free yogurt.
Diabetic Exchanges: 1½ vegetable; ¼ milk

REDUCED SODIUM: Use low-sodium broth.
Diabetic Exchanges: 1¼ vegetable; ¼ milk; ¼ fat

CHILLED CUCUMBER SOUP
with SPICY SALSA

The spicy salsa and the cool cucumber soup create an excellent contrast in tastes and mouth sensations. Use any mild salsa (homemade, page 280, or store-bought) for the timid.

> **5 cups peeled, cubed cucumber**
>
> **1 cup chicken or vegetable broth**
>
> **¼ cup 1-inch scallion pieces (green part only)**
>
> **2 tablespoons firmly packed cilantro leaves (fresh coriander)**
>
> **½ small clove garlic, minced**
>
> **1½ cups buttermilk**
>
> **Salt to taste**

> ***For the salsa***
>
> **½ cup tomato wedges**
>
> **1 jalapeño pepper, seeded (leave the seeds in if you want a spicier salsa)**
>
> **1 tablespoon sliced scallion (white and light green parts)**
>
> **1 tablespoon fresh lime or lemon juice**
>
> **Salt to taste**

1   To prepare soup: place the cucumber, broth, scallion, cilantro, and garlic in a blender or food processor container fitted with a steel blade. Cover and process until smooth. Stir in the buttermilk and salt to taste. Place in refrigerator at least 1 hour to chill.

2   To prepare salsa: place the tomato, jalapeño, scallion, juice, and salt in a blender or food processor container fitted with a steel blade. Cover and pulse until finely chopped.

3   Pour the soup into 4 individual bowls. Top with dollops of the salsa.

SERVES: 5
Diabetic Exchanges: 1 vegetable; ½ milk; ¼ fat

REDUCED SODIUM: Use low-sodium broth and no-salt-added buttermilk.
Diabetic Exchanges: 1 vegetable; ½ milk

Entrées

The entrées in this book are very flavorfully prepared dishes that are moderate- to low-fat. The portion sizes are not large, as a diabetic diet should not be excessively high in protein. (If your physician has recommended a high-protein diet for you, you may want to increase the size of the serving from those suggested here.) Entrées should be accompanied by at least one vegetable, but preferably more, and a carbohydrate, if your health professional allows. To help plan a balanced meal, menu suggestions are presented at the bottom of each entrée recipe.

GREAT SHAKES

Great Shakes are GREAT to keep on hand for those days you just have time to throw together a quick meal. Eating before you get too hungry is an important factor in maintaining a healthy diet. If you wait until you are famished, you will overeat. Therefore, always have items on hand that allow you to prepare quick, tasty meals. When I'm in a hurry I pull out my George Foreman grill and sprinkle one of the shakes on chicken, fish, pork, or vegetables. Then presto! Dinner is ready—usually before I've even finished preparing my salad. Shakes can also be used before baking, sautéing, or broiling. Each shake makes enough seasoning for several meals; just store the excess in tightly covered plastic containers or Ziploc style storage bags. You can also stir them into yogurt for a nice dip for vegetables or sauce for fish or chicken. Nutritionally I count them as free foods, except for the sodium content. For restricted-sodium diets, just leave out the salt.

HUNGARIAN

> **1 tablespoon garlic powder**
>
> **1 tablespoon Hungarian sweet paprika**
>
> **1½ teaspoons salt, or to taste**
>
> **1 teaspoon onion powder**
>
> **½ teaspoon ground black pepper**
>
> **¼ teaspoon ground ginger**

In a small bowl, stir together all the ingredients. Makes 2 tablespoons plus 2½ teaspoons

MEXICAN

> **2 tablespoons chili powder**
>
> **1 tablespoon garlic powder**
>
> **1½ teaspoons salt, or to taste**
>
> **1 teaspoon paprika**
>
> **1 teaspoon ground cumin**
>
> **½ teaspoon dried oregano**
>
> **½ teaspoon sugar**
>
> **¼ teaspoon ground red pepper**

In a small bowl, stir together all the ingredients. Makes 2½ tablespoons

Entrées

Herbal

 1 tablespoon garlic powder

 1 tablespoon dried parsley

 1½ teaspoons salt, or to taste

 1 teaspoon onion powder

 1 teaspoon dried basil

 ½ teaspoon dried rosemary

 ¼ teaspoon dried thyme

 ¼ teaspoon ground black pepper

Place all the ingredients in a food processor or blender container. Cover and process until the herbs are finely ground. Makes 1½ tablespoons

Cajun

 1 tablespoon garlic powder

 1½ teaspoons onion powder

 1½ teaspoons salt

 ½ teaspoon ground black pepper

 ½ teaspoon ground white pepper

 ¼ teaspoon ground red pepper (cayenne)

 ¼ teaspoon ground cumin

 ¼ teaspoon dried oregano

 ¼ teaspoon paprika

In a small bowl, stir together all the seasonings. Makes 2½ tablespoons

Curried

 1 tablespoon curry powder

 1 tablespoon garlic powder

 1½ teaspoons salt

 ½ teaspoon ground turmeric

 ½ teaspoon ground ginger

 ¼ teaspoon ground cinnamon

 ¼ teaspoon paprika

In a small bowl, stir together all the seasonings. Makes 3 tablespoons

Diabetic Exchanges: free

Poultry

I have lots of poultry and fish recipes since they are healthy choices in a diabetic diet. With the possible exception of roasted chicken, all dishes are prepared with skinned chicken parts. In general I prefer dark meat for stewing, since it is moister than white meat. However, white meat is lower in fat and cholesterol than dark. There is a world of difference between the serving size of chicken as purchased and the cooked edible part of the chicken. Here are some interesting figures: 2 pounds chicken parts as purchased (with skin and bones) = four 4-ounce servings of cooked chicken or 2 smallish thighs (no backbone); 2 smallish drumsticks; 1 small whole breast.

The nutritional analysis for recipes using chicken parts is for a combination of dark and white meat (except, of course, when the recipe calls specifically for only white or only dark meat). If you use only dark or only white, here are the figures for both—adjust your own calculations accordingly.

For 4 ounces—cooked, skinless, and boneless (the minerals are not too different):

	BREAST	THIGH
Calories	187	237
Protein	35g	29g
Carbohydrates	0	0
Fiber	0	0
Total fat	4g	12g
Saturated fat	1g	3g
Cholesterol	96mg	107mg
Diabetic Exchanges	4¼ very lean meat	5 very lean meat; ¼ fat

Entrées

EGGPLANT *and* CHICKEN PROVENÇAL

This an incredibly rich dish, even though it uses relatively little fat. The eggplant cooks down into a luxurious sauce for the chicken. I don't peel the eggplant because I like eating the skin and think it adds color to the dish. If you don't like the consistency of the skin, peel before cubing.

> **2 pounds chicken pieces**
> **1 tablespoon all-purpose flour**
> **⅛ teaspoon ground black pepper**
> **1½ teaspoons olive oil**
> **½ cup sliced leek (white and light green parts)**
> **3 cups cubed eggplant (1½-inch pieces)**
> **½ cup chopped red bell pepper**
> **2 cloves garlic, minced**
> **¼ cup water**
> **1 bay leaf**
> **¼ teaspoon dried rosemary, crumbled**
> **⅛ teaspoon dried thyme**
> **2 tablespoons chopped fresh parsley**
> **1½ tablespoons dry red wine**
> **Salt to taste**

1   Remove skin from the chicken; rinse and pat dry. On a piece of wax paper, combine the flour and black pepper. Dredge the chicken pieces in the flour.

2   In a 4-quart nonstick pot, heat the oil over medium-high heat. Add the chicken and cook until lightly browned, 3 to 4 minutes per side. Remove from pot.

3   Add the leek to the pot and cook, stirring, until softened, about 1 minute. Add the eggplant, bell pepper, and garlic. Cook, stirring, until the vegetables start to look cooked, about 5 minutes.

4 Add the water, bay leaf, rosemary, and thyme to the pot; bring to a boil. Add the browned chicken pieces and return to the boil. Reduce heat and simmer, covered, 30 minutes, stirring occasionally.

5 Add the parsley, wine, and salt. Simmer, uncovered, 10 minutes longer or until sauce has thickened.

SERVES: 4

Diabetic Exchanges: 4¾ very lean meat; 2 vegetable; ½ fat

REDUCED FAT/SATURATED FAT/CHOLESTEROL: Use only breast meat.
Diabetic Exchanges: 1 very lean meat; 3 vegetable; ½ fat

REDUCED PROTEIN: Use only 2 chicken thighs or drumsticks and reserve the unused flour-pepper mixture. Follow recipe through step 5 then remove the chicken from the pot and cut from the bone; set aside. Toss 1 cup coarsely chopped portobello mushrooms, 1 cup cubed yellow squash, and 1 cup frozen artichoke hearts with the the remaining flour/pepper mixture. Add to the pot when you add the parsley, wine, and salt. Simmer, uncovered, 15 minutes longer or until the squash is tender. Return chicken to pot and cook 2 minutes longer or until chicken is heated through.
Diabetic Exchanges: 1 very lean meat; 3 vegetable; ½ fat

MENU SUGGESTIONS: Arugula Salad; Polenta (page 266); Sliced Ripe Pears

Entrées

MOM'S ROASTED CHICKEN

When I was growing up, Friday night meant our special family dinner: Chopped Liver, Fresh Radishes, Celery, and Sour Pickles, followed by Chicken Noodle Soup (the noodles have to be extra thin), then Roasted Chicken, Roasted Potatoes, Wilted Cucumber Salad, and finally Fruit Salad and maybe cookies. Now let's talk portion size. Seven servings of protein is a lot at one meal. However, I would be uncomfortable putting one chicken on the table for more than 8 people. So pace yourself—take only 4 ounces of chicken, and it will come out to 4 exchanges.

One 6-pound roasting chicken

2 cups chopped onions

3 tablespoons Hungarian sweet paprika

3 cloves garlic

½ teaspoon ground ginger

¼ teaspoon ground black pepper

Salt to taste

1 cup water

1   Preheat oven to 350°F.

2   Thoroughly rinse the chicken, removing any visible fat. In a large roasting pan, combine the onions, paprika, garlic, ginger, black pepper, and salt. Rub this mixture all over the chicken. Place the chicken breast side down and roast 40 minutes.

3   Turn the chicken breast side up. Add the water, stirring up any browned bits from the bottom. Roast 1½ hours longer or until juices run clear when chicken is pricked with a fork (or when the plastic thermometer pops up).

4   Let stand 10 minutes before carving. Skim the fat off the drippings and serve as gravy for the chicken.

SERVES: 8

Diabetic Exchanges: 4¼ very lean meat; 2¾ lean meat; ¾ vegetable; 1¼ fat

REDUCED CHOLESTEROL/FAT: Remove skin before serving.

Diabetic Exchanges: 7 very lean meat; ¾ vegetable; ¼ fat

MENU SUGGESTIONS: Fresh Radishes and Hearts of Celery; Chicken Consommé with Chopped Fresh Parsley; Wilted Cucumber Salad; Roasted Red Bliss Potatoes; Baked Apple (page 335).

HIGH: **protein, cholesterol, magnesium, phosphorus, potassium,** *carbohydrate*

CHICKEN CREOLE

I find this dish to be only mildly spicy, but you may want to omit the ground red pepper if you do not like spicy foods. You can make the lower-protein variation with either white or brown rice. Also, if you have only tomatoes that are packed in thick purée you might want to add ¼ cup of water to the pot when you add the tomatoes; another alternative is to use a can of stewed tomatoes.

> **2 pounds cut-up chicken pieces**
> **Salt to taste**
> **¼ teaspoon ground black pepper**
> **1 tablespoon all-purpose flour**
> **1 tablespoon vegetable oil**
> **1 cup chopped onion**
> **1 cup chopped green bell pepper**
> **1 cup chopped celery**
> **2 cloves garlic, minced**
> **½ teaspoon paprika**
> **¼ teaspoon chili powder**
> **⅛ teaspoon dried thyme**
> **⅛ teaspoon ground cloves**
> **⅛ teaspoon ground red pepper**
> **1 bay leaf**
> **One 14- or 15-ounce can whole peeled tomatoes**

(continued)

1   Remove skin from the chicken; rinse and pat dry. Season the chicken with the salt and pepper. Dredge the chicken lightly in the flour.

2   In a 5- or 6-quart nonstick pot, heat the oil over medium-high heat. Add the chicken and cook 3 to 4 minutes per side or until chicken is browned. Remove from pot.

3   Add the onion, green pepper, celery, and garlic to the pot. Cook, stirring, until slightly softened, about 2 to 3 minutes.

4   Stir in the paprika, chili, thyme, cloves, red pepper, and bay leaf. Add the tomatoes with the canning liquid, breaking up the tomatoes with the side of a spoon.

5   Return the chicken to the pot. Bring to a boil. Reduce heat and simmer, covered, 35 minutes. Discard bay leaf before serving.

SERVES: 4
Diabetic Exchanges: 5½ very lean meat; 2 vegetable; 1 fat

REDUCED SATURATED FAT/CHOLESTEROL/PROTEIN: Use ¾ pound skinless chicken pieces; increase chili powder to 1 teaspoon; omit the all-purpose flour. Skip steps 1 and 2; add the oil to the pot and cook the vegetables until softened, about 4 minutes.

For white rice: continue with step 4, stirring in 1 cup of water after you've added the tomatoes. Add the chicken to the pot and cook, covered, 10 minutes. Stir in ⅔ cup converted white rice and simmer, covered, 20 minutes. Discard bay leaf; remove the chicken from the pot; remove bone(s) and cut chicken into bite-size pieces. Stir chicken pieces into the rice.
Diabetic Exchanges: 1½ bread; 3 very lean meat; 2 vegetable; ¾ fat

For brown rice: continue with step 4, stirring in 1¼ cups of water after you've added the tomatoes. Add ⅔ cup long-grain brown rice when you add the chicken and simmer, covered, 55 minutes longer. Discard bay leaf; remove the chicken from the pot; remove bone(s) and cut chicken into bite-size pieces. Stir chicken pieces into the rice.
Diabetic Exchanges: 1½ bread; 3 very lean meat; 2 vegetable; ¾ fat

REDUCED SODIUM: Use sodium-free canned tomatoes.
Diabetic Exchanges: 5½ very lean meat; 2¼ vegetable, 1 fat

MENU SUGGESTIONS: Lettuce, Tomato, and Red Onion Salad; Steamed Broccoli; Flan (page 320)

CHICKEN *with* FORTY CLOVES *of* GARLIC

Not really 40, but with plenty! It's very important to bake this dish a long time with low heat to bring out the sweetness of the roasted garlic.

> **1 small head garlic (16 medium cloves)**
>
> **3 pounds chicken pieces**
>
> **¼ teaspoon dried rosemary, crumbled**
>
> **⅛ teaspoon dried thyme**
>
> **⅛ teaspoon ground black pepper**
>
> **Salt to taste**
>
> **⅓ cup dry white wine**
>
> **⅓ cup water**

1   Preheat oven to 300°F.

2   Separate the garlic cloves, but do not peel them.

3   Remove skin from the chicken; rinse and pat dry. Arrange the chicken pieces, flesh side down, in a 9-by-13-inch nonreactive (enamel, glass, or stainless steel) baking pan. Sprinkle with the garlic cloves, rosemary, thyme, pepper, and salt. Add the wine and water to the pan. Cover tightly with heavy-duty aluminum foil.

4   Place in preheated oven and bake 2 hours. Carefully lift a corner of the foil to release the steam. Place chicken on serving platter with any pan juices and the garlic cloves.

SERVES: 6

Diabetic Exchanges: 4¾ very lean meat; ¼ fat

MENU SUGGESTIONS: Broccoli Fennel Velvet Soup (page 48); Whole Wheat Couscous Pilaf (page 264); Mixed Green Salad; Fresh Orange Slices

CHICKEN CHASSEUR

This is the French version of chicken Cacciatore, with more mushrooms and less tomato.

> **2 pounds chicken pieces**
> **Salt to taste**
> **1½ tablespoons all-purpose flour**
> **⅛ teaspoon ground black pepper**
> **2 teaspoons olive oil**
> **2 cups sliced mushrooms**
> **¼ cup minced shallots**
> **¾ cup water**
> **¼ cup dry white wine**
> **2 tablespoons chopped fresh parsley**
> **½ teaspoon tarragon**
> **2 tablespoons tomato paste**

1 Remove skin from the chicken pieces; rinse and pat dry. Season with salt, if using.

2 On a piece of wax paper combine the flour and black pepper. Lightly dredge the chicken in the mixture.

3 In a 6-quart nonstick pot, heat the oil over medium-high heat. Add the chicken and cook until browned, about 3 minutes. Turn and cook on second side, about 3 minutes. Remove the chicken from the pot.

4 Add the mushrooms and shallots. Cook, stirring, until softened, about 2 minutes. Stir in the water, wine, parsley, and tarragon. Bring to a boil.

5 Return the chicken to the pot. Return to the boil; reduce heat and simmer, covered, 20 minutes. Stir in the tomato paste; cook, uncovered, 20 minutes or until chicken is cooked through and sauce has thickened.

SERVES: 4
Diabetic Exchanges: ¼ bread; 4¾ very lean meat; ¾ vegetable; ½ fat

REDUCED SATURATED FAT/PROTEIN/CHOLESTEROL/SODIUM: Reduce chicken to 1 pound; increase mushrooms to 4 cups; add 1 cup sliced carrots when you return the chicken to the pot; use low-sodium tomato paste.

Diabetic Exchanges: 2¼ very lean meat; 1½ vegetable; ½ fat

MENU SUGGESTIONS: Chiffonade of Spinach Salad; Whole Wheat Couscous Pilaf (page 264); Green Beans Almondine; Fresh Kumquats

---

HIGH: **protein, cholesterol, magnesium, phosphorus, potassium,** *carbohydrate*

LOW: *sodium*

CHICKEN GUMBO

"Real" chicken gumbo starts with a roux (butter and flour) slowly cooked until deeply browned and uses filé powder. This version doesn't do either, but it does taste good—very good.

> **2 pounds chicken pieces**
> **Salt to taste**
> **1 tablespoon all-purpose flour**
> **2 teaspoons vegetable oil**
> **¾ cup chopped onion**
> **¾ cup chopped green bell pepper**
> **½ cup chopped celery**
> **2 cloves garlic, minced**
> **One 14- or 15-ounce can whole peeled tomatoes, undrained**
> **¼ cup water**
> **¼ teaspoon dried oregano**
> **¼ teaspoon Tabasco**
> **¼ teaspoon ground black pepper**
> **1 bay leaf**
> **2 cups sliced okra**

1   Remove skin from the chicken, rinse, and pat dry; season with salt if using. Dredge the chicken in the flour.

2 In a 4-quart nonstick saucepan, heat the oil. Add the chicken and cook until browned, about 3 minutes. Turn and cook on second side, about 3 minutes. Remove the chicken from the pot.

3 Add the onion, green pepper, celery, and garlic. Cook, stirring, until slightly softened, about 3 minutes. Stir in the tomatoes and water, breaking up the tomatoes with a wooden spoon. Bring to a boil.

4 Return the chicken to the pot, and stir in the oregano, Tabasco, pepper, and bay leaf. Return to the boil; reduce heat and simmer, covered, 30 minutes. Stir in the okra and cook, uncovered, 10 minutes or until chicken is cooked through and sauce has thickened. Discard bay leaf before serving.

SERVES: 4

Diabetic Exchanges: 4¾ very lean meat; 2¼ vegetable, ¾ fat

REDUCED FAT/SATURATED FAT/PROTEIN/CHOLESTEROL: Reduce chicken to 1 pound; omit flour. Stir in 1 additional cup of water (to equal 1¼ cups of water) after you've added the tomatoes in step 4. Add ⅔ cup long-grain brown rice when you add the chicken and simmer, covered, 45 minutes. Stir in the okra, simmer 10 minutes longer. Discard bay leaf; remove the chicken from the pot; remove bone(s) and cut chicken into bite-size pieces. Stir chicken pieces into the rice.

Diabetic Exchanges: 1½ bread; 2¼ very lean meat; 2¼ vegetable; ½ fat

REDUCED SODIUM: Use low-sodium tomatoes.

Diabetic Exchanges: 4¾ very lean meat; 2½ vegetable, ¾ fat

MENU SUGGESTIONS: Crispy Bread; Caesar Salad; Maple-Glazed Bananas (page 331)

CHICKEN CURRY

Even if you are not on a low-protein diet, you may like the low-protein variation because it adds vegetables to the chicken curry.

> **2 pounds chicken pieces**
> **Salt to taste**
> **2 teaspoons vegetable oil**
> **⅔ cup chopped onion**
> **2 cloves garlic, minced**
> **1 tablespoon curry powder**
> **1 teaspoon ground turmeric**
> **½ teaspoon ground ginger**
> **½ teaspoon ground cinnamon**
> **⅛ teaspoon ground red pepper**
> **½ cup water**

1   Remove skin from the chicken; rinse and pat dry. Season with salt, if using.

2   In a 3-quart nonstick pot, heat the oil over medium-high heat. Add the onion and garlic; cook, stirring, until translucent, about 2 minutes. Stir in the curry powder, turmeric, ginger, cinnamon, and red pepper until absorbed. Stir in the water.

3   Add the chicken pieces and bring to a boil. Reduce heat and simmer, covered, 30 minutes. Uncover and simmer 10 minutes longer.

SERVES: 4
Diabetic Exchanges: 4¾ very lean meat; ½ vegetable; ¾ fat

REDUCED SATURATED FAT/PROTEIN/CHOLESTEROL: Use 1 pound chicken pieces, 4 cups cauliflower florets, ¼ cup peas; and increase water to ¾ cup. Add the vegetables after you have simmered the chicken for 15 minutes, then continue simmering as directed above.
Diabetic Exchanges: ½ bread; 2½ very lean meat; 1¼ vegetable; ½ fat

MENU SUGGESTIONS: Spicy Cucumber Yogurt Salad (page 282), Brown Rice Pilaf (page 258), Lettuce and Tomato Salad; Mango Slices

COQ *au* VIN

This classic French dish is usually made with bacon and butter, but this version is just as rich as any you've tasted. I like to use legs or thighs as they remain much moister than breast meat. If the mushrooms are large, cut them into quarters.

> **2 pounds chicken pieces**
>
> **Salt to taste**
>
> **2 tablespoons all-purpose flour**
>
> **½ teaspoon paprika**
>
> **¼ teaspoon ground black pepper**
>
> **⅛ teaspoon ground nutmeg**
>
> **1 tablespoon vegetable oil**
>
> **2 cups (8 ounces) mushrooms, halved**
>
> **1 cup chopped onion**
>
> **2 cloves garlic, minced**
>
> **½ cup dry red wine**
>
> **⅓ cup chopped fresh parsley**
>
> **¼ teaspoon dried rosemary**
>
> **⅛ teaspoon dried thyme**

1   Remove skin from the chicken; rinse and pat dry. Season with salt, if using.

2   On a piece of wax paper, combine the flour, paprika, pepper, and nutmeg. Dredge the chicken in the flour mixture.

3   In a 6-quart nonstick pot, heat the oil over medium-high heat. Add the chicken pieces and cook 3 minutes; turn and cook 3 minutes longer. Remove chicken from pot.

4   Reduce heat to medium. Add the mushrooms, onion, and garlic to the pot and cook, stirring, until slightly softened, about 2 minutes. Stir in the wine, parsley, rosemary, and thyme. Return the chicken to the pot. Bring to a boil.

5   Reduce heat and simmer, covered, 45 minutes or until chicken is tender.

SERVES: 4

Diabetic Exchanges: ¼ bread; 4¾ very lean meat; ¾ vegetable; 1¼ fat

REDUCED SATURATED FAT/PROTEIN/CHOLESTEROL: Use only 1 pound of chicken pieces. Increase the mushrooms to 3 cups (12 ounces). Add 1 (additional) teaspoon of oil to the pot before adding the onion. After 20 minutes of simmering add 1 cup of carrot chunks (1-inch pieces) to the pot, cover, and continue simmering. Ten minutes after adding the carrots, add 2 cups of zucchini chunks (1-inch pieces) and any remaining flour mixture to the pot. Simmer, covered, 15 minutes longer.

Diabetic Exchanges: ¼ bread; 2½ very lean meat; 1¼ vegetable; 1½ fat

MENU SUGGESTIONS: Onion Soup; Parslied Rice; Steamed Haricots Verts; Tomato and Scallion Salad; Poached Pears

Entrées

SOUTHERN-STYLE CHICKEN *and* RICE

I learned how to make this chicken dish from my friend Sylvia Woods. It's a little spicy; reduce the ground black pepper to ¼ or ½ teaspoon if you are not sure about spicy foods. If you can't find Old Bay Seasoning, use any Cajun spice mix (but omit the ground black pepper). If you are not fond of garlic powder, you can mince 3 to 4 cloves of garlic and add them when you add the onion and bell pepper.

> **2 teaspoons Old Bay Seasoning**
> **¾ teaspoon ground black pepper**
> **½ teaspoon garlic powder**
> **Salt to taste**
> **3 pounds chicken pieces**
> **2 teaspoons vegetable oil**
> **1 cup chopped onion**
> **½ cup finely chopped green bell pepper**
> **2 cups water**
> **1½ cups converted rice**

1   In a small bowl, combine the Old Bay Seasoning, black pepper, garlic powder, and salt. Remove the skin from the chicken. Sprinkle spice mixture over the chicken and let stand 20 minutes or longer in the refrigerator.

2   In a 6-quart pot, heat the oil over medium-high heat. Add the chicken with all the seasonings. Cook, turning frequently, until seared on the outside, about 8 minutes. Remove from pot. Add the onion and green bell pepper and cook, stirring, until slightly softened, about 2 minutes.

3   Return chicken to pot. Add the water and bring to a boil. Reduce heat and simmer, covered, 20 minutes. Add the rice and return to the boil. Reduce heat and simmer, covered, 20 to 25 minutes longer or until the rice has absorbed the liquids. Remove from heat.

4 Remove the chicken pieces from the pot. Using a fork and sharp knife, cut the chicken away from the bones into bite-size pieces. Return the chicken to the pot, discarding the bones. Stir the chicken into the rice.

SERVES: 6
Diabetic Exchanges: 2 bread; 4¾ very lean meat; ½ vegetable; ½ fat

REDUCED SODIUM: For the Old Bay Seasoning substitute ½ teaspoon poultry seasoning, ¼ teaspoon paprika, ¼ teaspoon dry mustard, ⅛ teaspoon ground ginger, ⅛ teaspoon ground allspice, ⅛ teaspoon ground cinnamon, and a pinch celery seed. Do not use any salt in the seasoning of the chicken.
Diabetic Exchanges: 2 bread; 4¾ very lean meat; ½ vegetable; ½ fat

REDUCED PROTEIN/FAT/SATURATED FAT/CHOLESTEROL: Use only 1 pound of chicken leg and increase the water to 2¼ cups. Cook in a 4-quart pot. After the rice has cooked 10 minutes, stir in 2 cups sliced yellow squash. Simmer 10–15 minutes longer. Makes 4 servings.
Diabetic Exchanges: 3¼ bread; 2¼ very lean meat; 1 vegetable; ½ fat

MENU SUGGESTIONS: Fresh Vegetable Soup; Southern-Style Collards and Kale (page 227); Tomato and Onion Salad; Fruit Salad

BARBECUE CHICKEN

Serve this chicken warm or cold. Because I prefer dark meat, I use only thighs and legs. The baking time is for small pieces; if you are using large pieces you may have to bake them a little longer. If you are using breasts, you might need to bake them a little less. You can also serve this sauce with other meats or fish.

> **2 pounds chicken pieces**
> **Salt to taste**
> **⅓ cup chopped onion**
> **¼ cup water**
> **3 tablespoons ketchup**
> **1 tablespoon tomato paste**
> **1 tablespoon molasses**
> **1 tablespoon cider vinegar**
> **1 teaspoon steak sauce**
> **1 teaspoon Worcestershire sauce**
> **1 clove garlic, minced**

1 Remove skin from the chicken; rinse and pat dry. Season with salt, if using.

2 Preheat oven to 350°F.

3 In a small saucepan, combine the onion, water, ketchup, tomato paste, molasses, vinegar, steak sauce, Worcestershire sauce, and garlic. Bring to a boil over medium-high heat. Reduce heat and simmer, uncovered, 5 minutes, stirring occasionally; set aside.

4 Place chicken in the baking dish and brush top with barbecue sauce. Bake 20 minutes, turn the chicken, and brush second side with barbecue sauce; bake 10 minutes longer. Brush the chicken pieces with barbecue sauce again and bake 5 to 10 minutes longer or until chicken is no longer pink in the center.

SERVES: 4

Diabetic Exchanges: ½ other carbohydrate; 4¾ very lean meat; ½ vegetable; ¼ fat

REDUCED SATURATED FAT/CHOLESTEROL: Use only white meat.

Diabetic Exchanges: ½ other carbohydrate; 5 very lean meat; ½ vegetable; ½ fat

REDUCED SODIUM: Use low-sodium steak sauce, ketchup, and tomato paste.

Diabetic Exchanges: ½ other carbohydrate; 4¾ very lean meat; ½ vegetable; ½ fat

MENU SUGGESTIONS: Cole Slaw; Potato Salad; Collard Greens; Poached Peaches

CHICKEN GAI YANG

I first tasted this at Teachers, once my favorite local restaurant. Teachers is gone but I can order it from my now favorite Vietnamese restaurant, Saigon Grill. I'm not sure the soy sauce and sesame oil are authentic ingredients, but they taste good.

> **2 pounds chicken pieces**
>
> **Salt to taste**
>
> **3 tablespoons chopped cilantro leaves (fresh coriander)**
>
> **2 tablespoons fresh lime juice**
>
> **1 teaspoon soy sauce**
>
> **3 cloves garlic, minced**
>
> **1 teaspoon sesame oil**
>
> **⅛ teaspoon red pepper flakes**

1   Preheat broiler.

2   Remove skin from the chicken; rinse and pat dry. Season with salt, if using.

3   In a medium bowl, combine cilantro, lime juice, soy sauce, garlic, sesame oil, and pepper flakes. Add chicken and let stand 10 minutes or longer in the refrigerator, turning once.

4   Place the chicken pieces on a broiler tray. Brush with marinade. Broil 4 to 5 minutes per side or until chicken is browned. Brush other side of chicken with marinade and broil 4 to 5 minutes longer or until chicken is browned and cooked through.

SERVES: 4
Diabetic Exchanges: 4¾ very lean meat; 1 fat

REDUCED FAT/SATURATED FAT/CHOLESTEROL: Omit the sesame oil; use only white meat.
Diabetic Exchanges: 5 very lean meat; ¼ fat

REDUCED SODIUM: Use low-sodium soy sauce.
Diabetic Exchanges: 4¾ very lean meat; 1 fat

MENU SUGGESTIONS: Marinated Cucumber Salad; Brown Rice with Sliced Scallions; Steamed Broccoli; Fresh Strawberries

CHICKEN *with* FENNEL *and* ALMONDS

Fennel has a bulb (which is the part you will cook) that resembles a potbellied celery with thick stalks and feathery fronds that resemble dill. The flavor is similar to a mild licorice. If you do not like licorice, you can substitute celery for the fennel.

> **1¼ pounds skinless and boneless chicken breast (2 medium breasts)**
> **¼ teaspoon ground black pepper**
> **Salt to taste**
> **3 tablespoons sliced almonds**
> **1 tablespoon olive oil, divided**
> **3 cups sliced fennel**
> **2 cloves garlic, minced**
> **2 tablespoons fresh lemon juice**
> **1 tablespoon Dijon mustard**
> **¼ cup chopped fresh parsley**
> **2 tablespoons chopped fennel fronds**

1   Cut the chicken into ½-inch-wide strips. Sprinkle with pepper and salt, if using; set aside.

2   In a large nonstick skillet, toast the almonds over medium heat until browned, about 2 to 3 minutes. Remove from skillet and set aside.

3   In the skillet heat 2 teaspoons of the oil over medium-high heat. Add the sliced fennel and cook, stirring, until slightly softened and browned in places, about 3 to 4 minutes. Remove from skillet; set aside.

4   Add the remaining 1 teaspoon olive oil to the skillet. Add the chicken and garlic; cook, stirring, until chicken is browned on the outside and no longer pink in the center, about 4 minutes. Add the lemon juice and mustard to the skillet, and cook, stirring, until the chicken is coated.

5   Add the sliced fennel, parsley, and fennel fronds to the skillet; cook, stirring until warmed, about 1 minute. Sprinkle with the toasted almonds.

(continued)

SERVES: 4

Diabetic Exchanges: 4¾ very lean meat; ¾ vegetable; 1¼ fat

REDUCED FAT/SATURATED FAT/PROTEIN/CHOLESTEROL: Use only ¾ pound chicken breast, and increase the fennel to 5 cups.

Diabetic Exchanges: 3 very lean meat; 1½ vegetable; 1¼ fat

MENU SUGGESTIONS: Lentil Soup; Sautéed Baby Pattypan Squash or Sautéed Sliced Yellow Squash; Romaine Salad; Sliced Fresh Strawberries

HIGH: **protein, cholesterol, magnesium, phosphorus, potassium, sodium, *fiber, iron***
LOW: **saturated fat, cholesterol**

CHICKEN *with* MUNG BEAN SPROUTS

Look for black bean sauce in the Asian section of your local supermarket. It's a thick and salty sauce—a little bit goes a long long way. Serve this dish over brown or white rice.

⅔ cup chicken or vegetable broth

1½ tablespoons soy sauce

1 tablespoon mirin (rice wine) or dry sherry

1½ tablespoons cornstarch

2 teaspoons black bean sauce

About 1 pound skinless and boneless chicken breasts (2 breasts)

1 tablespoon vegetable oil

½ cup 2-inch scallion pieces (white and green parts)

2 large cloves garlic, minced

8 cups mung bean sprouts

1   In a small bowl, stir together the broth, soy sauce, mirin, cornstarch, and black bean sauce.

2   Cut the chicken into strips ¼ inch wide by 3 inches long.

3   In a large nonstick skillet, heat the oil over high heat. Add the scallion and garlic and cook, stirring, about 10 seconds. Add the chicken and sprouts. Cook, stirring, until chicken is cooked through, about 4 minutes.

4 Add the sauce and cook, stirring, until thickened, about 1 to 2 minutes longer.

SERVES: 4

Diabetic Exchanges: ¼ bread; 4½ lean meat; 2¾ vegetable; 1¼ fat

REDUCED SATURATED FAT/PROTEIN/CHOLESTEROL: Substitute 1 cake of firm tofu, cut into strips, for the chicken; cook until sprouts are cooked through and tofu is heated, about 2 minutes.
Diabetic Exchanges: ¼ bread; 1½ very lean meat; 2¾ vegetable; 1½ fat

REDUCED SODIUM: Use reduced-sodium broth and soy sauce; reduce black bean sauce to 1 teaspoon.
Diabetic Exchanges: ¼ bread; 4 protein; 2¾ vegetable; 1 fat

MENU SUGGESTIONS: Mandarin Soup; Steamed Brown Rice; Fresh Litchi Nuts

Entrées

CHICKEN *with* ROASTED RED PEPPER–GARLIC SAUCE

Homemade roasted red peppers are much sweeter than the ones you buy in a jar, although you can use the jarred ones in recipes when you're in a pinch. See page 26 for how to "roast" peppers. You can use this method with only one or as many as peppers as can comfortably fit on a pan that fits under your broiler. You can also roast any color pepper you like. If you don't have a Shake on hand you can use seasoned salt instead or Mrs. Dash.

> **⅔ cup roasted red pepper (2 medium red peppers, roasted)**
> **⅔ cup chicken or vegetable broth or water**
> **½ teaspoon sugar**
> **¼ teaspoon dried oregano**
> **2 cloves garlic, minced**
> **1 pound skinless and boneless chicken breast**
> **Cajun or Mexican Shake (see pages 69–70) or salt to taste**
> **2 teaspoons olive oil**

1   Place the roasted pepper in a blender container with the broth, sugar, oregano, and garlic. Cover and blend until smooth; set aside.

2   Place the chicken breasts between 2 pieces of wax paper. Using a meat pounder or other heavy object, pound the meat until ¼ inch thick all over. Season with Cajun or Mexican Shake, salt, or other seasoning.

3   In a large nonstick skillet, heat the oil over medium-high heat. Add as much of the chicken as will fit comfortably in the pan (if necessary, cook in 2 batches as you want the chicken to be sautéed, not steamed) and cook 2 to 3 minutes or until browned on bottom. Turn the chicken and cook 2 to 3 minutes longer or until cooked through. Remove to serving platter.

4   Add the red pepper sauce to the skillet; cook, stirring up the browned bits from the bottom of the pan. Heat about 1 minute or until sauce is warmed. Serve chicken with sauce.

Diabetic Exchanges: 3¾ very lean meat; ¼ vegetable; ½ fat

REDUCED SATURATED FAT/PROTEIN/CHOLESTEROL: Cook only ½ pound chicken breast (but the entire red pepper sauce recipe). Cut the chicken into strips and add 2 cups cooked whole wheat pasta (or 4 cups cooked spaghetti squash) and the chicken to the skillet with the sauce. Cook, stirring, until heated through, about 1 minute.
Diabetic Exchanges (with pasta): ¼ bread; 2 very lean meat; ¼ vegetable; ½ fat
Diabetic Exchanges (with spaghetti squash): 2 very lean meat; 2¼ vegetable; ½ fat

REDUCED SODIUM: Use salt-free Shake, homemade roasted red pepper, and low-sodium broth.
Diabetic Exchanges: 3¾ very lean meat; ¾ vegetable; ½ fat

MENU SUGGESTIONS: Crudités with Yogurt Dip; Broth-Sautéed Summer Squash; Salad of Baby Romaine and Grape Tomatoes; Fresh Apricots

MEXICAN CHICKEN *with* ORANGE *and* TOMATO SAUCE

This odd combination of ingredients makes a fresh and delicious sauce. For a little extra zip, increase the ground red pepper or add some minced jalapeño peppers; you can also season the chicken cutlets with Mexican Shake before cooking them.

> **1 pound skinless and boneless chicken breast**
>
> **Salt to taste or Mexican Shake (page 69)**
>
> **2 teaspoons vegetable oil**
>
> **1½ cups chopped tomatoes**
>
> **¾ cup orange segments, chopped**
>
> **1½ tablespoons chopped cilantro leaves (fresh coriander)**
>
> **¾ teaspoon ground cumin**
>
> **⅛ teaspoon ground red pepper**

1   Place the chicken breasts between 2 pieces of wax paper. Using a meat pounder or other heavy object, pound the meat until ¼ inch thick all over. Season with salt or Mexican Shake, if using.

2   In a large nonstick skillet, heat the oil over medium-high heat. Add as much of the chicken as will fit comfortably into the pan (if necessary, cook in 2 batches—you want the chicken to be sautéed, not steamed), and cook 2 to 3 minutes or until browned on bottom. Turn the chicken and cook 2 to 3 minutes longer or until cooked through. Remove to serving platter.

3   Add the tomatoes, orange, cilantro, cumin, and pepper to the skillet. Cook, stirring, until tomatoes are slightly softened, about 2 minutes. Serve chicken with sauce.

SERVES: 4
Diabetic Exchanges: 3¾ very lean meat; ¼ fruit; ¾ vegetable; ½ fat

REDUCED CARBOHYDRATE: Omit the orange and increase the chopped tomatoes to 2 cups.
Diabetic Exchanges: 3¾ very lean meat; ¾ vegetable; ½ fat

MENU SUGGESTIONS: Baked Tortilla Chips; Salsa; Mexican Rice; Cucumber Salad; Fresh Mango

SAUTÉED CHICKEN BREASTS *with* WILD RICE *and* MUSHROOMS

If it is not cranberry season, and you can't find frozen cranberries, you can substitute dried cranberries or chopped dried apricots but the carbohydrate count will be higher. If you don't have wild rice you can use brown rice.

> **1 tablespoon vegetable oil, divided**
>
> **1 pound skinless and boneless chicken breast, cut into ½-inch strips (1 large breast)**
>
> **2 tablespoons minced shallots**
>
> **3 cups coarsely chopped mushrooms**
>
> **2 cups cooked wild rice**
>
> **⅓ cup chopped cranberries**
>
> **¼ cup chopped fresh parsley**
>
> **¼ teaspoon ground black pepper**
>
> **Salt to taste**

1   In a large nonstick skillet, heat 2 teaspoons of the oil over high heat. Add the chicken strips and shallots; cook, stirring, until cooked through, about 3 to 4 minutes; remove from skillet.

2   Add the remaining 1 teaspoon of oil to the skillet. Add the mushrooms and cook, stirring, until softened, about 2 minutes.

3   Stir in the rice, cranberries, parsley, pepper, and salt. Return chicken strips to skillet; cook, stirring, until the chicken and rice is heated through.

SERVES: 4
Diabetic Exchanges: 1½ bread; 3¾ protein; 1 vegetable; ¾ fat

REDUCED PROTEIN: Omit the chicken; add 2 cups seitan when you stir in the rice.
Diabetic Exchanges: 1¾ bread; 1 lean meat; 1 vegetable; ¾ fat

MENU SUGGESTIONS: Kohlrabi and Jicama Slaw (page 294); Sautéed Fennel; Fresh Strawberries

SAUTÉED CHICKEN BREASTS
with ORANGE MUSTARD SAUCE

If you keep a few boneless chicken breasts in your freezer, you will have the ingredients on hand for this easy-to-prepare recipe—making it ideal for a delicious, last-minute dinner.

3 tablespoons white wine or vegetable broth

1½ tablespoons honey mustard

1½ tablespoons orange juice concentrate (undiluted)

1½ teaspoons minced ginger or ¼ teaspoon ground ginger

¼ teaspoon ground black pepper

2 teaspoons olive oil

1 pound skinless and boneless chicken breast, cut into ½-inch strips (1 large breast)

2 cloves garlic, minced

Salt to taste

1   In a small bowl, combine the wine, mustard, orange juice concentrate, ginger, and pepper; set aside.

2   In a large, nonstick skillet, heat the oil over high heat. Add only enough of the chicken strips to cook in a single layer to the skillet, cooking in batches if necessary; add garlic and cook until browned on each side, about 4 to 5 minutes altogether. Remove from skillet to serving plate. Cook remaining chicken strips if they did not all fit into the skillet; add to serving plate.

3   Deglaze the pan using the mustard-orange mixture, scraping up all the browned bits in the pan. Cook, stirring, about 30 seconds or until the sauce is bubbly all over. Pour over chicken.

SERVES: 4

Diabetic Exchanges: ¼ other carbohydrate; 3¾ very lean meat; ¼ fruit; ¾ fat

REDUCED SATURATED FAT/PROTEIN/CHOLESTEROL: Use only ½ pound of chicken. Increase oil to 1 tablespoon. Julienne 3 cups of one or any combination of the following: parsnip, carrot, sweet potato, butternut squash. In a large skillet, heat 2 teaspoons of the oil. Add the vegetables and cook, stirring, until they are cooked to desired texture, about 5 to 8 minutes; remove from skillet. Heat the remaining 1 teaspoon oil. Cook chicken and garlic as directed above. Deglaze pan with sauce. Return vegetables and chicken to pan and stir until coated with sauce. Season with salt if using.

Diabetic Exchanges (parsnip): ¾ bread; ¼ other carbohydrate, 2 very lean meat; ¼ fruit; ¾ fat

Diabetic Exchanges (carrot): ¼ other carbohydrate; 2 very lean meat; 2 vegetable; ¼ fruit; ¾ fat

Diabetic Exchanges (sweet potato): 1¼ bread; ¼ other carbohydrate; 2 very lean meat; ¼ fruit; ¾ fat

Diabetic Exchanges (butternut squash): ¼ other carbohydrate; 2 very lean meat; 2 vegetable; ¼ fruit; ¾ fat

MENU SUGGESTIONS: Mesclun Salad; Baked Sweet Potato; Steamed Haricots Verts; Fresh Strawberries

CHICKEN BREASTS
with GRAPEFRUIT SAUCE

There was a time when grapefruits were so sour your mouth would water and your face would scrunch just thinking of them. Now the growers are so successful at growing sweet grapefruits, you have to add lemon to the grapefruit juice to give this recipe the tartness I was looking for.

½ cup grapefruit juice

2 tablespoons fresh lemon juice

1 teaspoon grapefruit rind

½ teaspoon ground cardamom

¼ teaspoon ground black pepper

1 pound skinless and boneless chicken breast, cut into ½-inch strips (1 large breast)

1 tablespoon olive oil

2 cloves garlic, minced

2 tablespoons water

Salt to taste

1   In a medium bowl, combine the grapefruit and lemon juices, grapefuit rind, cardamom, and pepper. Add the chicken and let stand 20 minutes or longer in the refrigerator.

2   In a large, nonstick skillet, heat the oil over high heat. Add the chicken strips and garlic; cook until browned on each side, about 4 to 5 minutes altogether; remove from skillet to serving plate.

3   Deglaze the pan using the grapefruit mixture and water, scraping up all the browned bits in the pan. Cook, stirring, about 30 seconds or until the sauce is bubbly all over. Stir in salt, if using. Pour over chicken.

SERVES: 4

Diabetic Exchanges: 3¾ very lean meat; ¼ fruit; ¾ fat

REDUCED SATURATED FAT/PROTEIN/CHOLESTEROL: Use only ½ pound of chicken. Julienne 2 cups of snowpeas, ½ cup of carrot, and ½ cup jicama. In a large skillet, heat 2 teaspoons of the oil. Add the vegetables and cook, stirring, until they are cooked to desired texture, about 3 to 4 minutes; remove from skillet. Heat the remaining 1 teaspoon oil, and cook chicken and garlic as directed above; remove from pan. Deglaze pan with sauce. Season with salt if using.

SERVES: 4

Diabetic Exchanges: ¼ bread; 2 very lean meat; ¼ fruit; ½ vegetable; ¾ fat

MENU SUGGESTIONS: Arugula Salad; Brown Rice; Steamed Broccoli Florets; Poached Pear Slices

---

HIGH: **protein, cholesterol, magnesium, phosphorus, potassium**

LOW: **saturated fat, carbohydrate, fiber, *calcium, sodium***

GRILLED CHICKEN BREAST *with* MUSTARD DILL SAUCE

This is a very basic grilled chicken recipe. It makes an excellent sandwich filler or salad topper. The sauce is also a suitable dip for crudités. If you do not have a grill, heat a little oil in a non-stick skillet and cook the chicken on top of the stove. Don't broil it or it will be dry.

> **1 pound chicken cutlets (breast)**
> **1 tablespoon olive oil**
> **2 cloves garlic, minced**
> **½ teaspoon paprika**
> **¼ teaspoon ground pepper**
> **Salt to taste**

For the sauce (²⁄₃ cup)

> **2 tablespoons snipped fresh dill**
> **1 tablespoon Dijon mustard**
> **1 teaspoon prepared white horseradish**
> **¼ teaspoon Tabasco**
> **⅛ teaspoon Worcestershire sauce**
> **½ cup plain yogurt**

(continued)

1   Place each chicken cutlet between 2 pieces of wax paper and using a heavy weight (such as a meat pounder or the bottom of a skillet), pound until ¼ inch thick. Remove from the wax paper.

2   In a small bowl, combine the olive oil, garlic, paprika, and pepper. Lightly brush the top of each cutlet with some of this mixture. Sprinkle with salt, if using. Stack the cutlets one on top of the other and let stand 20 minutes or longer in the refrigerator.

3   Preheat grill. Cook the chicken cutlets 2 to 3 minutes per side or until cooked through and no longer pink in the middle.

4   For the sauce: in a small bowl, stir together the dill, mustard, horseradish, Tabasco, and Worcestershire sauce; fold in the yogurt. Serve each chicken breast topped with a quarter of the sauce.

SERVES: 4

Diabetic Exchanges: 3¾ very lean meat; 1 fat

REDUCED FAT: Reduce oil to 2 teaspoons; use nonfat yogurt.

Diabetic Exchanges: 3¾ very lean meat; ½ fat

MENU SUGGESTIONS: V-8 Juice; Sliced Cucumber Salad; Garlic Sautéed Spinach; Angel Food Cake

HIGH: **protein, cholesterol, phosphorus, sodium,** *calcium, iron, magnesium*

LOW: **fat, saturated fat, carbohydrate, fiber, calcium,** *cholesterol*

CHICKEN YAKITORI

This chicken dish is popular even with people who don't usually eat Japanese food, and the best part is that it's easy to prepare at home.

> **1 pound skinless and boneless chicken breast**
>
> **2 tablespoons soy sauce**
>
> **1 tablespoon mirin or dry sherry**
>
> **2 teaspoons minced ginger**
>
> **1 teaspoon vegetable oil**
>
> **1 teaspoon sugar**
>
> **2 cloves garlic, minced**

1 Cut the chicken into 1-inch cubes.

2 In a large bowl, stir together the soy sauce, mirin, ginger, oil, sugar, and garlic. Add the chicken and let stand 20 minutes or longer in the refrigerator.

3 Preheat broiler. String the chicken on eight 6-inch skewers. Cook 2 to 3 minutes or until chicken is browned. Brush with any remaining marinade and cook on second side until cooked through.

SERVES: 4

Diabetic Exchanges: 4 very lean meat; ¼ fat

REDUCED PROTEIN: Substitute a 15-ounce cake of firm tofu, cut into cubes, for the chicken.
Diabetic Exchanges: ½ bread; 2¼ lean meat; ¼ fat

REDUCED SODIUM: Use low-sodium soy sauce.
Diabetic Exchanges: ¼ bread; 3½ very lean meat; ¼ fat

MENU SUGGESTIONS: Miso Soup; Marinated Carrot and Cucumber Salad; Sticky Rice; Peach Slices

GRILLED CHICKEN KEBABS *with* LEMON, THYME, *and* ROSEMARY

The vegetables take longer to grill than the chicken so I string them on separate skewers. I serve one vegetable skewer and one chicken skewer to each person. These kebabs are just as good served cold. When I use wooden skewers for this recipe I soak them in water at least one hour to prevent them from burning. But don't worry if they do char, it won't affect the food.

> **1 pound skinless and boneless chicken breast**
> **1½ tablespoons fresh lemon juice**
> **1 tablespoon olive oil**
> **1 teaspoon Dijon mustard**
> **2 cloves garlic, minced**
> **½ teaspoon finely chopped fresh rosemary or ¼ teaspoon dried rosemary**
> **¼ teaspoon chopped fresh thyme leaves or ⅛ teaspoon dried thyme**
> **⅛ teaspoon ground black pepper**
> **1 cup red and/or green bell pepper cubes (1-inch pieces)**
> **1 medium onion, cut into 8 wedges**
> **Salt to taste**

1   Cut the chicken breast into 1-inch cubes.

2   In a large bowl, combine the lemon juice, olive oil, mustard, garlic, rosemary, thyme, and pepper. Add chicken and vegetables; toss until coated. Sprinkle with salt, if using, and let stand 20 minutes or longer in the refrigerator. String the chicken pieces on four 6-inch or 8-inch skewers and the vegetables on four 8-inch skewers.

3   Preheat grill or broiler. Line a pan with foil and grease with oil. Place the vegetable skewers in the pan and cook 4 minutes. Turn the vegetable kebabs and add the chicken kebabs to the pan. Cook the chicken 2 to 3 minutes per side or until cooked through and no longer pink in the middle (don't turn the vegetable kebabs when you turn the chicken).

SERVES: 4

Diabetic Exchanges: 3¾ very lean meat; ¾ vegetable; ¾ fat

REDUCED PROTEIN: Use only half the chicken; increase red peppers to 2 cups and add 2 cups sliced zucchini.

Diabetic Exchanges: 2 very lean meat; 1 vegetable; ¾ fat

MENU SUGGESTIONS: Gazpacho Variation (page 65); Cooked Brown or White Rice; Arugula Salad; Mini Pavlovas (page 330)

CHICKEN *en* BROCHETTE *with* ORANGE MARMALADE *and* SHERRY MARINADE

Try to find metal skewers that are square instead of round—the chicken and vegetables will stay in place better. Don't make the mistake of turning the cooked brochettes with your unprotected hands—the metal skewers get HOT!!! Use potholders, no matter how clumsy they may feel.

1¼ pounds skinless and boneless chicken breast

1 medium mild onion (about 10 ounces), such as Vidalia or Wala Wala

⅓ cup sweet orange marmalade, divided

1 tablespoon dry sherry, divided

1 teaspoon Dijon mustard

¾ teaspoon low sodium soy sauce, divided

1 clove garlic, minced

¼ teaspoon ground ginger

Salt and pepper to taste

1 Cut the chicken and onion into 1½-inch chunks.

2 In a large bowl, stir together ¼ cup of the marmalade, 2 teaspoons of the sherry, the mustard, ½ teaspoon of the soy sauce, garlic, and ginger. Add the chicken and toss with the marinade. Add the onion and toss to coat. Let stand at least 20 minutes or longer in the refrigerator.

3 Heat grill or broiler.

4 String the onion and chicken pieces alternately onto four 12-inch skewers; brush with the marinade; sprinkle with salt and pepper if desired. Place the skewers on the grill or across the top edges of a 9-by-13-inch baking pan lined with foil. Cook the chicken 4 inches from the heat 4 minutes per side until the chicken is cooked through.

5 While the chicken is cooking, in a small bowl combine the remaining orange marmalade (1 tablespoon plus 1 teaspoon), 1 teaspoon sherry, and ¼ teaspoon soy sauce. Microwave on high for 30 seconds or until the marmalade has melted. Using a clean basting brush, brush the cooked brochettes with the heated glaze. (If you do not have a microwave, just combine the glaze in a small saucepan and bring to a boil over high heat.)

SERVES: 4 (1 skewer per person)
Diabetic Exchanges: 1 other carbohydrate; 4¾ very lean meat; 1 vegetable

REDUCED PROTEIN/SODIUM: Use only ¾ pound chicken breast; omit soy sauce. Prepare recipe as written. Add peeled sweet potato (12 ounces), cut into pieces, and 1 large green bell pepper (10 ounces), cut into pieces, to the marinade with the chicken and onion. String the vegetables alternately on skewers with the chicken pieces. Cook as directed above.
Diabetic Exchanges: 1 bread; 1 other carbohydrate; 2¾ very lean meat; 2 vegetable

MENU SUGGESTIONS: Two-Cabbage Salad; Wheat Berries with Scallions; Zucchini Sauté; Sliced Strawberries

Entrées

STUFFED CHICKEN BREASTS *with* SPINACH *and* FETA CHEESE

Presentation of this dish is quite lovely; the pinwheel of chicken and spinach slices arranged on a platter looks very impressive. Don't forget to spoon the cooking liquid over the slices.

> **2 teaspoons olive oil**
>
> **1 tablespoon minced shallot**
>
> **1 package frozen chopped spinach, thawed and drained**
>
> **½ cup crumbled feta cheese**
>
> **2 tablespoons plain dry bread crumbs**
>
> **½ teaspoon dried oregano**
>
> **⅛ teaspoon dried thyme**
>
> **⅛ teaspoon ground pepper**
>
> **Salt to taste**
>
> **1¼ pounds boneless and skinless chicken breast (2 whole breasts, halved)**
>
> **Paprika to taste**
>
> **2 tablespoons water**
>
> **2 tablespoons white wine**

1   Preheat oven to 350°F.

2   In a medium nonstick skillet, heat the oil over medium-high heat. Add the shallot and cook, stirring, until translucent, about 30 seconds. Remove from heat. Stir in the spinach, feta, bread crumbs, oregano, thyme, pepper, and salt.

3   Pound the chicken breasts between 2 pieces of wax paper until ¼ inch thick. Remove wax paper. Place ¼ of the spinach mixture on each chicken breast. Spread to within ¼ inch of the edge of the breast. Roll starting at the pointy bottom. Fasten with toothpicks.

4   Place the breasts in a 9-inch-square baking pan. Lightly sprinkle paprika over the rolls. Pour the water and wine into the baking pan. Cover with aluminum foil and bake 25 to 30 minutes or until cooked through.

5   Cut the rolled chicken breasts crosswise into ½-inch slices. Arrange on serving platter, pouring the cooking liquid over the sliced rolls.

SERVES: 4

Diabetic Exchanges: ¼ bread; 4¾ very lean protein; ½ lean meat; ½ vegetable; 1¼ fat

REDUCED SODIUM: Omit the feta cheese.

Diabetic Exchanges: ¼ bread; 4¾ very lean meat; ½ vegetable; ½ fat

MENU SUGGESTIONS: Minted Pea Soup; Tomato and Onion Salad; Steamed Asparagus; Bread Pudding

CHICKEN POT PIE

This is a great thing to do with leftover chicken. It's homey and filling and much better (and healthier) than the pies you find in the freezer case of your supermarket.

⅓ cup plus 1½ tablespoons all-purpose flour, divided

Salt to taste

2 tablespoons butter or margarine

2 teaspoons water

2 teaspoons vegetable oil

1 cup coarsely chopped celery

1 cup sliced mushrooms

½ cup chopped onion

½ cup chopped zucchini

½ cup chopped carrot

1 clove garlic, minced

1 cup chicken or vegetable broth

2 cups cubed cooked chicken

¼ cup fresh or frozen peas

¼ cup chopped fresh parsley

2 tablespoons snipped fresh dill

⅛ teaspoon ground black pepper

1 Preheat oven to 375°F.

2 In a medium bowl, mix together ⅓ cup of the flour and salt, if using. Using a pastry cutter or two sharp knives, cut the butter into the flour until mixture resembles coarse cornmeal. Sprinkle the water over the surface of the flour and stir until mixture forms a ball. Cover and chill 20 minutes.

3 In a large nonstick skillet, heat the oil over medium-high heat. Add the celery, mushrooms, onion, zucchini, carrot, and garlic; cook, stirring, until vegetables are slightly softened, about 3 minutes. Stir in the remaining 1½ tablespoons flour until absorbed. Stir in the broth; cook, stirring, until mixture has thickened.

4   Stir in the chicken, peas, parsley, dill, pepper, and additional salt, if using. Spoon into a 1½-quart baking dish (a casserole or soufflé dish works well).

5   Roll the dough out between two pieces of wax paper until 1 inch larger than the circumference of the baking dish. Lift carefully and place over chicken mixture. Prick with a fork to vent. Bake 40 minutes or until the crust is golden and the filling is heated through.

SERVES: 4
Diabetic Exchanges: ¾ bread; 3 very lean meat; 1½ vegetable; 2 fat

REDUCED PROTEIN: Use only 1 cup cubed chicken; increase mushrooms to 2 cups sliced mushrooms; when you sauté the onion, increase zucchini to 1 cup and peas to ½ cup.
Diabetic Exchanges: ¾ bread; 1½ very lean meat; 2 vegetable; 2 fat

REDUCED SODIUM: Use low-sodium broth, fresh peas cooked in unsalted water, and unsalted butter.
Diabetic Exchanges: ¾ bread; 3 very lean meat; 1½ vegetable; 1¾ fat

MENU SUGGESTIONS: Chicken Soup; Mixed Green Salad; Chocolate Pudding

Entrées

TURKEY FAJITAS

These make a great last-minute meal. They do not take long to make. You can prepare the filling in advance and just reheat when you are ready; and you can use anything you have on hand. Of course, chicken is just as good as turkey—or you could substitute shrimp or tofu for the poultry and use julienned zucchini or yellow squash instead of or in addition to the peppers and onions.

> ½ **pound turkey cutlets**
> 1 **tablespoon vegetable oil, divided**
> 1 **tablespoon lime juice**
> 1 **tablespoon chopped cilantro leaves (fresh coriander)**
> 1½ **teaspoons chili powder**
> ½ **teaspoon oregano**
> ½ **teaspoon ground cumin**
> 2 **large cloves garlic, minced**
> **Salt to taste**
> 1 **cup julienned red bell pepper**
> 1 **cup julienned yellow bell pepper**
> 1 **cup sliced onion**
> 4 **(7-inch) flour tortillas**
> ¼ **cup salsa (homemade, page 24, or store-bought)**

1   Cut the turkey into ¼-inch-thick strips; place in a medium bowl.

2   In another medium bowl, stir together 2 teaspoons of the oil, the lime juice, cilantro, chili powder, oregano, cumin, garlic, and salt. Remove 2 teaspoons of the chili mixture and add to the bowl with the turkey; toss. Add the vegetables to the remaining chili mixture in the bowl and toss to coat; let marinate 15 minutes or longer in the refrigerator.

3   In a large nonstick skillet, heat the remaining 1 teaspoon oil over medium-high heat. Cook the turkey 4 minutes, stirring constantly, until no longer pink in the center; remove from pan. Add the vegetables and cook, stirring, until slightly softened, about 3 minutes or to desired doneness.

4 Warm the tortillas on a grill or in an oven or microwave oven. Place a quarter of the turkey in the center of each tortilla, top with a quarter of the vegetables, then with 1 tablespoon salsa. Fold one side over the vegetables, then roll to form a tube.

SERVES: 4

Diabetic Exchanges: 1¾ bread; 1¾ very lean meat; 1½ vegetable; 1½ fat

REDUCED SATURATED FAT/PROTEIN/CHOLESTEROL: Use 6 ounces baked tofu (you can use barbecue- or Mexican-flavored, if you like) instead of the turkey, cut into long strips.
Diabetic Exchanges: 1¾ bread; ½ lean meat; 1½ vegetable; 1¼ fat

REDUCED CARBOHYDRATE: Omit the tortilla and serve as stir-fry.

SERVES: 2

Diabetic Exchanges: 4 very lean meat; 2¾ vegetable; 1½ fat

MENU SUGGESTIONS: Gazpacho (page 65); Chopped Salad; Sliced Mango

Entrées

TURKEY PICADILLO

I used to make picadillo with ground beef, but found that turkey is just as good, and better for you. The reduced-protein variation doesn't use any turkey at all, but substitutes cooked bulgur—a good choice for any vegetarians in the household, too.

1 pound ground turkey

1 cup chopped onion

½ cup finely chopped green bell pepper

3 cloves garlic, minced

¼ teaspoon dried oregano

⅛ teaspoon ground cloves (or more to taste)

3 cups chopped tomatoes

½ cup water

¼ cup tomato paste

15 small pimiento-stuffed olives, sliced

¼ cup raisins

⅛ teaspoon ground red pepper

2 teaspoons distilled white vinegar

Salt to taste

1   In a large nonstick skillet, cook the turkey with the onion, green pepper, and garlic over medium-high heat until the turkey is no longer pink, about 6 minutes. Stir in the oregano and cloves.

2   Stir in the tomatoes, water, tomato paste, olives, raisins, and ground red pepper.

3   Cook, stirring occasionally, for 15 minutes. Stir in the vinegar and salt, if using, and cook until heated through.

SERVES: 4

Diabetic Exchanges: 2¾ lean meat; ½ fruit; 2¾ vegetable; ½ fat

REDUCED SODIUM: Omit the olives and use low-sodium tomato paste.
Diabetic Exchanges: 2¾ lean meat; ½ fruit; 2¾ vegetable; ¼ fat

REDUCED PROTEIN: In 2 teaspoons of olive oil over medium-high heat, sauté the onion, green pepper, and garlic until slightly softened, about 2 minutes. Cook according to recipe until the tomato sauce has thickened, about 10 minutes. Add 1½ cups cooked bulgur to the sauce and cook, stirring, until heated through, about 3 minutes.
Diabetic Exchanges: ¾ bread; ½ fruit; 2¾ vegetable; ¾ fat

MENU SUGGESTIONS: V-8 juice; Brown Rice with Scallion; Cucumber and Red Pepper Salad; Fresh Pineapple

Entrées

TWENTY-MINUTE TURKEY BLACK BEAN CHILI

Who says diabetics don't know how to party? This chili is easy, quick, and divine! If you don't have espresso powder, you can use plain instant coffee—or just skip it entirely. You can use pinto beans or kidney beans instead of the black beans—or no beans at all. Serve this with chopped onions, or sliced scallions, yogurt or sour cream, and/or shredded Cheddar cheese—or with nothing at all!

> 1¼ pounds ground turkey
>
> 1 cup chopped onion
>
> 2 cloves garlic, minced
>
> 3 tablespoons mild chili powder
>
> 1 teaspoon ground cumin
>
> ½ teaspoon dried oregano
>
> 1½ cups cooked (from dried or canned, drained) black beans
>
> ¾ cup water
>
> One 8-ounce can tomato sauce
>
> One 4- to 5-ounce can chopped chilies (including canning liquid)
>
> 2 tablespoons tomato paste
>
> 1 bay leaf
>
> ½ teaspoon sugar
>
> ¼ teaspoon instant espresso or coffee (decaffeinated, if desired)
>
> Salt to taste

1   In a large nonstick skillet, cook the turkey, onion, and garlic over medium-high heat, crumbling the turkey until it is no longer pink, about 7 minutes.

2   Stir in the chili powder, cumin, and oregano. Stir in the beans, water, tomato sauce, chilies, tomato paste, bay leaf, sugar, espresso, and salt.

3   Cook, stirring occasionally, until the mixture has thickened, about 10 minutes; discard bay leaf before serving.

SERVES: 6

Diabetic Exchanges: ½ bread; 2½ lean meat; 1¾ vegetable; ¼ fat

REDUCED PROTEIN: Omit turkey; sauté the onion and garlic in 1 tablespoon vegetable oil. Use only 2 tablespoons of chili powder and ½ can of chilies. Add 1 tablespoon molasses. Continue with recipe. Serve on 3 cups cooked spaghetti squash.

SERVES: 4

Diabetic Exchanges: ¾ bread; 4½ vegetable; ¾ fat

REDUCED CARBOHYDRATE: Omit the beans; use only 2 tablespoons of chili and ½ can of chilies, and simmer 5 minutes longer.

SERVES: 4

Diabetic Exchanges: 3½ lean meat; 2¾ vegetable; ½ fat

REDUCED SODIUM: Use cooked-from-scratch black beans (without salt); low-sodium tomato sauce and tomato paste. Omit the canned chilies, add ¼ cup chopped green bell pepper when you add the onion, and add ground red pepper to taste.

SERVES: 6

Diabetic Exchanges: ¾ bread; ¼ other carbohydrate/sugar; 2½ lean meat; 1¼ vegetable; ¼ fat

MENU SUGGESTIONS: Baked Tortilla Chips; Lettuce and Tomato Salad; Blood Orange Wedges

Entrées

VEGETABLE STEW
with TURKEY MEATBALLS

The sauce without the balsamic vinegar is perky—add the vinegar and it becomes complex and murkier. Taste the sauce before you add the vinegar and make your decision then. I like the vinegar version. You can, of course, substitute any ground meat for the turkey.

1 pound ground turkey

3 tablespoons flavored or plain dry bread crumbs

2 tablespoons minced onion

¼ teaspoon dry oregano

Salt to taste

2 teaspoons olive oil

½ cup chopped onion

½ cup chopped carrot

2 cloves garlic, minced

2 cups chopped zucchini

One 15-ounce can crushed tomatoes

⅓ cup water

2 tablespoons chopped fresh parsley

1 teaspoon dried basil

½ teaspoon sugar

⅛ teaspoon ground pepper

1 tablespoon balsamic vinegar (optional)

1   In a medium bowl, combine the turkey, bread crumbs, minced onion, oregano, and salt. Form into 1-inch balls; set aside.

2   In a 3-quart nonstick saucepan, heat the oil over medium-high heat. Add the chopped onion, carrot, and garlic. Cook, stirring, until slightly softened, about 2 minutes. Add the zucchini; cook, stirring, until tender-crisp, about 2 minutes. Add the tomatoes, water, parsley, basil, sugar, and pepper; bring to a boil. Add the turkey balls, return to the boil, reduce heat, and simmer, uncovered, 20 minutes. Taste, stir in the vinegar, if using, and cook 2 minutes longer.

SERVES: 4 (makes 5 cups)

Diabetic Exchanges: ¼ bread; 3 very lean meat; 2½ vegetable; 1¼ fat

REDUCED FAT/SATURATED FAT/PROTEIN/CHOLESTEROL: Make only half as many turkey balls. Stir in 4 cups cooked spaghetti squash when you add the vinegar.

REDUCED SODIUM: Use low-sodium crushed tomatoes.

Diabetic Exchanges: ¼ bread; 3 very lean meat; 2½ vegetable; 1¼ fat

MENU SUGGESTIONS: Crusty Whole Wheat Bread; Mesclun Salad; Strawberries with Rhubarb

Fish

How many times have you heard or read that fish is good for you? Well, it's true. In addition to being low-calorie, generally low-fat, and a great source of protein, it is also an excellent source of omega fatty acids, antioxidants thought to prevent heart disease.

The problem with many traditional recipes for fish is that they are frequently cooked with lots of fat or served with high-fat sauces. The recipes here are low to moderate fat—and delicious!

Although each of these recipes was tested with a specific fish, you can certainly substitute one similar type of fish for another.

THE ULTIMATE DIABETES COOKBOOK

BLACKENED TUNA

The trick to blackened anything is to have the skillet really hot before you throw on the fish. (I usually disconnect my smoke alarm before starting this dish—not that I recommend disconnecting smoke alarms as a habit—and if you do, don't forget to reconnect it as soon as the smoke has cleared from the air.) I like my tuna warm in the middle but not cooked. I find the easiest way to achieve this is to use a thin tuna steak and cook it for only one minute. The thicker tuna steaks take too long for the middle to get warm.

> **1 pound tuna steaks, ½ inch thick**
>
> **1 tablespoon melted butter**
>
> **2 teaspoons Cajun Shake (page 70) or blackening seasonings (available in the spice section of the supermarket)**

1   Lightly brush both sides of the tuna with butter. Sprinkle with the spice mix.

2   Heat a large nonstick skillet 3 minutes over high heat. Add the fish and cook 30 seconds per side for rare; 1 to 2 minutes for medium to well done.

SERVES: 4

Diabetic Exchanges: 3¾ very lean meat; ½ fat

REDUCED SATURATED FAT/CHOLESTEROL: Substitute olive oil for the melted butter.

Diabetic Exchanges: 3¾ very lean meat; ¾ fat

REDUCED SODIUM: Use low-sodium seasoning.

Diabetic Exchanges: 3¾ very lean meat; ½ fat

MENU SUGGESTIONS: Watercress and Endive Salad; Roasted Root Vegetables; Steamed Green Beans; Baked Pears

Cilantro Tuna Burgers

Serve these as patties or as a sandwich (I recommend a nice crispy French roll with Dijon mustard). If you are eating this as a patty, my testers all agree that tomato salsa is a perfect accompaniment (you can use the salsa on page 24 if you want to make it homemade).

> **1 pound fresh tuna, cubed**
> **½ cup 1-inch scallion pieces (light and dark parts)**
> **½ cup lightly packed cilantro leaves (fresh coriander)**
> **¼ cup lightly packed fresh parsley leaves**
> **¼ cup plain dry bread crumbs**
> **2 tablespoons fresh lime juice**
> **2 egg whites**
> **2 cloves garlic, minced**
> **⅛ teaspoon ground red pepper**
> **Salt to taste**
> **1 teaspoon olive oil**

1　Place the tuna, scallion, cilantro, parsley, bread crumbs, lime juice, egg whites, garlic, pepper, and salt in a food processor container. Cover and process until everything is minced.

2　Form into four 4-inch patties.

3　In a large nonstick skillet, heat the oil over medium-high heat. Add the patties and cook 3 minutes on one side, then turn and cook 2 to 3 minutes longer or until cooked through.

SERVES: 4
Diabetic Exchanges: ¼ bread; 4 very lean meat; ¼ vegetable; 1 fat

REDUCED PROTEIN: Prepare a quarter of the tuna burger recipe (¼ pound tuna, 2 tablespoons scallion, 2 tablespoons cilantro, 1 tablespoon parsley, 1 tablespoon lime juice, ½ egg white, ½ clove garlic, pinch pepper). After step 1 do the following: in a large nonstick skillet heat 2 teaspoons of olive oil over medium-high heat. Add 2 cups of sliced zucchini and cook, stirring, until slightly softened, about 3 minutes; remove from skillet. Add the tuna mixture and cook, stirring and breaking up the mixture into coarse crumbles, until no longer pink, about 2 minutes. Return the zucchini to the skillet and add 3 cups cooked farfalle (bowties) or other similar-size pasta, 2 tablespoons water, and ⅛ teaspoon ground black pepper. Cook, stirring, until mixture is heated through.

Diabetic Exchanges: 2¼ bread; 1¼ very lean meat; ½ vegetable; ½ fat

MENU SUGGESTIONS: Gazpacho (page 65); Cabbage Salad with Lemon Dressing; Fresh Melon Wedges

PASTA *with* TUNA SAUCE

This is a convenient sauce to make because I always have all the ingredients on hand. It makes a fair amount of sauce (6 servings) and I like to freeze some for nights when I'm feeling lazy. As for pasta, I tend to like penne or rigatoni. However, long pasta is fine if you prefer twirling to spearing.

> **2 teaspoons olive oil**
>
> **1 cup chopped onion**
>
> **2 cloves garlic, minced**
>
> **One 28-ounce can whole tomatoes in thick purée**
>
> **⅓ cup chopped fresh parsley**
>
> **¼ cup water**
>
> **1 tablespoon tomato paste**
>
> **1 teaspoon dried oregano**
>
> **1 teaspoon dried basil**
>
> **1 teaspoon sugar**
>
> **¼ teaspoon ground black pepper**
>
> **Salt to taste**
>
> **12 ounces dried pasta**
>
> **One 6½-ounce can water-packed tuna, drained**
>
> **2 teaspoons chopped capers**

1   In a 2-quart nonstick saucepan, heat the oil over medium-high heat. Add the onion and garlic, and cook, stirring, 2 minutes, or until the onion is slightly softened. Stir in the tomatoes with the purée, breaking them up with the back of a spoon. Stir in the parsley, water, tomato paste, oregano, basil, sugar, pepper, and salt. Bring to a boil. Reduce heat and simmer, uncovered, 20 to 25 minutes or until thickened.

2   While the sauce is simmering, cook the pasta according to package directions, drain.

3   Add the tuna and capers to the tomato sauce. Cook 3 minutes, or until heated through. Place the cooked pasta in a large bowl, pour the sauce over the pasta, and toss.

SERVES: 6

Diabetic Exchanges: 2¾ bread; 1 very lean meat; 1½ vegetable; ¼ fat

REDUCED PROTEIN: Omit the tuna and capers and serve this as a marinara sauce.
Diabetic Exchanges: 2¾ bread; 1¾ vegetable; ¼ fat

REDUCED SODIUM: Use low-sodium tomatoes, tomato paste, and tuna. Omit capers.
Diabetic Exchanges: 2½ bread; 1 very lean meat; 1¾ vegetable; ¼ fat

MENU SUGGESTIONS: Melon and Prosciutto; Arugula Salad; Sautéed Spinach with Garlic; Fresh or Stewed Cherries

HIGH: **fat, protein, cholesterol, magnesium, phosphorus, potassium**

LOW: **fiber, iron, *carbohydrate, sodium***

POACHED SALMON *with* TWO SAUCES

If you're in a hurry, you can purchase cooked salmon and serve it with one or both of these sauces.

6 cups water

1 cup dry white wine

½ cup celery leaves

2 bay leaves

½ teaspoon dried thyme

¼ teaspoon dried rosemary

6 whole black peppercorns

Salt to taste

1½ pounds fresh salmon fillet

Horseradish Mustard Sauce

⅔ cup plain yogurt

2 teaspoons mayonnaise

1½ tablespoons prepared white horseradish

2 teaspoons Dijon mustard

Dilled Cucumber Sauce

⅔ cup plain yogurt

2 teaspoons mayonnaise

¼ cup minced cucumber

1 tablespoon snipped fresh dill

Salt to taste

1   In a large skillet, bring water and wine to a boil over medium-high heat. Add the celery, bay leaves, thyme, rosemary, peppercorns, and salt, if using. Reduce heat and simmer, uncovered, 5 minutes.

2   Add the salmon and simmer, covered, 5 to 7 minutes or until cooked through. (While the fish is poaching, prepare the sauces.)

3   Horseradish Mustard Sauce: in a medium bowl, stir together the yogurt and mayonnaise, then stir in the horseradish and mustard.

4   Dilled Cucumber Sauce: in a medium bowl, stir together the yogurt and mayonnaise, then add cucumber, dill, and salt, if using.

5   If serving warm, remove fish from pot and serve. If serving chilled, place the fish on platter and put in the refrigerator to chill at least 1½ hours. Either way, serve the fish with the two sauces on the side.

SERVES: 6
Diabetic Exchanges: 3¼ lean meat; 1¼ fat; ¼ milk

REDUCED FAT: Use fat-free yogurt; omit the mayonnaise or use fat-free mayonnaise.
Diabetic Exchanges: 3¼ lean meat; ¼ milk; ¾ fat

REDUCED CARBOHYDRATE: Eat the poached salmon without the sauces.
Diabetic Exchanges: 3¼ lean meat; ¾ fat

MENU SUGGESTIONS: Crudités; Tossed Green Salad or Julienned Celeriac Salad; Crispy Whole Wheat Rolls; Fresh Fruit Salad

Entrées

HIGH: **fat, protein, cholesterol, magnesium, phosphorus, potassium**
LOW: **carbohydrate, fiber**

ROASTED SALMON
with BLACK SESAME SEEDS

You can find black sesame seeds in the Asian section of the supermarket. They do not taste exactly like the more familiar white ones. They are milder and really just add a little crunch and visual excitement to the salmon. The amount of time you will need to roast the salmon will depend on how thick it is.

> **1 teaspoon Dijon mustard**
> **1 teaspoon honey**
> **1 teaspoon soy sauce**
> **1 clove garlic, minced**
> **1¼ pounds salmon fillet**
> **1 tablespoon black sesame seeds**

1   Preheat oven to 400°F.

2   In a small bowl, stir together the mustard, honey, soy sauce, and garlic.

3   Rinse and pat dry the salmon. Place in a 9-by-9-inch square baking pan lined with aluminum foil.

4   Spoon the mustard mixture over the top of the salmon and spread with the back of the spoon so that the entire top of the salmon is coated in the sauce. Sprinkle with the sesame seeds.

5   Bake 15 to 25 minutes or until desired doneness.

6   To serve, cut into 4 pieces.

SERVES: 4
Diabetic Exchanges: 4 lean meat; 1 fat

REDUCED SODIUM: Substitute low-sodium soy sauce.
Diabetic Exchanges: 4 lean meat; 1 fat

MENU SUGGESTIONS: Bean Sprout Salad; Steamed Spinach; Brown Rice with Scallions; Grapefruit Wedges

THE ULTIMATE DIABETES COOKBOOK

Asian Salmon Burgers

For lunch, serve these on rolls with Dijon mustard, with sliced raw onion and coleslaw on the side. For dinner, serve them as patties with vegetables and brown rice on the side.

1 tablespoon sesame seeds

1 pound fresh salmon chunks (skinless and boneless)

⅓ cup 1-inch scallion pieces (light and dark parts)

¼ cup plain dry bread crumbs

2 egg whites

1 tablespoon soy sauce

2 cloves garlic, minced

1 teaspoon ground ginger

1 teaspoon chili (hot sesame) oil

1 teaspoon vegetable oil

1   In a dry skillet, toast the sesame seeds over medium heat, stirring constantly, until lightly browned, 3 minutes.

2   Place the salmon, scallion, bread crumbs, egg whites, soy sauce, garlic, ginger, chili oil, and toasted sesame seeds in a food processor container fitted with a steel blade. Cover and process until everything is minced.

3   Form into four 3-inch patties.

4   In a large nonstick skillet, heat the oil over medium-high heat. Add the patties and cook 2 minutes on one side, then turn and cook 2 minutes longer.

SERVES: 4

Diabetic Exchanges: ¼ bread; ¼ very lean meat; 3 lean meat; ½ fat

REDUCED FAT: Omit the chili oil; add ¼ teaspoon ground black pepper; omit the vegetable oil and broil or grill the burgers.

Diabetic Exchanges: ¼ bread; ¼ very lean meat; 3 lean meat

(continued)

REDUCED SODIUM: Use low-sodium soy sauce.

Diabetic Exchanges: ¼ bread; ¼ very lean meat; 3 lean meat; ½ fat

MENU SUGGESTIONS: Asparagus Vinaigrette; Garlic Sautéed Broccoli Rabe; Brown Rice with Sesame Seeds; Clementines

---

HIGH: **protein, phosphorus, potassium**
LOW: **fiber, calcium**

SWORDFISH KEBABS
with LIME *and* SOY MARINADE

You could probably use grouper, tuna, or salmon cubes for this kebab as well. Just be sure not to overcook them. Start cooking the onions first. When you turn the onions, add the fish to the grill, then turn the fish while the onions cook on the second side.

> **2 tablespoons fresh lime juice**
> **1 tablespoon soy sauce**
> **1 tablespoon mirin or dry sherry**
> **1 tablespoon minced ginger**
> **1½ teaspoons plum sauce**
> **1½ teaspoons sesame oil**
> **1 teaspoon honey**
> **¼ teaspoon chili oil (optional)**
> **2 cloves garlic, minced**
> **1 pound swordfish steak, cubed**
> **1 medium onion, cut into 8 wedges**

1   In a large bowl, stir together the lime juice, soy sauce, mirin, ginger, plum sauce, sesame oil, honey, chili oil, and garlic. Add the swordfish and onion; toss to coat. Let stand 20 minutes or longer in the refrigerator.

2   Preheat broiler or grill.

3   String the swordfish cubes onto four 8-inch metal skewers. Brush with any remaining marinade. String the onion onto two 8-inch skewers.

4   Grill or broil the onion 4 inches from the heat for 4 minutes. Turn and brush second side with marinade. Place the fish kebabs on the grill for 2 minutes, turn the fish, and cook 2 to 3 minutes longer or until fish and onion are cooked.

SERVES: 4

Diabetic Exchanges: 3¼ very lean meat; ¼ vegetable; 1¼ fat

REDUCED FAT: Omit the sesame and chili oils.

Diabetic Exchanges: 3¼ very lean meat; ¼ vegetable; ¾ fat

REDUCED SODIUM: Use reduced-sodium soy sauce.

Diabetic Exchanges: 3¼ very lean meat; ¼ vegetable; 1¼ fat

MENU SUGGESTIONS: Steamed Butternut Squash; Sautéed Zucchini; Poached Oranges

Entrées

GRILLED SWORDFISH PUTTANESCA

Serve this dish with pasta on the side; the sauce is good on both the pasta and the fish. This sauce can also be served on any kind of mild-flavored fish, such as tuna, halibut, or even a stronger fish like bluefish.

> **1½ teaspoons olive oil**
> **½ cup chopped onion**
> **2 cloves garlic, minced**
> **One 14½-ounce can whole peeled tomatoes in thick purée**
> **1 teaspoon sugar**
> **⅛ teaspoon red pepper flakes**
> **2 anchovies, mashed**
> **⅓ cup chopped black olives**
> **⅓ cup chopped fresh parsley**
> **1 tablespoon capers**
> **Salt to taste**
> **1½ pounds swordfish steak, about ½ inch thick**

1   Preheat grill or broiler.

2   In a medium nonstick skillet, heat the oil over medium-high heat. Add the onion and garlic, and cook, stirring, 2 minutes until the onion is slightly softened. Stir in the tomatoes with purée, breaking them up with the side of a spoon, the sugar, and the pepper flakes. Bring to a boil; reduce heat and simmer, covered, 10 minutes. Stir in the anchovies, olives, parsley, capers, and salt. Simmer, uncovered, 5 minutes.

3   While the sauce is simmering, place the fish on the grill or on a pan in the broiler. Cook 2 to 3 minutes, then turn and cook second side 2 to 3 minutes longer. Serve with sauce on the side.

SERVES: 6

Diabetic Exchanges: 3¼ very lean meat; ¾ vegetable; 1 fat

REDUCED PROTEIN/SATURATED FAT/CHOLESTEROL: Grill 8 ounces of swordfish until well done. Prepare the sauce adding ½ cup water when you add the tomatoes. Flake the swordfish and add to the sauce when you add the parsley. Serve over 3 cups of cooked pasta.

SERVES: 4

Diabetic Exchanges: 1¼ bread; 1 very lean meat; ¾ vegetable; ½ fat

REDUCED SODIUM: Use low-sodium tomatoes; omit the anchovies and capers.

SERVES: 4

Diabetic Exchanges: 3½ very lean meat; 1 vegetable; 1 fat

MENU SUGGESTIONS: Caesar Salad; Sautéed Escarole; Penne; Sabayon

BAKED HALIBUT *with* HORSERADISH CRUST

I love this way of preparing fish—the crust is delicate and the Dijon mustard adds a nice "zip" while helping to hold the crumbs on the fish. This would work with cod or scrod, Chilean sea bass, monkfish, or any firm-fleshed white fish.

1 tablespoon olive oil

⅓ cup plain dry bread crumbs

2 teaspoons prepared (white) horseradish

¼ teaspoon paprika

1 pound halibut fillet

⅛ teaspoon ground black pepper

Salt to taste

2 teaspoons Dijon mustard

1   Preheat oven to 400°F.

2   In a small bowl, combine the oil and bread crumbs. Stir in the horseradish and paprika.

3   Cut the halibut into 4 pieces; season with pepper and salt. Place in a lightly greased 9-inch-square baking pan. Spread the mustard on top of the fish, then pat on the crumbs.

4   Bake 10 minutes or until the fish flakes with a fork.

SERVES: 4

Diabetic Exchanges: ½ bread; 3½ very lean meat; ¾ fat

MENU SUGGESTIONS: Cauliflower Soup; Okra with Tomatoes (page 232), Cucumber and Red Pepper Salad; Baked Pears

HALIBUT *with* SAUTÉED TOMATOES

Make this recipe only when you have ripe tasty tomatoes. You can also use this recipe with any white-fleshed fish. This is a mild sauce for the fish. If you like, you can add a pinch of ground red pepper to provide a little gusto.

> **1 tablespoon olive oil**
> **3 tablespoons minced shallots**
> **3 cups tomato wedges**
> **⅓ cup chopped fresh parsley**
> **1 tablespoon balsamic vinegar**
> **¼ teaspoon ground black pepper**
> **Salt to taste**
> **1¼ pounds halibut fillet, cut into 4 pieces**

1   In a large nonstick skillet, heat the oil over medium-high heat. Add the shallots and cook, stirring, 1 minute or until softened. Add the tomatoes, parsley, vinegar, pepper, and salt. Cook, stirring, until the tomatoes are softened, about 2 minutes.

2   Place the halibut in the skillet, flesh side down. Spoon the tomato mixture over the halibut. Cook 3 minutes. Turn the halibut pieces and cook 2 to 3 minutes longer or until the fish flakes when tested with a fork.

SERVES: 4
Diabetic Exchanges: 4¼ very lean meat; 1 vegetable; ¾ fat

REDUCED PROTEIN: Omit the halibut. Cut 1 medium (1 pound) eggplant in half crosswise then into wedges. Sauté in the oil with the shallots until browned in places, about 4 to 5 minutes. Add remaining ingredients, cooking about 10 minutes until all the vegetables are soft and cooked through. Serve with 2 tablespoons of grated Parmesan cheese.

SERVES: 2
Diabetic Exchanges: 2½ vegetable; ¾ fat

MENU SUGGESTIONS: Sliced Fennel Salad; Wild Rice; Green Beans; Sliced Strawberries with Orange Liqueur

ROASTED COD
with MOROCCAN FLAVORS

This is a really easy, tasty method of preparing any firm, mild fish.

> **1¼ pounds cod**
>
> **Salt to taste**
>
> **¼ cup lightly packed fresh parsley leaves**
>
> **¼ cup lightly packed cilantro leaves (fresh coriander)**
>
> **1 tablespoon olive oil**
>
> **1 tablespoon tomato paste**
>
> **1 tablespoon fresh lemon juice**
>
> **3 cloves garlic, minced**
>
> **1 teaspoon distilled white vinegar**
>
> **1 teaspoon paprika**
>
> **¼ teaspoon ground cumin**
>
> **⅛ teaspoon ground red pepper**

1   Preheat oven to 400°F.

2   Season the cod with salt to taste; let stand 10 minutes or longer in the refrigerator.

3   In a food processor container, combine the parsley, cilantro, olive oil, tomato paste, lemon juice, garlic, vinegar, paprika, cumin, and pepper. Cover and process until finely chopped.

4   Place the cod in a 9-by-13-inch baking pan lined with greased aluminum foil. Spread the seasoning paste over the fish. Bake 15 to 20 minutes or until fish flakes when pricked with a fork.

SERVES: 4

Diabetic Exchanges: 2¾ very lean meat; ¾ fat

REDUCED PROTEIN/CHOLESTEROL: Slice one 15-ounce cake of tofu crosswise into 8 slices. Spread spice paste over top and place on baking pan lined with greased foil. Bake 15 minutes. *Diabetic Exchanges:* ½ bread; 2¼ very lean meat; 1¾ fat

MENU SUGGESTIONS: Ethiopian Kale (page 229); Green Salad; Yellow Rice; Grapes

HIGH: **protein, cholesterol, magnesium, phosphorus, potassium,** *calcium*

LOW: **saturated fat, fiber, calcium, sodium,** *cholesterol*

SOUTHWESTERN CHILEAN SEA BASS

Chilean sea bass has become so popular that overfishing is becoming a problem, but this sauce would be equally good on scrod, cod, halibut, or similar.

1¼ pounds Chilean sea bass

Salt to taste

2 teaspoons olive oil

¾ cup finely chopped red bell pepper

5 cloves garlic, minced

2 teaspoons minced seeded jalapeño pepper

1 teaspoon paprika

1 teaspoon chili powder

¼ cup dry white wine

1 Rinse the sea bass and pat dry. Season with salt.

2 In a large nonstick skillet, heat the oil over medium-high heat. Add the pepper, garlic, and jalapeño pepper, and cook, stirring, until slightly softened, about 3 minutes. Stir in the paprika and chili powder until absorbed.

3 Add the wine to the skillet, then the sea bass. Cover and simmer 6 to 8 minutes or until the fish flakes when pricked with a fork. Place fish on serving platter and pour the sauce over it.

SERVES: 4

Diabetic Exchanges: 3½ very lean meat; ¼ vegetable; ¾ fat

REDUCED PROTEIN: Substitute cubed firm tofu (1-pound package), cut into 1-inch cubes. Increase the chili powder to 1½ teaspoons. Cook, uncovered, until all the liquid has evaporated, 6 to 8 minutes, turning the cubes so they absorb the spices on all sides.

Diabetic Exchanges: ¼ bread; 2¼ very lean meat; ¼ vegetable; 1¾ fat

MENU SUGGESTIONS: Guacamole with Baked Chips; Mixed Greens; Yellow Rice; Flan (page 320)

Entrées

GRILLED MARLIN *with* STRAWBERRY-PEPPER SAUCE

Marlin is a relatively new arrival to the fish store. As a conservation measure, it used to be illegal to sell fresh marlin. This is a wonderful, mild-flavored fish, and the unusual combination of fish and strawberries makes this a real winner. The nutritional calculations for this recipe were done with tuna, as I could not find marlin in the database.

¾ cup diced strawberries

2 tablespoons minced green bell pepper

1 tablespoon minced ginger

1 tablespoon minced onion

1 teaspoon fresh lime juice

1 pound marlin

Salt to taste

Ground black pepper to taste

2 teaspoons butter

1   In a medium bowl, stir together the strawberries, bell pepper, ginger, onion, and lime juice; let stand 20 minutes or longer in the refrigerator.

2   Rinse the marlin and pat dry. Season with salt and pepper if desired.

3   In a large nonstick skillet, heat the butter over medium-high heat. Add the marlin and cook 2 to 3 minutes per side or until fish flakes when pricked with a fork. (Cooking time will depend on thickness of the piece of marlin.)

4   Serve with sauce on top or pass the sauce separately.

SERVES: 4

Diabetic Exchanges: 2½ lean meat; ¼ fruit

MENU SUGGESTIONS: Tricolore Salade (page 271); Quinoa Pilaf; Steamed Green Beans; Tuilles (page 329)

MAHI MAHI *with* TOMATO *and* ROASTED RED PEPPER COULIS

Coulis is just a purée by a fancier name. The red pepper is not overwhelming in this sauce. If you want yours more red-peppery, add more. You can also use this sauce on grilled or sautéed chicken. For the reduced-protein variation, you can buy prepared polenta in Italian specialty markets or sometimes in supermarkets. If you cannot locate prepared polenta, you can find a recipe for it on page 266.

> **1½ tablespoons olive oil, divided**
> **¼ cup chopped onion**
> **3 cloves garlic, minced, divided**
> **¾ cup chopped tomato**
> **1¼ pounds mahi mahi fillet**
> **Salt to taste**
> **Ground black pepper to taste**
> **¼ cup roasted red pepper (½ medium)**

1 Preheat broiler.

2 In a 1-quart nonstick saucepan, heat ½ tablespoon of the oil over medium-high heat. Add the onion and 1 clove garlic. Cook, stirring, until onion is slightly softened, about 1 minute. Add the tomato and cook, stirring frequently, until tomato is cooked through, about 4 minutes.

3 While the tomato is cooking, in a small bowl, stir together the remaining 1 tablespoon oil and 2 cloves garlic. Brush over the fish fillet; season with salt and pepper. Cook the fish 6 inches from the heat for 6 minutes or until fish flakes when lifted with a fork.

4 While the fish is cooking, place the tomato mixture in a blender container with the roasted red pepper. Cover and blend until smooth Serve with fish.

SERVES: 4
Diabetic Exchanges: 3¾ very lean meat; ¼ vegetable; 1 fat

(continued)

REDUCED SATURATED FAT/PROTEIN/CHOLESTEROL: Prepare the sauce, and serve it over 2 cups cooked polenta sprinkled with 2 tablespoons grated Parmesan cheese.
Diabetic Exchanges: 2 bread; ¼ vegetable; 1 fat

MENU SUGGESTIONS: Asparagus Soup; Tabouli (page 299); Steamed Broccoli; Angel Food Cake

HIGH: **protein, magnesium, phosphorus, potassium**
LOW: **saturated fat, fiber, sodium**

CARIBBEAN GROUPER

This recipe would be very good with any number of firm-fleshed fish. I can see substituting salmon steaks, Chilean sea bass, monkfish, swordfish, halibut, or scrod—and I'm sure I'm forgetting other fish that would taste great prepared this way.

1 tablespoon olive oil

1 tablespoon minced fresh ginger

2 cloves garlic, minced

1¼ pounds fresh grouper

Salt to taste

Ground black pepper to taste

2 tablespoons water

2 tablespoons dry white wine or orange juice

2 tablespoons fresh lime juice

2 tablespoons pineapple or orange juice

1 teaspoon cornstarch

3 drops Tabasco

2 tablespoons finely chopped mango

1 tablespoon chopped cilantro leaves (fresh coriander)

1 tablespoon thinly sliced scallion

1   In a large bowl, mix the oil, ginger, and garlic. Add the fish and toss to coat, then sprinkle with salt and pepper. Let stand 20 minutes or longer in the refrigerator.

2   Heat a large nonstick skillet over high heat. When a drop of water sizzles across the pan, add the fish and cook 3 minutes, then turn and cook the other side 2 to 3 minutes or to desired doneness.

3   While the fish is cooking, in a small bowl, stir together the water, wine, lime juice, pineapple or orange juice, cornstarch, and Tabasco. Stir in the mango and cilantro.

4   Remove fish from the skillet to a serving platter. Deglaze pan with the mango mixture; cook, stirring, until mixture comes to a boil and has thickened. Pour over the fish. Sprinkle with scallion.

SERVES: 4

Diabetic Exchanges: 3¾ very lean meat; ¼ fruit; ¾ fat

MENU SUGGESTIONS: Carrot Soup; Whole Wheat Couscous Pilaf (page 264); Sautéed Red Pepper and Zucchini Strips; Maple-Glazed Bananas (page 331)

MONKFISH COZUMEL

Monkfish is called *lotte* in France. It's a chewy fish, frequently compared with lobster. Monkfish has a tough membrane that should be removed before cooking. Any firm white-fleshed fish would also do well with this sauce.

> **2 teaspoons olive oil**
> **¾ cup chopped onion**
> **½ cup chopped green bell pepper**
> **1 teaspoon ground coriander**
> **¼ teaspoon ground cumin**
> **⅛ teaspoon ground red pepper**
> **Salt to taste**
> **1½ cups chopped tomatoes**
> **2 tablespoons water**
> **1 tablespoon fresh lime juice**
> **1 pound monkfish**
> **1 tablespoon chopped cilantro leaves (fresh coriander)**

1 In a large nonstick skillet, heat the oil over medium-high heat. Add the onion and green pepper; cook, stirring, until onion is slightly softened, about 3 minutes. Stir in the ground coriander, cumin, red pepper, and salt until absorbed.

2 Stir in the tomatoes, water, and lime juice. Cover and cook, stirring occasionally, 5 minutes. Add the fish to the skillet. Cover and cook over medium heat 10 minutes or until fish flakes when pricked with a fork.

3 Remove the fish to a serving platter. Stir the cilantro into the sauce and cook 1 minute. Pour sauce over fish.

SERVES: 4

Diabetic Exchanges: 2¼ very lean meat; 1¼ vegetable; ½ fat

REDUCED PROTEIN: Omit fish; add 2 cups cooked black beans to sauce when you would add fish, and follow the rest of the recipe.

Diabetic Exchanges: 1 bread; 1½ vegetable; ½ fat

MENU SUGGESTIONS: Sliced Cucumber Salad; Quinoa Pilaf; Steamed Snap Peas; Apple Brown Betty (page 334)

HIGH: **protein, magnesium, sodium**
LOW: **carbohydrate, fiber, calcium, iron,** *cholesterol*

Cajun Turbot

I am so impressed when this fish comes out of the broiler—it looks so "professional"—just like from a good restaurant! If you don't want to make the Cajun Shake you can buy a Cajun blend in the spice section of the supermarket.

> **2 teaspoons Cajun Shake (page 70)**
> **1 tablespoon tomato paste**
> **2 tablespoons water**
> **2 teaspoons olive oil**
> **1 pound turbot fillets**

1   Preheat broiler.

2   In a small bowl, combine the shake, tomato paste, water, and olive oil. Spread on fish.

3   Broil 5 to 8 minutes, or until fish flakes when pricked with fork.

SERVES: 4
Diabetic Exchanges: 2½ very lean meat; ¾ fat

REDUCED PROTEIN/CHOLESTEROL: Cut 2 cakes of tofu in half so that you have four cakes about ¾ inch thick; brush both sides with the Cajun mixture. Broil until browned, about 3 to 4 minutes per side.
Diabetic Exchanges: ½ bread; 2¼ lean meat; ½ fat

REDUCED SODIUM: Use the low-sodium version of the Cajun Shake and low-sodium tomato paste.
Diabetic Exchanges: 2½ very lean meat; ¾ fat

MENU SUGGESTIONS: Coleslaw; Peas; Cauliflower with Preisel (page 215); Sliced Peaches

Entrées

BAKED BLUEFISH
with ARTICHOKE HEARTS

The first fish I ever ate and enjoyed, when I was well into my twenties, was bluefish. I know some people think it is too fishy. For those people I suggest using any fish they prefer as the vegetables are very versatile and would be suitable to any mild fish. Bluefish range in size from small enough to feed two to huge. The cooking times will differ greatly depending on which one you've purchased. I prefer the smaller fish fillets.

> **1 pound bluefish fillets**
> **Salt to taste**
> **2 tablespoons slivered almonds**
> **2 teaspoons olive oil**
> **1 cup julienned red bell pepper**
> **½ cup sliced onion**
> **2 cloves garlic, minced**
> **1 cup halved cherry tomatoes**
> **½ cup (frozen and thawed, or canned) artichoke hearts, cut into eighths**
> **2 tablespoons chopped fresh basil or ½ teaspoon dried basil**

1 Preheat oven to 375°F.

2 Rinse the bluefish and pat dry. Season with salt, if using. Place in a greased 9-by-13-inch baking pan.

3 Toast the almonds by placing on a piece of foil and putting in the oven for 8 to 12 minutes or until they are lightly browned. Watch out that they don't burn! Remove from oven; set aside.

4 In a medium nonstick skillet, heat the oil over medium-high heat. Add the bell pepper, onion, and garlic. Cook, stirring, until tender-crisp, about 3 minutes. Add the cherry tomatoes, artichokes, and basil. Cook, stirring, until slightly softened, about 1 minute. Spoon the vegetable mixture over the fillets.

5 Bake, uncovered, 10 to 20 minutes or until the fish flakes when pricked with a fork.

6 Sprinkle with the toasted almonds.

SERVES: 4

Diabetic Exchanges: 2¾ very lean meat; 1¼ vegetable; 1½ fat

REDUCED PROTEIN: Slice 1 medium eggplant lengthwise into four ¾-inch-thick slices. Season with salt and pepper to taste. Combine ½ cup broth and 1 minced clove garlic. Pierce eggplant slices all over with a fork; brush with broth mixture . Broil 3 minutes per side or until eggplant is browned. Remove from oven and sprinkle each slice with 1 tablespoon of shredded mozzarella cheese. Prepare the recipe omitting steps 2 and 3 (as you will be omitting the fish and almonds), spoon the vegetable mixture over the mozzarella cheese, and bake at 375°F for 10 minutes or until cheese has melted and veggies are warm.

SERVES: 4

Diabetic Exchanges: ½ very lean meat; 3 vegetable; 1 fat

MENU SUGGESTIONS: White Beans with Beets (page 30); Tossed Green Salad; Sautéed Mushrooms; Asian Pear

Entrées

SEA BASS *with* LEEKS

Sea bass is a fish you often find in Chinese restaurants, which is why this combination of ingredients is such a natural fit. Of course, if you can't find sea bass, any mild-flavored fillet will do.

½ cup vegetable broth

1 tablespoon mirin or dry sherry

2 teaspoons soy sauce

2 teaspoons cornstarch

½ teaspoon sugar

1¼ pounds sea bass fillets

Salt and ground black pepper to taste

2 teaspoons vegetable oil

1 cup sliced leeks

1 tablespoon minced ginger

1   Preheat broiler.

2   In a small bowl, stir together the broth, mirin, soy sauce, cornstarch, and sugar.

3   Season the fish with salt and pepper. Broil 5 minutes or until fish flakes with a fork.

4   While the fish is broiling prepare the sauce. Heat the oil in a small saucepan, add the leeks and ginger, and cook, stirring, until leeks are cooked, about 2 to 3 minutes. Add the soy sauce mixture and cook, stirring until sauce comes to a boil and is thickened, about 1 minute.

5   Pour sauce over fish.

SERVES: 4
Diabetic Exchanges: 4 very lean meat; ¾ vegetable; 1 fat

REDUCED SODIUM: Use low-sodium soy sauce and low-sodium broth.
Diabetic Exchanges: 4 very lean meat; ¾ vegetable; 1 fat

MENU SUGGESTIONS: Julienned Zucchini and Yellow Squash; Green Salad; Brown Rice; Cantaloupe Slices

BROCCOLI-STUFFED SOLE

I confess that I use frozen chopped broccoli rather than cook it from fresh. I like to serve stuffed fish to company, because it looks as though I've worked really hard—when in fact I haven't. Of course this is a great way to serve any flat fish like Dover sole, lemon sole, or flounder.

1 teaspoon olive oil

¼ cup chopped onion

1 clove garlic, minced

1 cup chopped cooked broccoli (fresh, or thawed frozen)

2 teaspoons butter

1 tablespoon all-purpose flour

⅓ cup chicken or vegetable broth

¼ teaspoon dried tarragon

Salt to taste

4 small fillets of sole (1 pound)

1 tablespoon white wine or (additional) broth

1   Preheat oven to 350°F.

2   In a medium nonstick skillet, heat the oil over medium-high heat. Add the onion and garlic and cook, stirring, until softened, 1 minute. Stir in broccoli.

3   In a 1-quart saucepan melt the butter. Stir in the flour until absorbed. Stir in the broth, and bring to a boil, stirring constantly. Add to the broccoli mixture with tarragon, and salt; set aside.

4   Season the fish with salt. Place a quarter of the broccoli mixture on each fillet and roll up. Place fish, seam down, in an 8-inch-square baking dish. Add wine; cover with foil. Bake 30 minutes or until fish flakes when tested with a fork.

SERVES: 4

Diabetic Exchanges: 2¾ very lean meat; 1 vegetable; ¾ fat

(continued)

REDUCED PROTEIN: Make Broccoli-Stuffed Tomato, omitting the flounder. Stir ½ cup shredded Cheddar into the broccoli mixture. Stuff into 4 hollowed-out medium tomato shells. Bake 20 minutes.

Diabetic Exchanges: ½ lean meat; 2 vegetable; 1½ fat

REDUCED SODIUM: Use low-sodium broth and unsalted butter.

Diabetic Exchanges: 2¾ very lean meat; 1 vegetable; ½ fat

MENU SUGGESTIONS: Tomato Soup; Leafy Salad; Parslied New Potatoes; Steamed Asparagus; Fresh Raspberries

THE ULTIMATE DIABETES COOKBOOK

LEMON SOLE *with* WHITE WINE

This is a very simple method for preparing any fillet of fish. I find the Herbal Shake a nice complement to the wine, but you can use any seasoning shake in the book (pages 69–70) or any commercially prepared seasoning, too.

> **1 pound lemon sole**
> **Herbal Shake (page 70)**
> **2 teaspoons butter**
> **3 tablespoons white wine**

1   Sprinkle the sole with the shake.

2   In a large nonstick skillet, melt the butter over medium-high heat. Add the fish and cook 1 to 2 minutes per side. When the fish is just cooked, add the wine to the skillet and shake the pan so the fish is surrounded by the wine. Remove fish to serving platter, pouring any pan juices over the fish.

SERVES: 4

Diabetic Exchanges: 3 very lean meat; 1¼ fat

REDUCED SATURATED FAT: Substitute olive oil for the butter.

Diabetic Exchanges: 3 very lean meat; 1½ fat

REDUCED SODIUM: Use a salt-free seasoning such as Mrs. Dash or prepare the Herbal Shake without salt; use unsalted butter.

Diabetic Exchanges: 3 very lean meat; 1¼ fat

MENU SUGGESTIONS: Chilled Yogurt Basil Soup (page 66); Mixed Vegetable Salad; Green Beans with Dill and Mustard Sauce; Poached Pears

SALMON-STUFFED FLOUNDER

Be sure to use small fillets of fish because large ones will overwhelm the filling. Use lemon sole, or any mild-flavored fillet—whichever fish has the smallest fillets. You can also omit the fish fillet and bake the salmon mixture as patties (be sure to grease the pan so they don't stick); you will want to double or triple the recipe if you are serving just the salmon.

¼ **pound salmon**

1 **egg white**

2 **tablespoons snipped fresh chives, divided**

1 **tablespoon dry sherry**

Salt to taste

1 **pound flounder fillets**

Freshly ground black pepper to taste

2 **tablespoons dry white wine**

1 **tablespoon chopped onion**

½ **cup lightly packed watercress sprigs, chopped**

¼ **cup chopped fresh parsley**

1 **tablespoon olive oil**

1 **tablespoon fresh lime juice**

1 Preheat oven to 350°F.

2 For the salmon mousse: in a food processor container fitted with a steel blade, combine the salmon, egg white, 1 tablespoon of the chives, sherry, and salt. Cover and process until smooth.

3 Rinse the fish fillets and pat dry; season with salt and pepper. Place the flounder skin side up, on wax paper. Put a quarter of the salmon mixture on the wider end of the fish fillets, then roll the fish to encase the salmon. Place the rolls in a lightly greased 9-inch-square baking pan, seam side down. Add wine and onion to the pan. Cover pan with aluminum foil and bake 18 to 20 minutes or until fish is cooked throughout.

4 Remove fish from pan and put on a serving platter; keep in a warm oven while you prepare the sauce. Pour the pan juices (with the onion) into a blender container. Add the watercress, parsley, olive oil, and lime juice. Cover and blend until smooth. Pour over fish rolls.

Diabetic Exchanges: 3¼ very lean meat; ¾ lean meat; 1 fat

REDUCED FAT/SATURATED FAT/PROTEIN/CHOLESTEROL: Make Salmon-Stuffed Zucchini: prepare the salmon filling as described in step 2. Cut 2 medium zucchini in half lengthwise. Scoop out the center, leaving hollow "boats." Fill each boat with a quarter of the salmon mixture. Bake 15 minutes or until salmon is cooked through. To prepare sauce: place the watercress, parsley, lime juice, and ⅓ cup warm chicken or vegetable broth in a blender container. Cover and process until smooth. Pass the sauce with the zucchini.
Diabetic Exchanges: ¼ bread; 1 lean meat; 1 fat

MENU SUGGESTIONS: Broccoli Vinaigrette; Bulgur; Ratatouille; Bing Cherries

ORANGE ORANGE ROUGHY

This is a wonderful way to serve a mild-flavored fish fillet. This fish is relatively new to the market since they live so deep that it wasn't until recently that modern fishing techniques allowed harvesting of such deep waters. They are native to New Zealand, have a delicate flavor, and are now widely available.

> **1 pound orange roughy fillets**
>
> **3 tablespoons orange juice**
>
> **2 tablespoons water**
>
> **1 tablespoon white wine, or additional orange juice**
>
> **½ teaspoon crushed coriander seed**
>
> **¼ teaspoon grated orange rind**
>
> **1 teaspoon canola oil**
>
> **1 teaspoon butter**
>
> **Salt to taste**
>
> **1 tablespoon chopped cilantro leaves (fresh coriander)**

1   Rinse and pat dry the fish fillets.

2   In a shallow bowl, combine the orange juice, water, wine, coriander seed, and orange rind. Add the fish fillets and let marinate 20 minutes or longer in the refrigerator.

3   In a large nonstick skillet, heat the oil and butter. Add the fish and cook 2 minutes per side or until fish flakes when pricked with a fork. Remove fish from skillet, place on serving platter, and season with salt.

4   Deglaze the skillet with the marinating mixture. Pour over fish and sprinkle with cilantro.

SERVES: 4

Diabetic Exchanges: 2½ very lean meat; ½ fat

MENU SUGGESTIONS: Chicken Broth with Scallion Slices; Mixed Salad; Baked Sweet Potato; Sliced Strawberries

Red Rainbow Trout
with Sweet Pepper Salsa

Red rainbow trout looks just like salmon. You can substitute almost any fish for the trout, as the salsa has a lovely versatile flavor. If you are no fan of mint, the relish is quite good even without it.

> ⅔ **cup finely chopped orange or red bell pepper**
> ⅓ **cup finely chopped onion**
> ¼ **cup finely diced orange**
> 2 **tablespoons finely chopped lime pulp**
> 1 **tablespoon chopped cilantro leaves (fresh coriander)**
> 1 **teaspoon finely chopped fresh mint**
> ¼ **teaspoon ground cumin**
> 1¼ **pounds red rainbow trout, boned**
> **Salt to taste**
> **Ground black pepper to taste**
> **Cajun Shake (page 70) or seasoning to taste**

1   In a small bowl, combine the bell pepper, onion, orange, lime, cilantro, mint, and cumin. Let stand at least 30 minutes for the flavors to meld.

2   Preheat broiler.

3   Sprinkle trout with salt, pepper, and Cajun seasoning. Place skin side down on a broiler pan. Cook 5 to 6 minutes or until fish flakes when pricked with fork, or to desired doneness.

4   Divide the fish among 4 plates, topped with the salsa.

SERVES: 4
Diabetic Exchanges: 4¼ very lean meat; ¼ fruit; ½ vegetable; 1 fat

MENU SUGGESTIONS: Sautéed Zucchini with Dill; Whole Wheat Couscous Pilaf (page 264); Arugula and Grape Tomato Salad; Sliced Anjou Pears

SEA TROUT *with* SNOW PEAS *and* MINT

Some years ago the fish industry felt that some of the catch would be more popular if they had nicer names. So they changed this fish's name from weakfish to sea trout. I was pleasantly surprised to find the flavor so mild because it smelled fishy as it was cooking. The combination of snow peas and mint is just right.

> **1¼ pounds sea trout**
> **Salt to taste**
> **Ground black pepper to taste**
> **2 teaspoons vegetable oil**
> **1 cup sliced onion**
> **1 cup julienned snow peas**
> **2 teaspoons minced ginger**
> **2 cloves garlic, minced**
> **2 tablespoons mirin or dry sherry**
> **1 tablespoon chopped fresh mint**

1   Season the sea trout with salt and pepper; let stand 10 minutes or longer in the refrigerator.

2   In a large nonstick skillet, heat the oil over medium-high heat. Add the onion, snow peas, ginger, and garlic. Cook, stirring, until tender-crisp, about 3 minutes. Remove from the skillet.

3   Add the fish to the skillet. Cook skin side down 3 minutes. Turn and cook 4 minutes longer or until fish flakes when pricked with a fork (you can remove the skin while the second side is cooking).

4   Remove the fish from the skillet and place on a serving platter. Return the vegetables to the skillet; add the mirin and chopped mint. Cook, stirring, until heated through, about 1 minute. Pour over fish fillets.

SERVES: 4
Diabetic Exchanges: ¼ bread; 3½ very lean meat; ¾ vegetable; 1½ fat

MENU SUGGESTIONS: Boston Lettuce Salad, Herbed Orzo (page 252); Steamed Broccoli; Grapefruit and Pear Salad

CITRUS GLAZED RED SNAPPER *with* SESAME SEEDS

This glaze would work well with many different fish: flounder, sole, tuna, swordfish, sea bass, or any other mild-flavored fish. Don't forget to grate the zest before you cut the lemon and orange to squeeze the juice.

> **4 red snapper fillets (5 ounces each)**
> **Salt and ground black pepper to taste**
> **2 teaspoons sesame seeds**
> **2 teaspoons vegetable oil**
> **⅓ cup fresh orange juice**
> **1 tablespoon fresh lemon juice**
> **1 teaspoon sesame oil**
> **½ teaspoon grated orange rind**
> **¼ teaspoon grated lemon rind**

1   Season the fillets with salt and pepper; set aside.

2   In a large nonstick skillet, cook the sesame seeds over medium-high heat, stirring constantly, until lightly browned, about 4 to 5 minutes. Be careful not to burn them. Remove seeds from skillet.

3   Heat the oil in the skillet. Add the fillets and cook skin side down for 2 minutes, then turn and cook 2 minutes longer. Remove from skillet.

4   Add the orange juice, lemon juice, sesame oil, orange and lemon rinds to the skillet, to deglaze the pan. Pour sauce over the fillets; sprinkle with sesame seeds.

SERVES: 4
Diabetic Exchanges: 3¾ very lean meat; ¼ fruit; 1 fat

MENU SUGGESTIONS: Summery Yellow Squash Soup; Baked Dumpling Squash; Steamed Green Beans; Fresh Strawberries

HIGH: protein, cholesterol, iron, magnesium, phosphorus, potassium, *carbohydrate*
LOW: saturated fat, fiber

CIOPPINO

Sort of a soup, sort of a stew. You can vary this by adding or deleting any fish or shellfish you like.

> **2 teaspoons vegetable oil**
> **1 cup chopped onion**
> **½ cup chopped green bell pepper**
> **2 cloves garlic, minced**
> **One 14- to 15-ounce can diced tomatoes**
> **½ cup water**
> **2 tablespoons dry red wine**
> **1 bay leaf**
> **1 teaspoon dry basil**
> **¼ teaspoon ground black pepper**
> **⅛ teaspoon dried thyme**
> **Salt to taste**
> **12 clams**
> **½ pound shrimp, peeled and deveined**
> **½ pound cod, halibut, or other white fish**
> **2 tablespoons chopped fresh parsley**

1   In a 4-quart nonstick saucepan, heat the oil over medium-high heat. Add the onion, green pepper, and garlic. Cook, stirring, until vegetables are slightly softened, about 2 minutes.

2   Stir in the tomatoes; stir in the water, wine, bay leaf, basil, pepper, thyme, and salt. Bring to a boil. Reduce heat and simmer, uncovered, 15 minutes.

3   Add the clams. Simmer, covered, 3 minutes. Add the shrimp, cod or halibut, and parsley. Cover and simmer 5 minutes or until fish are cooked and clams have opened. Discard bay leaf before serving.

Diabetic Exchanges: 3¼ very lean meat; 1½ vegetable; ½ fat

REDUCED PROTEIN: Add ½ cup converted rice when you add the tomatoes; simmer 20 minutes, covered. Omit the cod and clams, add shrimp and ¼ cup peas, cover, and simmer 5 to 7 minutes longer or until shrimp is cooked.

Diabetic Exchanges: 1¼ bread; 1¾ very lean meat; 1½ vegetable; ½ fat

REDUCED SODIUM: Use low-sodium tomatoes.

Diabetic Exchanges: 3¼ very lean meat; 1¾ vegetable; ½ fat

MENU SUGGESTIONS: Crusty Bread; Fresh Spinach and Mushroom Salad; Fruit Tart

Pan-Seared Cajun Shrimp

I like to leave the tails on the shrimp for a pretty presentation: arrange the shrimp in a pinwheel with the tails facing the outside of a serving platter; place lemon or lime wedges and fresh parsley in the center of the pinwheel. If you love spicy food, use more of the Cajun spice mix; if you can't tolerate spice, use less.

> 1¼ pounds jumbo shrimp
>
> 1 tablespoon olive oil
>
> 1½ teaspoons Cajun spice mix
> (available in most supermarkets; or Cajun Shake, page 70)
>
> Salt to taste
>
> 2 tablespoons chopped fresh parsley
>
> 1 tablespoon fresh lemon juice

1   Remove the shells and devein the shrimp; rinse and pat dry.

2   In a large bowl, combine the oil, Cajun spice mix, and salt, if using. Add the shrimp and toss until covered with the spice mixture. Let stand 10 minutes.

3   In a large nonstick skillet, cook the shrimp over medium-high heat until just cooked, about 2 to 3 minutes per side. Stir in the parsley and lemon juice.

SERVES: 4

Diabetic Exchanges: 4 very lean meat; ¾ fat

REDUCED PROTEIN/CHOLESTEROL: Make Pan-Seared Cajun Shrimp with Wild Rice: reduce the shrimp to ¾ pound large shrimp. When the shrimp are cooked, stir in 2 cups of cooked wild (or brown or white) rice. Stir until heated through; add extra (low-sodium) Cajun spice, if desired.

Diabetic Exchanges: 1 bread; 2½ very lean meat; ¾ fat

REDUCED SODIUM: Prepare the homemade Cajun Shake, omitting the salt.

Diabetic Exchanges: 4 very lean meat; ¾ fat

MENU SUGGESTIONS: Endive, Radicchio, and Watercress Salad; White and Wild Rice; Garlicky Baby Green Beans; Black and Red Plums

GINGER SHRIMP *with* BROWN RICE *and* SCALLIONS

You can use short- or long-grain brown rice, but I prefer the short-grain for its chewier texture.

>   1 tablespoon vegetable oil
>
>   1 pound extra-large or jumbo shrimp, peeled and deveined
>
>   1½ tablespoons minced ginger
>
>   3 cloves garlic, minced
>
>   ½ cup sliced scallions (green and white parts)
>
>   3 cups cooked brown rice
>
>   1½ tablespoons soy sauce
>
>   1 tablespoon hoisin sauce

1   In a nonstick wok or large skillet, heat the oil over high heat. Add the shrimp, ginger, and garlic. Cook, stirring, until shrimp are no longer translucent, about 3 minutes.

2   Stir in the scallions and cook, stirring, 30 seconds, or until just slightly softened.

3   Stir in the rice, soy sauce, and hoisin sauce. Cook, stirring, until rice is heated through.

SERVES: 4

Diabetic Exchanges: 2¼ bread; 2 very lean meat; ¼ vegetable; ¾ fat

REDUCED PROTEIN/CHOLESTEROL: Omit the shrimp. Sauté the scallion, ginger, and garlic until softened, about 1 minute. Add 2 cups cooked chickpeas and the rice with the soy and hoisin sauces.

Diabetic Exchanges: 3½ bread; ¼ very lean meat; ¼ vegetable; ¾ fat

REDUCED SODIUM: Use low-sodium soy sauce.

Diabetic Exchanges: 2¼ bread; 2 very lean meat; ¼ vegetable; ¾ fat

MENU SUGGESTIONS: Mixed Green Salad; Sautéed Yellow Squash; Fresh Fruit Salad

GARLIC SAUTÉED SCALLOPS

Don't be deceived by the simplicity of this recipe—it is full-flavored. Serve it with good bread, so you can sop up any sauce on the plate. I also serve this as an appetizer for 8.

> **1 pound sea scallops**
> **Salt and ground black pepper to taste**
> **1½ tablespoons butter**
> **3 cloves garlic, minced**
> **1 tablespoon fresh lemon juice**
> **1 tablespoon chopped fresh parsley**

1   Rinse the scallops and pat dry. Season with salt and pepper.

2   In a large nonstick skillet, melt the butter over medium-high heat. Add the garlic and cook, stirring, 30 seconds. Add the scallops. Cook, stirring, until opaque and cooked through, about 3 to 4 minutes or until scallops are lightly browned.

3   Add the lemon juice and parsley; cook, stirring, about 30 seconds longer.

SERVES: 4
Diabetic Exchanges: 2¾ very lean meat; 1 fat

REDUCED SATURATED FAT/CHOLESTEROL: Substitute olive oil for the butter.
Diabetic Exchanges: 2¾ very lean meat; 1 fat

MENU SUGGESTIONS: Crusty Bread; Watercress and Endive Salad; Green Beans with Mustard; Poached Pear

HIGH:	**protein, iron, phosphorus, potassium,** *carbohydrate, magnesium*
LOW:	**fat, saturated fat, fiber, sodium,** *cholesterol, calcium*

ZUPPA DE CLAMS

I first tasted this dish in a very well known seafood (now defunct) restaurant in Hoboken, New Jersey, called the Clam Broth House. It's been a favorite ever since. Sometimes I add some red pepper flakes, for a little zip.

4 pounds littleneck clams

1½ teaspoons olive oil

½ cup chopped onion

2 cloves garlic, minced

2 cups chopped tomatoes

1 tablespoon tomato paste

¼ teaspoon dried basil

¼ teaspoon dried oregano

⅛ teaspoon dried thyme

⅛ teaspoon ground black pepper

Salt to taste

1   Thoroughly rinse the clams and discard any that don't close when tapped.

2   In a 6-quart nonstick pot, heat the oil over medium-high heat. Add the onion and garlic and cook, stirring, until the onion is slightly softened, about 2 minutes. Add the tomatoes, tomato paste, basil, oregano, thyme, pepper, and salt. Cook, uncovered, 3 minutes or until tomatoes give up their juice.

3   Add the clams, increase the heat to high, and cook, covered, 5 to 7 minutes or until the clams have opened. Discard any clams that don't open in the allotted cooking time.

SERVES: 4
Diabetic Exchanges: 2 very lean meat; 1¼ vegetable; ½ fat

REDUCED PROTEIN: Prepare only 1 pound of clams, using the rest of the ingredients as listed. Serve over 4 cups cooked pasta.
Diabetic Exchanges: 2½ bread; ½ very lean meat; 1¼ vegetable; ¼ fat

MENU SUGGESTIONS: Garlic Bread; Caesar Salad; Ripe Nectarines

Mussels *in* Saffron Tomato Broth

If you have some mussels that do not open in the allotted cooking time, discard them.

> **3 pounds farm-raised mussels**
>
> **1½ teaspoons olive oil**
>
> **¾ cup finely sliced leek (white and light green parts)**
>
> **3 cloves garlic, minced**
>
> **¾ cup finely chopped tomato**
>
> **⅔ cup water**
>
> **⅓ cup dry white wine, vegetable broth, or clam juice**
>
> **¼ cup chopped fresh parsley**
>
> **⅛ teaspoon saffron threads**
>
> **⅛ teaspoon ground black pepper**
>
> **Salt to taste**

1   Thoroughly rinse and debeard (pull off any stringy-looking stuff) the mussels; discard any mussels that do not close when tapped.

2   In a 6-quart nonstick pot, heat the oil over medium-high heat. Add the leek and garlic; cook, stirring, until slightly softened, 1 to 2 minutes. Add the tomato, water, wine, parsley, saffron, pepper, and salt, if using. Bring to a boil, reduce heat, and simmer, covered, 5 minutes.

3   Add the mussels. Cover and cook on high heat, 4 to 7 minutes or until all or most of the mussels have opened. Serve in soup bowls with the saffron broth.

SERVES: 4
Diabetic Exchanges: 2 lean meat; ¾ vegetable; ½ fat

REDUCED PROTEIN/CHOLESTEROL: Use only 1 pound of mussels and serve over 4 cups cooked whole-wheat pasta shells.

SERVES: 4
Diabetic Exchanges: 2 bread/starch; ½ lean meat; ¾ vegetable; ½ fat

MENU SUGGESTIONS: Marinated Tomato Salad; French Bread; Fresh Blueberries

Beef

Although you are probably better off choosing a chicken or fish dish, there is still a place for beef in a diabetic menu plan. Despite high fat and cholesterol, don't forget that beef is a good source of iron and vitamins as well—not to mention plain old good taste. Watch portion sizes and choose leaner cuts of beef and you will be just fine.

HIGH: **protein, cholesterol, phosphorus**
LOW: **fiber, sodium**

MOM'S HUNGARIAN BRAISED POT ROAST

My mom was a fabulous cook—the only problem was that she only had one recipe. Everything she cooked had onion, garlic, paprika, and kosher salt. That's how she cooked roast beef, roast chicken, duck, or turkey—that's even how she cooked roast pork. It's also how she made chicken and meatball fricassee, chicken paprikash, and hotdog goulash—each and every one of which was delicious! By the way, Mom would have wanted you to know this freezes beautifully. You can slice the meat before freezing, store it in the gravy, then just pop it into the oven to heat when you want to serve it.

> **1 tablespoon vegetable oil**
>
> **2 cups chopped onions**
>
> **2 cloves garlic, minced**
>
> **2 tablespoons Hungarian sweet paprika**
>
> **½ teaspoon ground black pepper**
>
> **Salt to taste**
>
> **2 pounds first-cut brisket**
>
> **2 cups water, and additional water, if necessary**

(continued)

Entrées

1   In a 6-quart nonstick pot, heat the oil over medium-high heat. Add the onions and garlic and cook, stirring, until slightly softened, about 2 minutes. Stir in the paprika, black pepper, and salt, if using.

2   Add the brisket to the pot and cook until slightly browned on bottom, about 2 minutes. Turn and brown slightly on the other side, about 2 minutes.

3   Add the water to the pot. Bring to a boil; reduce heat and simmer, covered, 2 hours, turning occasionally. Uncover and cook 1 to 2 hours longer, turning occasionally, until tender when pierced with a fork, adding additional water if necessary.

4   Slice and serve with pan juices on the side.

SERVES: 6
Diabetic Exchanges: 3½ very lean meat; 1 vegetable; 3¼ fat

MENU SUGGESTIONS: Mushroom Barley Soup; Cucumber Salad; Parslied Carrots; Baked Apples (page 333)

GARLICKY TENDERLOIN TIPS

Although this recipe calls for tenderloin (also known as filet mignon), any tender cut of meat will do. Sirloin or boneless rib steak would work well. The red wine and water make a nice sauce for the steak, but you can omit them and still have a splendid main course.

1 pound beef tenderloin (filet mignon) or other tender cut, cut into 1-inch cubes

¼ teaspoon ground black pepper

Salt to taste

1 tablespoon olive oil

4 cloves garlic, minced

3 tablespoons water

3 tablespoons red wine

1   Season beef with pepper and salt; let stand 10 minutes.

2   In a large nonstick skillet, heat the oil over high heat. Add the beef cubes and garlic and cook, turning until all sides are seared and meat is at desired doneness (3 to 4 minutes for rare; 9 to 10 minutes for well done). Remove beef from skillet. Add the water and wine to deglaze the pan. Pour the sauce over the beef cubes.

SERVES: 4

Diabetic Exchanges: 3 lean meat; 1¾ fat

REDUCED FAT/SATURATED FAT/CHOLESTEROL/PROTEIN: In a large nonstick skillet, heat 1½ teaspoons of the olive oil, sauté 2 cups sliced zucchini; ½ cup red pepper cubes; 1 cup green pepper cubes; and 1 cup of thick sliced onion over medium-high heat for 5 minutes or until tender-crisp.

Remove from skillet. Heat the remaining 1½ teaspoons oil and cook ½ pound of cubed beef with garlic to desired doneness. Remove beef to serving platter with vegetables. Deglaze pan with water and wine and pour sauce over beef and vegetables.

SERVES: 4

Diabetic Exchanges: 1½ lean meat; 1½ vegetable; 1¼ fat

MENU SUGGESTIONS: Snap Pea Soup with Rosemary (page 54); Arugula Salad; Twice-Baked Potato; Broth-Sautéed Zucchini; Baked Apples (page 333)

Braised Beef *with* Red Wine

Although not exactly beef bourguignon, I would say this is a first cousin. Because it is rich and filling, I look forward to this kind of meal on a cold winter's day, curled up reading a book while the house fills with the aroma of stewing beef.

> 1 pound stewing beef, cubed
>
> 1 tablespoon all-purpose flour
>
> 1 tablespoon vegetable oil, divided
>
> 3 cups sliced mushrooms
>
> 1½ cups coarsely chopped onions
>
> 1½ to 2 cups water
>
> ½ cup sliced carrot
>
> 1 bay leaf
>
> ¼ teaspoon dried rosemary
>
> ¼ teaspoon dried thyme
>
> ⅓ cup red wine
>
> 2 tablespoons chopped fresh parsley
>
> ¼ teaspoon ground black pepper
>
> Salt to taste

1   Dredge the beef in the flour.

2   In a 2-quart pot, heat 2 teaspoons of the oil over medium-high heat. Add the beef and cook, turning, until browned on all sides, about 5 minutes. Remove beef from pot. Add remaining teaspoon of oil, then add mushrooms and onions. Cook, stirring, until softened, about 4 minutes.

3   Add 1½ cups water; bring to a boil over medium-high heat. Add the beef, carrot, bay leaf, rosemary, and thyme; return to the boil. Reduce heat and simmer, covered, 1½ hours. Uncover and simmer 40 minutes longer or until beef is almost tender.

4   Add the wine, parsley, pepper, and salt; return to the boil. Reduce heat and simmer, covered, 30 to 40 minutes longer or until beef is tender, adding more water if necessary. Discard bay leaf before serving.

SERVES: 4

Diabetic Exchanges: 3 meat; 1¾ vegetable; 3¾ fat

LOW PROTEIN: Decrease beef to ½ pound; add 2 cups celery cut into 1-inch pieces when you add the carrot. Add 2 cups sliced zucchini when you add the wine.

Diabetic Exchanges: 1 bread; 1½ lean meat; 2¼ vegetable; 2½ fat

MENU SUGGESTIONS: Onion Soup; Marinated Tomato Salad; Crusty Bread; Cantaloupe

MEDITERRANEAN BEEF STEW

I like to serve this rich stew with couscous or noodles. It would also be delicious if you used lamb instead of beef.

2 teaspoons olive oil, divided

1¼ pounds beef cubes

1 cup chopped onion

2 cloves garlic, minced

1½ cups water

2 cups cubed eggplant

1 cup chopped tomato

2 tablespoons tomato paste

1 teaspoon sugar

½ teaspoon ground cinnamon

¼ teaspoon dried oregano

¼ teaspoon ground allspice

¼ teaspoon ground black pepper

⅛ teaspoon ground cloves

¼ teaspoon grated lemon rind

Salt to taste

1   In a 3-quart nonstick saucepot, heat 1 teaspoon of the oil over medium-high heat. Add the beef and cook, turning often, until browned on all sides, about 5 minutes. Remove beef from pot; set aside. Add the remaining teaspoon of oil, then the onion and garlic. Cook, stirring, until onion is slightly softened, about 2 minutes.

2   Add the water and bring to a boil. Return beef to pot. Reduce heat and simmer, covered, 1½ to 2 hours or until beef is tender.

3   Add the eggplant, tomato, tomato paste, sugar, cinnamon, oregano, allspice, black pepper, and cloves. Cook, uncovered, 30 minutes.

4   Stir in the lemon rind and salt.

SERVES: 4

Diabetic Exchanges: 3¾ lean meat; 1½ vegetable; 3 fat

REDUCED PROTEIN: Omit the beef. Increase oil to 1 tablespoon and sauté 4 cups cubed eggplant with the onion and garlic. Add ½ cup beef broth. Go to step 3, adding 1¾ cups cooked chickpeas.

Diabetic Exchanges: 1½ bread; ½ very lean meat; 1¾ vegetable; ¾ fat

MENU SUGGESTIONS: Sliced Tomato with Mozzarella; Couscous with Sautéed Onions; Sautéed Spinach; Poached Pears

Santa Fe Beef Stew

I love this Southwestern stew! Don't be intimidated by the relatively long list of ingredients—it's really not hard to make. It's also not too spicy; if you like more heat, add some Tabasco sauce or ground red pepper.

2 teaspoons vegetable oil

1 cup chopped onion

½ cup chopped green bell pepper

2 cloves garlic, minced

One 14- or 15-ounce can whole peeled tomatoes packed in juice, undrained

1 pound stewing beef, cut into 1-inch cubes

1 cup water

¼ cup canned chopped green chilies, undrained

1 tablespoon dark brown sugar

1 teaspoon cider vinegar

½ teaspoon chili powder

½ teaspoon ground cumin

¼ teaspoon dried oregano

⅛ teaspoon ground black pepper

2 tablespoons chopped cilantro leaves (fresh coriander)

Salt to taste

1   In a 2-quart nonstick saucepan, heat the oil over medium-high heat. Add the onion, green pepper, and garlic. Cook, stirring, until vegetables are slightly softened, about 3 minutes.

2   Add the tomatoes with canning liquid, breaking up with the back of a spoon. Add the beef, water, chilies, brown sugar, vinegar, chili powder, cumin, oregano, and black pepper. Bring to a boil; reduce heat and simmer, covered, 1½ hours. Stir in the cilantro and salt. Simmer, uncovered, 40 minutes longer or until the beef is tender.

SERVES: 4

Diabetic Exchanges: ¼ other carbohydrate; 3 lean meat; 1¾ vegetable; ½ fat

REDUCED FAT/SATURATED FAT/PROTEIN/CHOLESTEROL: Substitute 1 cup black beans for the beef; omit the water and use 2 cups broth instead.

SERVES: 6

Diabetic Exchanges: 2 bread; ¼ other carbohydrate; 1¾ vegetable; ½ fat

REDUCED SODIUM: Use low-sodium tomatoes, omit the green chilies, and add 1 to 2 seeded jalapeño peppers, chopped.

Diabetic Exchanges: ¼ other carbohydrate; 3 lean meat; 1¾ vegetable; ½ fat

MENU SUGGESTIONS: Salsa with Baked Tortilla Chips; Israeli Salad (page 283); Noodles; Fresh Strawberries

Ropa Vieja (Shredded Beef *in* Tomato Sauce)

This is my favorite dish to order when I go to a Cuban or Asian-Cuban restaurant. Now I make it at home. Don't be discouraged by the long time it takes for the meat to become tender—the result is well worth the wait.

12 cups water

1¼ pounds flank steak

1 cup chopped onion

2 cloves garlic

1 bay leaf

1 tablespoon olive oil

½ cup finely chopped onion

⅓ cup finely chopped green bell pepper

2 cloves garlic, minced

One 8-ounce can tomato sauce

3 tablespoons tomato paste

2 tablespoons dry red wine

1 tablespoon red wine vinegar

½ teaspoon ground cumin

¼ teaspoon dried oregano

¼ teaspoon ground black pepper

Salt to taste

1   In a 6-quart pot, bring the water to a boil over medium-high heat. Add the steak and return to the boil. Boil 10 minutes, discarding any scum that forms on the surface. Add the chopped onion, whole cloves of garlic, and bay leaf. Return to the boil. Reduce heat and simmer, uncovered, 2½ to 3 hours or until the beef is tender. Remove beef from pot (reserving 1 cup of the cooking liquid) and let cool about 30 minutes. When it is cool enough to handle, shred the beef along the grain, cutting the shreds in half if very long.

2 In a large nonstick skillet, heat the oil over medium-high heat. Add the finely chopped onion, bell pepper, and the minced garlic. Cook, stirring, until slightly softened, about 3 minutes. Add the shredded beef, reserved 1 cup of cooking liquid, tomato sauce, tomato paste, wine, vinegar, cumin, oregano, pepper, and salt. Cook, stirring frequently, until mixture is thick, about 30 minutes.

SERVES: 4

Diabetic Exchanges: 4¼ very lean meat; 2¾ vegetable; 2½ fat

REDUCED SODIUM: Use salt-free tomato sauce and paste.

Diabetic Exchanges: 4¼ very lean meat; 2¾ vegetable; 2½ fat

MENU SUGGESTIONS: Shredded Iceberg Lettuce with Sliced Tomatoes and Onions; Baked Plantain; Sautéed Okra; Flan (page 320)

Entrées

BARBECUE BEEF

You'll love how tender and tasty the beef is after the long slow simmering. You can also make this with lamb or pork, or shred the meat and serve it on a bun, if you like.

1½ pounds boneless lean beef, cubed

2 cups water

1 cup chopped red onion

3 cloves garlic, minced

¼ cup ketchup

1 tablespoon cider vinegar

1 tablespoon dark brown sugar

½ teaspoon Worcestershire sauce

⅛ teaspoon Tabasco

Salt to taste

1   Place the beef in a 3-quart saucepan. Add the water, onion, and garlic. Bring to a boil over high heat. Reduce heat and simmer, covered, 2 hours or until beef is tender, adding more water if necessary.

2   Remove the beef from the pot and shred. Return to the pot, with any remaining cooking liquid.

3   Stir in the ketchup, vinegar, brown sugar, Worcestershire sauce, Tabasco, and salt. Cook, uncovered, over medium heat until mixture is thickened, about 30 to 45 minutes.

SERVES: 5

Diabetic Exchanges: ¼ other carbohydrate; 3½ meat; ½ vegetable; 3½ fat

REDUCED FAT/SATURATED FAT/PROTEIN/CHOLESTEROL: Substitute 1 cup dry red kidney beans for the beef. Cook 1 to 1½ hours or until beans are tender. Proceed with recipe as written. *Diabetic Exchanges:* 1½ bread; ¼ other carbohydrate; ½ vegetable

MENU SUGGESTIONS: Tomato Soup; Baked Acorn Squash; Sautéed Spinach; Rice Pudding

Herbed Meat Loaf

Meat loaf is one of my favorite comfort foods (which is why you'll find more than one meat loaf recipe in this book). In addition to making a perfect entrée, there's usually enough left for sandwiches. You can double this recipe and really have lots of leftovers. You can slice the cold meat loaf and wrap each slice in plastic wrap, then place in a freezer baggie. This way you can just pull out as much as you need for sandwiches or to reheat for another meal.

> **1½ pounds ground beef**
>
> **One 8-ounce can tomato sauce**
>
> **½ cup finely chopped onion**
>
> **⅓ cup chopped fresh parsley**
>
> **¼ cup quick-cooking oats**
>
> **1 egg white**
>
> **1 clove garlic, minced**
>
> **1 teaspoon dried oregano**
>
> **½ teaspoon dried basil**
>
> **¼ teaspoon ground black pepper**
>
> **⅛ teaspoon dried thyme**
>
> **Salt to taste**

1   Preheat oven to 350°F.

2   In a large bowl, combine the beef, tomato sauce, onion, parsley, oats, egg white, garlic, oregano, basil, pepper, thyme, and salt. Pat into an 8-by-4¾-inch loaf pan. Bake for 50 minutes or until meat is cooked through.

SERVES: 6 (makes 1 loaf)
Diabetic Exchanges: 3¼ lean meat; ¾ vegetable; 2¼ fat

REDUCED SODIUM: Use low-sodium tomato sauce.
Diabetic Exchanges: 3¼ lean meat; ¾ vegetable; 2¼ fat

MENU SUGGESTIONS: Vegetable Soup; Garlic Mashed Potatoes; Steamed Green Beans; Tapioca Pudding

SHEPHERD'S PIE

Shepherd's pie is also known as cottage pie. It is a classic English comfort food. Traditionally shepherd's pie is prepared with ground lamb or beef or a combination thereof. The mushrooms are not traditional—they're my idea. You can omit them, of course.

> **1 pound potatoes (2 to 3 medium)**
> **1 pound ground beef**
> **1 cup sliced mushrooms**
> **¾ cup chopped carrot**
> **½ cup finely chopped onion**
> **1 tablespoon all-purpose flour**
> **½ cup beef broth**
> **¼ cup fresh or frozen peas**
> **2 tablespoons snipped fresh dill**
> **¼ teaspoon dried marjoram or oregano**
> **¼ teaspoon ground black pepper, divided**
> **Salt to taste**
> **¼ cup milk**

1   Preheat oven to 350°F.

2   Peel the potatoes and cut into 1-inch cubes. Cook the potatoes in boiling water (salted if desired) 20 minutes or until the potatoes are soft.

3   While the potatoes are cooking, in a large nonstick skillet, cook the beef, mushrooms, carrot, and onion, breaking up the beef, about 4 minutes. The beef should no longer be pink. Stir in the flour until absorbed.

4   Add the broth, peas, dill, marjoram, ⅛ teaspoon of the pepper, and salt. Spoon into a 1½-quart baking dish.

5 Drain the potatoes, then return the potatoes to the pot and mash with milk, the remaining ⅛ teaspoon pepper, and salt until smooth. Spoon the potatoes around the edge of the baking dish and decorate attractively using the tines of a fork. Bake 30 minutes or until potatoes are browned and meat mixture is hot.

SERVES: 6
Diabetic Exchanges: 1 bread; 2 lean meat; ¾ vegetable; 1½ fat

REDUCED FAT/SATURATED FAT/PROTEIN/CHOLESTEROL/POTASSIUM: Use only ½ pound of meat; increase mushrooms to 2 cups; carrots to 1 cup; and add 1 cup diced zucchini when you cook the meat. For the crust, use ¼ cup instant polenta, 1 cup water, and salt to taste. Prepare polenta according to package directions. Spread over the top of the meat mixture in the baking dish. Bake 30 minutes.

SERVES: 5
Diabetic Exchanges: 1 bread; 1¼ lean meat; 1 vegetable; 1 fat

MENU SUGGESTIONS: Lettuce and Tomato Salad; Fresh Blueberries

Entrées

STUFFED GREEN PEPPERS

I like these very much. The recipe now calls for *cooked* rice because the first time I tested it, I called for raw rice and we had to eat "crunchy" stuffed peppers—not fun. So save a little rice from your Chinese takeout or substitute any cooked grain that you may have around the house and you won't have a problem.

> **2 medium to small green or red bell peppers**
>
> **¾ pound ground lean beef**
>
> **½ cup cooked white or brown rice**
>
> **¼ cup chopped onion**
>
> **1 clove garlic, minced**
>
> **¼ teaspoon ground pepper**
>
> **Salt to taste**
>
> **One 8-ounce can tomato sauce, divided**
>
> **One 8-ounce can stewed tomatoes**
>
> **¼ teaspoon ground ginger**
>
> **¼ teaspoon Tabasco (or less to taste)**

1   Preheat oven to 375°F.

2   Cut the peppers in half through the stem; remove seeds and white pith; cook in boiling water 4 minutes; remove from water and drain well.

3   In a medium bowl, combine the beef, rice, onion, garlic, pepper, salt, and ½ cup of the tomato sauce. Divide the meat among the bell pepper halves. Place in an 8-inch-square baking pan.

4   Stir together the remaining tomato sauce, stewed tomatoes, ginger, and Tabasco; pour over the peppers. Bake 50 minutes.

SERVES: 4

Diabetic Exchanges: ¼ bread; 2¾ very lean meat; 2½ vegetable; ¼ fat

REDUCED SATURATED FAT/PROTEIN/CHOLESTEROL: Omit meat. Sauté onion and garlic in 1 teaspoon olive oil. Stir in ½ teaspoon chili, until absorbed. Stir in 1 cup cooked brown rice, ½ cup cooked chickpeas, and ½ cup shredded Cheddar cheese. Continue recipe, baking 20 minutes.

Diabetic Exchanges: 1 bread; ½ lean meat; 2½ vegetable; ¾ fat

REDUCED SODIUM: Use low-sodium tomato sauce and stewed tomatoes.

Diabetic Exchanges: ¼ bread; 2¾ very lean meat; 2½ vegetable; ¼ fat

MENU SUGGESTIONS: Vegetable Soup; Sautéed Zucchini; Fresh Strawberries

Entrées

Veal

Since veal comes from calves, it's not too unexpected that the nutritional values are somewhat similar to beef (which comes from cows—just in case anyone didn't know that). It's interesting that although, pound for pound, veal is slightly lower in calories, fat, and saturated fat than beef, beef is lower in cholesterol and sodium.

HIGH: protein, fiber, cholesterol, magnesium, phosphorus, potassium, *carbohydrate*

LOW: sodium, *saturated fat*

ROSEMARY VEAL STEW

This stew just melts in your mouth. The rosemary is a very prominent flavor. If you're not a rosemary fan, substitute ¼ teaspoon dried thyme.

> 1¼ pounds veal cubes (boneless veal for stew)
> 1 tablespoon all-purpose flour
> 1 tablespoon vegetable oil
> 1 cup chopped onion
> 2 cloves garlic, minced
> 1 cup water
> 1 cup sliced carrots
> ⅓ cup chopped fresh parsley
> ½ teaspoon dried rosemary, crumbled
> ¼ teaspoon ground black pepper
> 3 cups whole green beans, trimmed (¾ pound)
> Salt to taste

1   On a piece of wax paper, dredge the veal in the flour.

2   In a 6-quart nonstick pot, heat the oil over high heat. Add the veal and cook until browned all over, about 5 to 7 minutes. Add the onion and garlic to the pot and cook, stirring, until slightly softened, about 1 minute.

3 Add the water and bring to a boil. Reduce heat and simmer, covered, 45 minutes.

4 Add the carrots, parsley, rosemary, and pepper. Simmer, covered, 10 minutes longer.

5 Add the green beans. Simmer, covered, 7 minutes or until desired doneness. Add salt to taste.

SERVES: 4

Diabetic Exchanges: ½ bread; 4 very lean meat; 2½ vegetable; 1 fat

REDUCED SATURATED FAT/PROTEIN/CHOLESTEROL: Reduce veal to ½ pound and add 1 cup cooked chickpeas when you add the green beans.

Diabetic Exchanges: 1 bread; 2 very lean meat, 2½ vegetable; ¾ fat

MENU SUGGESTIONS: Tomato Juice; Couscous; Tossed Green Salad; Bread Pudding

HERBED VEAL *and* SPINACH MEAT LOAF

This meat loaf has quite a garlicky kick. I love it this way, but you may choose to use less garlic. I thaw the spinach and use half the package, but I don't drain it or squeeze it dry the way I do for most recipes. In this recipe you want the liquid from the spinach. I use white-wine Worcestershire sauce here, but if you only have regular Worcestershire on hand, that will be fine.

> **1¼ pounds ground veal**
>
> **Half a 10-ounce package frozen chopped spinach, thawed**
>
> **⅓ cup plain dry bread crumbs**
>
> **2 egg whites**
>
> **3 cloves garlic, minced**
>
> **1 teaspoon dried oregano**
>
> **1 teaspoon dried basil**
>
> **1 teaspoon white-wine or regular Worcestershire sauce**
>
> **½ teaspoon dried thyme**
>
> **¼ teaspoon ground black pepper**
>
> **Salt to taste**

1   Preheat oven to 350°F.

2   In a large bowl, combine all the ingredients. Shape into a loaf 6 by 4 by 2 inches.

3   Place in an 8-inch-square baking pan. Bake 50 to 60 minutes or until cooked through.

SERVES: 4

Diabetic Exchanges: ½ bread; 4¼ very lean meat; ¼ vegetable; 1½ fat

MENU SUGGESTIONS: Vegetable Soup; Dilled New Potatoes; String Beans; Minted Grapefruit Segments

VEAL *with* PEPPERS *and* TOMATOES

For those people not happy eating veal, this recipe can be made with sliced turkey or chicken cutlets. If you have fresh basil on hand, use 1 tablespoon chopped instead of the dried.

> **1 pound veal scallops (thinly sliced boneless veal)**
>
> **⅛ teaspoon ground black pepper**
>
> **Salt to taste**
>
> **2 tablespoons all-purpose flour**
>
> **2 teaspoons olive oil**
>
> **1 cup sliced green bell pepper**
>
> **¾ cup sliced onion**
>
> **2 cloves garlic, minced**
>
> **2 cups tomato wedges**
>
> **¼ cup vegetable or beef broth or water**
>
> **¼ teaspoon dried basil**

1 Cut the veal into strips ¾ inch wide. Season with pepper and salt. Dredge in the flour.

2 In a large nonstick skillet, heat the oil over medium-high heat. Add the veal and cook, stirring, until cooked through, about 4 minutes. Remove from skillet.

3 Add the green pepper, onion, and garlic to the skillet; cook, stirring, until vegetables are slightly softened, about 3 minutes. Add the tomatoes, broth, and basil. Cook, stirring, until tomatoes are cooked, about 4 minutes. Return the veal to the skillet and cook, stirring, 1 minute or until veal is heated and sauce has thickened.

SERVES: 4
Diabetic Exchanges: ¼ bread; 3¾ lean meat; 1¾ vegetable; 1¼ fat

REDUCED PROTEIN: Prepare half of the recipe and serve with 3 cups cooked white rice.
Diabetic Exchanges: 2 bread; 2 lean meat; ¾ vegetable; ¾ fat

REDUCED SODIUM: Use water instead of broth.
Diabetic Exchanges: ¼ bread; 3¾ meat; 1¾ vegetable; 1¼ fat

MENU SUGGESTIONS: Minted Pea Soup; Grilled Cauliflower; Pasta with Olive Oil; Watermelon Wedges

VEAL *with* SHIITAKE MUSHROOMS

Any mushroom will do, although I like the texture of the shiitake mushrooms best in this recipe.

> **1½ pounds veal scallops (thinly sliced boneless veal)**
>
> **Salt and freshly ground black pepper to taste**
>
> **2 tablespoons all-purpose flour**
>
> **1 tablespoon olive oil, divided**
>
> **2 cloves garlic, minced**
>
> **2 cups halved shiitake mushrooms**
>
> **1 cup chicken or vegetable broth**
>
> **2 tablespoons Madeira or Marsala**

1   Pound the veal with a meat tenderizer (pointy mallet) or pierce all over with a fork.

2   Season with salt and pepper, if using. Let stand 20 minutes or longer in the refrigerator.

3   Dredge the veal in the flour to cover lightly.

4   In a large nonstick skillet, heat 2 teaspoons of the oil. Add the veal and cook until browned all over, about 5 minutes.

5   Remove veal from the skillet and set aside.

6   Add the remaining 1 teaspoon olive oil to the skillet. Add the garlic and cook, stirring, 10 seconds. Add the mushrooms and cook, stirring, until oil is absorbed. Add the broth and Madeira or Marsala. Cook until the mushrooms have softened, about 4 minutes.

7   Return the veal to the skillet. Cook until veal is heated through and sauce has thickened.

SERVES: 6

Diabetic Exchanges: 3½ very lean meat; ¼ vegetable; 1 fat

REDUCED SODIUM: Use low-sodium broth.

Diabetic Exchanges: 3½ very lean meat; ¼ vegetable; 1 fat

REDUCED SATURATED FAT/PROTEIN/CHOLESTEROL: Omit veal (skip steps 1 and 2). Increase mushrooms to 6 cups. Dredge the mushrooms in the flour (skip steps 4 and 5). Cook the mushrooms and garlic in the tablespoon of olive oil until oil is absorbed. Add 1¼ cups broth and the wine. Simmer 5 minutes until sauce has thickened. Season to taste with salt and pepper. Serve over Polenta (see page 266).

SERVES: 4

Diabetic Exchanges: 1¼ bread; ¾ vegetable; 1 fat

MENU SUGGESTIONS: Leek and Roasted Red Pepper Vinaigrette; Parslied New Potatoes; Steamed Broccoli; Fresh Plums

Entrées

Lamb

———

For those who love it, lamb is the most delicious meat of all. On the other hand it is also one of the least liked meats. Be sure to check with guests before you serve it to make sure they are among the fans—not the detractors. I've never met a baby lamb that was not tender. It is one of the few meats that you can get as tender a cut in the supermarket as you can from a fine butcher. You will find that lamb is very commonly used in dishes from Mediterranean countries and also from India. It blends well with strong spices.

HIGH: **fat, saturated fat, protein, fiber, cholesterol, phosphorus, potassium**
LOW: **sodium**

GREEK-STYLE BRAISED LAMB *and* GREEN BEANS

The green beans are intended to be overcooked and mushy in this recipe—if you want yours tender-crisp, add them during the last 5 to 7 minutes of cooking. Keep an eye on the stew during the last 15 minutes of cooking. If the liquid is almost completely gone, add ¼ cup more water; the sauce should be rich, but not abundant.

> **2 teaspoons olive oil**
> **1 pound lamb, cubed**
> **1 cup chopped onion**
> **2 cloves garlic, minced**
> **½ teaspoon ground paprika**
> **½ teaspoon ground turmeric**
> **¼ teaspoon ground ginger**
> **¼ teaspoon ground cinnamon**
> **3 cups water**

3 cups halved green beans
⅓ cup chopped fresh parsley
¼ teaspoon ground black pepper
Salt to taste

1   In a 3-quart nonstick saucepot, heat the oil over medium-high heat. Add the lamb, onion, and garlic, and cook, turning occasionally, until the lamb and onion are browned, about 10 minutes. Stir in the paprika, turmeric, ginger, and cinnamon until absorbed. Add the water and bring to a boil. Reduce heat and simmer, uncovered, until the lamb is fairly tender, 1 to 1½ hours.

2   Add the green beans. Return to the boil; simmer, covered, until the green beans are very tender, about 30 minutes longer, stirring occasionally. Stir in the parsley, pepper, and salt.

SERVES: 4
Diabetic Exchanges: 2¾ lean meat; 1¾ vegetable; 3½ fat

REDUCED FAT/SATURATED FAT/PROTEIN/CHOLESTEROL: Use only ½ pound of lamb and add 2 cups sliced zucchini when you add the green beans.
Diabetic Exchanges: 1½ lean meat; 1¾ vegetable; 2 fat

MENU SUGGESTIONS: Whole Wheat Couscous Pilaf (page 264); Shredded Kohlrabi and Jicama Slaw (page 294); Maple-Glazed Bananas (page 331)

Entrées

ROAST LEG of LAMB

As far as I am concerned there is nothing more delicious or festive than a perfectly cooked leg of lamb. If you want to please traditionalists, you might have some mint jelly (available in some supermarkets or gourmet stores) to pass on the side. Don't forget to count carbohydrates for the jelly if you choose to use it.

½ leg of lamb, about 4 pounds
½ cup chopped fresh parsley
4 cloves garlic, minced
½ teaspoon dried rosemary
¼ teaspoon ground black pepper
Salt to taste

1   Preheat oven to 350°F.

2   Place the lamb in a 9-by-13-inch baking pan.

3   Combine the parsley, garlic, rosemary, pepper, and salt. Rub all over the lamb.

4   Roast 1 hour and 10 minutes for rare, or longer to desired doneness.

SERVES: 6

Diabetic Exchanges: 5¾ very lean meat; 1 fat

MENU SUGGESTIONS: Snap Pea soup with Rosemary (page 54); Oven-Roasted Potatoes; Lemon Asparagus (page 204); Boston Lettuce Salad; Chocolate-Dipped Strawberries (page 332)

HIGH: **calorie, fat, saturated fat, protein, carbohydrate, fiber, cholesterol, iron, magnesium, phosphorus, potassium**

LOW: **sodium**

LAMB *and* CHICKPEA STEW

I cube shoulder chops for this recipe. The result is a lovely tender stew. I also throw the bones from the lamb into the pot to give the reduced-protein variation more flavor.

3 cups water

1 pound lamb shoulder, cubed

1½ cups chopped onions

2 cloves garlic, minced

½ teaspoon ground cinnamon

½ teaspoon ground allspice

¼ teaspoon ground black pepper

Salt to taste

3 cups cubed butternut squash (1-inch pieces)

1 cup cooked chickpeas

2 tablespoons chopped fresh mint

1 In a 3-quart saucepot, bring the water to a boil over medium-high heat. Add the lamb, onions, garlic, cinnamon, allspice, pepper, and salt. Return to the boil. Reduce heat and simmer, uncovered, until the lamb is fairly tender, 1 to 1½ hours.

2 Add the squash and chickpeas. Return to the boil. Reduce heat and simmer, covered, until the squash is very tender, about 40 minutes longer, stirring occasionally. Stir in the mint.

SERVES: 4

Diabetic Exchanges: ¾ starch; ¼ very lean meat; 2¾ lean meat; 3 vegetable; 2¾ fat

REDUCED FAT/SATURATED FAT/PROTEIN/CHOLESTEROL: Use only ½ pound of lamb and ½ cup chickpeas; double the cinnamon and allspice. Add 2 cups carrot chunks (1-inch pieces) when you add the squash.

Diabetic Exchanges: ½ bread; 1½ lean meat; 4 vegetable; 1½ fat

MENU SUGGESTIONS: Fresh Fennel and Belgian Endive Salad with Balsamic Vinaigrette; Couscous with Scallions; Scallion Raita (page 52); Fresh Melon Salad

HIGH: **fat, saturated fat, protein, fiber, cholesterol, iron, magnesium, phosphorus, potassium, *carbohydrate, sodium***

LOW: **sodium, *saturated fat, cholesterol***

Curried Lamb *with* Vegetables

The secret to making this dish is not to overcook the okra. That way it doesn't become slimey. If you can't stand the thought of okra, leave it out and substitute a cup of sliced zucchini.

1 tablespoon vegetable oil

4 cups coarsely chopped cabbage

1 cup chopped onion

1 tablespoon minced ginger

3 cloves garlic, minced

1 tablespoon curry powder

1½ cups water

¾ pound lamb, cubed

½ cup sliced carrot

1 cup sliced okra

1 cup sliced yellow squash

¼ cup green peas (fresh or frozen)

2 tablespoons chopped cilantro leaves (fresh coriander)

Salt to taste

1   In a 3-quart nonstick saucepan, heat the oil over medium-high heat. Add the cabbage, onion, ginger, and garlic. Cook, stirring, until slightly softened, about 4 minutes. Stir in the curry powder until absorbed.

2   Add water and bring to a boil. Add the lamb and carrot; return to the boil. Reduce heat and simmer, uncovered, 1 hour and 15 minutes, stirring occasionally. Add the okra, squash, peas, cilantro, and salt. Cook, uncovered, 10 minutes longer.

SERVES: 4

Diabetic Exchanges: ¼ bread; 3 lean meat; 2¼ vegetable; 2¼ fat

REDUCED FAT/SATURATED FAT/PROTEIN/CHOLESTEROL: Omit the lamb. Add 1½ cups cooked chickpeas and substitute 1 cup chicken or vegetable broth for the water. Cook, uncovered, 30 minutes. Add okra, squash, peas, cilantro, and salt. Cook, uncovered, 10 minutes.
Diabetic Exchanges 1¼ bread; ¼ very lean meat; 2¼ vegetable; 1 fat

MENU SUGGESTIONS: Dal; Rice Pilaf; Raita (page 52); Mango and Pineapple Slices

---

HIGH: **fat, saturated fat, protein, cholesterol, iron, magnesium, phosphorus, potassium, calcium**

LOW: *cholesterol*

AFGHAN LAMB *with* SPINACH

When I served this dish to my acupuncturist, Robert Easter, he confessed that of all meats, lamb was his least favorite (I forgot to take my own advice to check preferences before cooking lamb). He was a good sport and tried it anyway—then he came back for seconds. He liked it!

1 pound lamb cubes

1 tablespoon all-purpose flour

2 teaspoons olive oil

1 cup chopped onion

2 cloves garlic, minced

1 teaspoon ground turmeric

¼ teaspoon ground cinnamon

¼ teaspoon ground cardamom

⅛ teaspoon ground nutmeg

⅛ teaspoon ground red pepper

One 14- to 15-ounce can diced tomatoes

½ cup water

4 cups lightly packed spinach leaves

¼ cup plain yogurt

½ teaspoon grated lemon rind

Salt to taste

(continued)

Entrées

1   Preheat oven to 350°F.

2   Dust the lamb cubes with the flour.

3   In a 3-quart nonstick ovenproof dutch oven or pot, heat the oil over medium-high heat. Add the lamb and cook until browned on all sides, about 5 minutes. Remove lamb from the pot and set aside.

4   Add the onion and garlic to the pot; cook, stirring, until slightly softened, about 2 minutes. Stir in the turmeric, cinnamon, cardamom, nutmeg, and pepper until absorbed. Stir in the tomatoes and water; then return lamb to the pot. Cover and place in oven for 1½ to 2 hours or until the lamb is soft.

5   Remove the pot from the oven and stir in the spinach until it is wilted. Stir in the yogurt, lemon rind, and salt.

SERVES: 4
Diabetic Exchanges: 2¾ lean meat; 2 vegetable; ¼ milk; 2½ fat

REDUCED SODIUM: Use low-sodium tomatoes.
Diabetic Exchanges: 2¾ lean meat; 2 vegetable; ¼ milk; 2½ fat

REDUCED FAT/SATURATED FAT/PROTEIN/CHOLESTEROL: Substitute 1 pound firm tofu cut into 1-inch cubes for the lamb and flour. Skip steps 2 and 3. Sauté onion and garlic in oil. Substitute beef or vegetable broth for the water. Bake 1 hour.
Diabetic Exchanges: 1½ very lean meat; 2 vegetable; 1¼ fat

MENU SUGGESTIONS: Green Salad; Pita Bread; Steamed Green Beans; Fresh Strawberries

SHISH KEBAB

I make this on my George Foreman Grill—it's easy and quick. If you are not a fan of lamb, you can substitute chicken or beef, but if you're using beef, be sure to use a tender cut, such as sirloin or filet mignon.

> **1 tablespoon fresh lemon juice**
>
> **1 tablespoon olive oil**
>
> **2 teaspoons red wine vinegar**
>
> **2 cloves garlic, minced**
>
> **½ teaspoon dried oregano**
>
> **⅛ teaspoon ground black pepper**
>
> **1 pound lamb, cut into 1-inch cubes**
>
> **1 medium green pepper, cored, seeded, and cut into 8 pieces**
>
> **2 small tomatoes, quartered**
>
> **1 medium onion, cut into 8 wedges**
>
> **Salt to taste**

1　In a large bowl, combine the lemon juice, olive oil, vinegar, garlic, oregano, and pepper. Add lamb and vegetables; toss until coated. Sprinkle with salt, if using. Let stand 20 minutes or longer in the refrigerator. String the lamb cubes onto four 8-inch skewers and the vegetables onto four 8-inch skewers. Brush with any extra marinade.

2　Preheat grill or broiler. Line a pan with foil and grease with oil. Place the vegetable skewers in the pan and cook 4 minutes. Turn the vegetable kebabs and add the lamb kebabs to the pan. Cook the lamb 2 to 3 minutes per side or until cooked to desired doneness (don't turn the vegetable kebabs when you turn the lamb).

SERVES: 4

Diabetic Exchanges: 3¼ very lean meat; 1 vegetable; 2 fat

REDUCED FAT/SATURATED FAT/PROTEIN/CHOLESTEROL: Use only half the lamb and double the vegetables.

Diabetic Exchanges: 1¾ very lean meat; 1¾ vegetable; 1¼ fat

MENU SUGGESTIONS: Greek Salad; Yellow Rice; Fresh Strawberries

LAMB TIKKA

This is such an easy, tasty way to prepare lamb that it has become one of my "regular" meals.

> **1 teaspoon coriander seeds**
> **¼ cup plain yogurt**
> **2 teaspoons fresh lemon juice**
> **1 teaspoon curry powder**
> **1 teaspoon chili powder**
> **Salt to taste**
> **1¼ pounds lamb cubes**

1   In a plastic bag, pound the coriander seeds with a heavy object until the seeds are crushed.

2   In a medium bowl, stir together the yogurt, lemon juice, curry powder, chili powder, crushed coriander seeds, and salt. Add the lamb and marinate, turning occasionally, 2 hours in the refrigerator.

3   Preheat broiler.

4   String the lamb onto four 8-inch skewers. Cook 6 inches from the heat for 3 minutes. Turn and cook 3 minutes longer for medium-rare, or until desired doneness.

SERVES: 4
Diabetic Exchanges: 4 very lean meat; ¼ milk; 1¼ fat

REDUCED FAT/SATURATED FAT/PROTEIN/CHOLESTEROL: Substitute 15 to 16 ounces firm tofu cut into 1-inch cubes for the lamb. Grill until tofu starts to brown, then turn, about 3 minutes per side.
Diabetic Exchanges: 1½ very lean meat; ¾ vegetable; 1 fat

MENU SUGGESTIONS: Cucumber Salad; Rice Pilaf; Curried Okra; Pineapple Slices

Pork

The pork industry likes to refer to pork as "the other white meat," indicating that pork is as healthy for you as chicken, and removing itself from its old image as a fatty food. Depending on the cut, the analogy is correct. However, it does not apply to bacon or other obviously fatty or untrimmed cuts of pork. The other difference is that pork can be tough and dry if not cooked properly (chicken can be dry too, but is seldom tough). You must cook pork just until it loses the pink in the center. No longer. Or, as with any other stewing meat, cook until it becomes tender, about an hour to an hour and a half.

HIGH: **fat, saturated fat, protein, cholesterol, phosphorus, potassium**

LOW: **carbohydrate, fiber, sodium**

SPICE-CRUSTED ROAST LOIN *of* PORK

This recipe wins rave reviews from everyone. You can use a boneless pork roast or tenderloin for this amazingly tasty dish. When cooking pork it's very important not to overcook it or it will be dry.

2-pound boneless pork roast

1 tablespoon coriander seeds

1 tablespoon molasses

2 cloves garlic, minced

½ teaspoon anise seed

½ teaspoon ground cardamom

¼ teaspoon ground allspice

¼ teaspoon ground black pepper

⅛ teaspoon dried mint, crumbled

(continued)

Entrées

1   Score the roast with slashes 1 inch apart.

2   Place the coriander seeds in a plastic bag. Pound with a meat pounder, the back of a heavy skillet, or any heavy object until the seeds are thoroughly crushed.

3   In a small bowl stir together the molasses, crushed coriander seeds, garlic, anise seed, cardamom, allspice, pepper, and mint. Brush all over the roast. Cover and refrigerate at least 1 hour.

4   Preheat oven to 350°F. Bake 1 hour and 15 minutes or until meat thermometer reads 160°F.

SERVES: 6

Diabetic Exchanges: ¼ other carbohydrate; 4¼ very lean meat; 2¾ fat

MENU SUGGESTIONS: Mixed Green Salad; Baked Sweet Potato; Sautéed Green Beans; Fresh Pineapple Slices

ROAST LOIN *of* PORK *with* FRESH HERBS

The herbs complement the taste of the pork beautifully. You can use a boneless pork roast or tenderloin. If you can't find fresh herbs, you can use ½ teaspoon each of dried thyme, rosemary, and mint.

> **1¾ pounds boneless pork roast**
>
> **Ground black pepper to taste**
>
> **Salt to taste**
>
> **1½ teaspoons fresh thyme leaves, chopped**
>
> **1½ teaspoons chopped fresh rosemary**
>
> **1 teaspoon chopped fresh mint**
>
> **2 cloves garlic, minced**
>
> **1 teaspoon olive oil**
>
> **⅓ cup chopped fresh parsley**

1   Preheat oven to 350°F.

2   Score the roast with slashes 1 inch apart. Season with pepper and salt; let stand 20 minutes or longer in the refrigerator.

3   In a small bowl, combine the thyme, rosemary, mint, and garlic. Stir in the oil, then the parsley. Spread over pork roast. Place in a 9-inch-square baking pan. Bake 1 hour to 1 hour and 15 minutes or until meat thermometer reads 160°F.

SERVES: 6

Diabetic Exchanges: 4 very lean meat; ¾ fat

MENU SUGGESTIONS: Zucchini Escarole Soup (page 47); Orzo with Peppers; Wedge of Iceberg Lettuce; Papaya Slices

APPLE PORK CHOPS

A rich, special-occasion dish. These chops should not be overcooked or they will be dry. You can use pork chops with or without the bone.

> **4 small pork chops, ½ inch thick**
> **(about 1½ pounds with the bone or 1 pound boneless)**
> **Salt to taste**
> **¼ teaspoon ground black pepper**
> **2 tablespoons all-purpose flour**
> **1 tablespoon vegetable oil**
> **1 cup sliced onion**
> **2 cups sliced apples**
> **¼ teaspoon dried thyme**
> **¼ cup apple juice**

1   Season the chops with salt and pepper; dredge lightly in flour.

2   In a large nonstick skillet, heat the oil over medium-high heat. Add the pork chops. Cook 4 minutes per side or until juices run clear when a small slit is cut in the meat. Remove from skillet.

3   Add the onion and cook until slightly softened, about 1 minute, add the apples and thyme; cook until slightly softened, about 2 minutes. Add the apple juice; return the pork chops to the skillet, and cook, turning the chops once, until sauce has thickened.

SERVES: 4

Diabetic Exchanges: ¼ bread; 3 lean meat; ½ fruit; ½ vegetable; 1½ fat

MENU SUGGESTIONS: Puréed Squash and Turnip; Green Beans; Green Salad; Poached Orange

BONELESS PORK CHOPS
with LEEKS *and* ORANGE JUICE

The hint of sweetness enhances the flavor of the pork. Cook the chops until just done; over-cooking leaves you with a very tough piece of meat.

> **4 boneless pork chops, ½ inch thick (about 1 pound)**
>
> **Salt to taste**
>
> **¼ teaspoon ground black pepper**
>
> **1 tablespoon cornstarch**
>
> **2 teaspoons vegetable oil**
>
> **½ cup chopped leek (white and light green parts)**
>
> **1 clove garlic, minced**
>
> **⅓ cup orange juice, white wine, or water**
>
> **2 tablespoons water**
>
> **1 teaspoon light or dark brown sugar**
>
> **½ teaspoon ground ginger**
>
> **½ teaspoon grated orange rind**

1   Season the chops with salt and pepper and dredge lightly in cornstarch.

2   In a large nonstick skillet, heat the oil over medium-high heat. Add the pork chops. Cook 4 minutes per side or until juices run clear when a small slit is cut in the meat. Remove from skillet.

3   Add the leek and garlic and cook until softened, about 1 minute. Stir in the juice, water, brown sugar, ginger, and orange rind; return the pork chops to the skillet and cook, turning the chops once, until sauce is thickened, 1 to 2 minutes.

SERVES: 4

Diabetic Exchanges: ¼ bread; 3¾ very lean meat; ½ vegetable; 1 fat

MENU SUGGESTIONS: Couscous with Zucchini and Scallion (page 265); Cucumber Salad; Grapefruit Segments with Mint

BRAISED PORK CHOPS
with RED ONION

You can make this with veal chops instead of pork chops and yellow or white onions instead of red.

> **4 boneless pork chops, ½ inch thick (about 1 pound)**
>
> **Salt to taste**
>
> **¼ teaspoon ground black pepper**
>
> **2 tablespoons all-purpose flour**
>
> **1 tablespoon vegetable oil**
>
> **2 cups sliced red onions**
>
> **¼ cup chopped fresh parsley**
>
> **¼ teaspoon dried rosemary, crumbled**
>
> **⅛ teaspoon dried thyme**
>
> **⅓ cup water**
>
> **2 tablespoons red wine**

1   Season the chops with salt and pepper; dredge lightly in flour.

2   In a large nonstick skillet, heat the oil over medium-high heat. Add the pork chops. Cook 4 minutes per side or until juices run clear when a small slit is cut in the meat. Remove from skillet.

3   Add the onions, parsley, rosemary, and thyme and cook until slightly softened, about 2 minutes. Add the water and wine; return the pork chops to the skillet and cook, turning the chops once, until sauce is thickened, 1 to 2 minutes.

SERVES: 4

Diabetic Exchanges: ¼ bread; 3¾ lean meat; 1 vegetable; 1½ fat

MENU SUGGESTIONS: Zucchini Escarole Soup (page 47); Orzo with Peppers; Wedge of Iceberg Lettuce; Papaya Slices

SZEKELE GOULASH

This is an authentic Hungarian dish—you will be amazed at how good this combination of flavors is, unless of course you're Hungarian—then you already know! The original recipe would be made with sour cream, not yogurt, but you really can't tell the difference.

2 teaspoons vegetable oil

1 pound pork, cubed

¾ cup chopped onion

2 cloves garlic, minced

1 tablespoon Hungarian paprika

1½ cups diced tomatoes

1¼ cups water

2 tablespoons tomato paste

1-pound package sauerkraut, drained

¼ teaspoon ground black pepper

¼ cup plain yogurt

1   In a 3-quart nonstick pot, heat the oil over medium-high heat. Add half the pork and cook until browned all over, about 5 minutes. Remove from pot. Repeat with remaining pork, removing from pot.

2   Add the onion and garlic to the pot. Cook, stirring, until slightly softened, about 2 minutes. Stir in the paprika until absorbed.

3   Add the pork, tomatoes, water, and tomato paste to the pot; bring to a boil. Reduce heat and simmer, covered, for 1 hour and 15 minutes. Add the sauerkraut and pepper; cook, uncovered, 25 minutes or until pork is tender.

4   Stir in the yogurt (do not allow to boil); remove from heat and serve immediately.

SERVES: 4

Diabetic Exchanges: 3½ lean meat; 1¾ vegetable; ½ fat

REDUCED SODIUM: Use low-sodium sauerkraut and tomato paste.

Diabetic Exchanges: 3½ lean meat; 1¾ vegetable; ½ fat

MENU SUGGESTIONS: Cucumber Salad; Spaetzle or other dumpling; Apricot Halves)

SHREDDED PORK *with* GARLIC SAUCE

This is a classic Szechuan preparation of pork or beef. Julienning is defined as cutting into matchstick-size pieces. In this recipe, it just means cut into thin strips, about 3 inches long.

⅓ cup chicken or vegetable broth

1 tablespoon soy sauce

1 tablespoon mirin or dry sherry

1½ teaspoons cornstarch

1 teaspoon sugar

1 tablespoon vegetable oil, divided

1 pound boneless pork, "julienned"

1 tablespoon minced ginger

2 cloves garlic, minced

1 cup "julienned" celery

½ cup "julienned" green bell pepper

½ cup "julienned" carrot

¼ cup "julienned" scallions

¼ teaspoon chili oil

1   In a small bowl, stir together the broth, soy sauce, mirin, cornstarch, and sugar.

2   In a nonstick wok or large nonstick skillet, heat 1 teaspoon of the oil over high heat. Add the pork, ginger, and garlic; cook, stirring, until pork is no longer pink inside, about 6 minutes. Remove from skillet.

3   Add the remaining 2 teaspoon of oil. Add the celery, bell pepper, carrot, and scallions. Cook, stirring, until vegetables are tender-crisp, about 3 minutes. Return pork to skillet.

4   Add the broth mixture and cook, stirring, until sauce comes to a boil and thickens, about 2 minutes. Stir in the chili oil.

SERVES: 4

Diabetic Exchanges: 4½ lean meat; ¾ vegetable; 1 fat

REDUCED FAT/SATURATED FAT/PROTEIN/CHOLESTEROL: Substitute a 15-ounce package of firm tofu cut into strips for the pork, skip step 2 and add ginger, scallions, and garlic in step 3. Add tofu just before you add the broth mixture in step 4.

Diabetic Exchanges: 1½ very lean meat; ¾ vegetable; 1¾ fat

REDUCED SODIUM: Use low-sodium soy sauce.

Diabetic Exchanges: 4½ lean meat; ¾ vegetable; 1 fat

MENU SUGGESTIONS: Chicken Broth; Steamed Rice; Orange Wedges

Entrées

HIGH: **protein, cholesterol, phosphorus, potassium, sodium**

LOW: **fiber, calcium**

HOLIDAY BAKED HAM

I love the look of the scored ham studded with whole cloves. My mom used to do hers this way and decorated it with rings of pineapple with maraschino cherries in the center—a not-too-subtle hint that I grew up in the fifties! You can use regular preserves for the glaze, but I used the fruit-only no-added-sugar kind. Chinese mustard is spicier than yellow, brown, or Dijon. It's the mustard you get at a Chinese restaurant or in packets when you order in. If you don't have any, use Dijon.

> **½ shank-end smoked cooked ham (about 6 pounds)**
>
> **30 whole cloves**
>
> **¼ cup apricot spread**
>
> **2 tablespoons plum sauce**
>
> **1 tablespoon mirin or dry sherry**
>
> **1½ teaspoons prepared Chinese mustard (available in Asian markets or the Asian section of your supermarket)**

1   Preheat oven to 375°F.

2   Score the ham and stud with the cloves. Place in roasting pan and bake, uncovered, 45 minutes.

3   In a small bowl, stir together the apricot spread, plum sauce, mirin, and Chinese mustard. Brush onto ham and bake 30 minutes longer.

SERVES: 8

Diabetic Exchanges: ½ other carbohydrate; 5½ very lean meat; 1¼ fat

MENU SUGGESTIONS: Green Salad; Mashed Butternut Squash and Turnip; Peas with Dill; Fresh Strawberries

THE ULTIMATE DIABETES COOKBOOK

Side Dishes

Unless your physician or nutritionist has put you on a very low carbohydrate diet, side dishes should be an important part of your daily food intake. Choose at least one or more vegetables that are lower in carbohydrates for each meal (that means fewer of these starchy vegetables: artichokes, brussels sprouts, carrots, corn, kale, okra, onions [and the onion family such as leeks, scallions, chives], parsnips, peas, red peppers, tomatoes, turnips, and winter squash). Choose the starchy vegetables and other complex carbohydrates (potatoes, grains, beans) according to your eating plan.

If you don't have time to prepare one of the recipes in this chapter, defrosting a simple box of frozen vegetables is good in a pinch. My favorite trick for instant cooked vegetables is to wrap a portion of green beans or asparagus or similar in a wet paper towel, then microwave for 1 minute or until desired doneness—voilà, perfectly cooked vegetables!

Vegetables

Mom always said, "Eat your vegetables," and now the government is saying it too. At least five a day (that's a combination of fruits and vegetables). Vegetables are great. They provide vitamins, minerals, and fiber and they are not too calorific. If you don't prepare them using fat, they are low in fat and have no cholesterol. What more could a person ask for? Don't forget that not all vegetables are low in carbohydrates. Potatoes, corn, winter squash, beans, and peas all are high in starch and counted as bread exchanges. There are also vegetables that are higher in starch but still count as vegetables. They are listed in the introduction on page 16.

LOW: fat, protein, cholesterol, calcium, iron, magnesium, phosphorus, sodium, saturated fat

LEMON ASPARAGUS

Thin or thick is always a debate when choosing asparagus. It's strictly a matter of taste. I prefer spears as thin as possible. The main point is that if you've chosen thick, you'll have to cook them longer than I suggest here. To prepare fresh asparagus, hold the spear with one hand in the center of the stalk and the other at the end. Bend until the stalk breaks in two; discard the bottom.

> 1 tablespoon butter
> 1 pound thin asparagus
> 1½ tablespoons fresh lemon juice
> ⅛ teaspoon ground black pepper
> Salt to taste

1   In a large nonstick skillet, melt the butter over medium-high heat. Add the asparagus and cook, stirring, until tender-crisp, about 3 to 4 minutes (or more if your asparagus is thicker).

2   Add the lemon juice, pepper, and salt. Toss until asparagus spears are coated.

SERVES: 4
Diabetic Exchanges: 1 vegetable; ½ fat

REDUCED SATURATED FAT/CHOLESTEROL/SODIUM: Use olive oil instead of butter.
Diabetic Exchanges: 1 vegetable; ¾ fat

MUNG BEAN SPROUTS
with SCALLIONS

A friend and I liked these so much that we polished off the whole recipe, even though it's supposed to serve four.

> **2 tablespoons water**
>
> **1 tablespoon soy sauce**
>
> **1 tablespoon mirin or dry sherry**
>
> **1 teaspoon cornstarch**
>
> **2 teaspoons vegetable oil**
>
> **4 cups fresh mung bean sprouts**
>
> **⅓ cup thinly sliced scallions (white and green parts)**
>
> **2 cloves garlic, minced**
>
> **1 teaspoon minced ginger**

1   In a small bowl, stir together the water, soy sauce, mirin, and cornstarch.

2   In a nonstick skillet or wok, heat the oil over high heat. Add the bean sprouts, scallions, garlic, and ginger. Cook, stirring, until tender-crisp, about 1 to 2 minutes. Add the soy sauce mixture. Cook, stirring, until mixture thickens, about 1 minute longer.

SERVES: 4
Diabetic Exchanges: 1½ vegetable; ½ fat

REDUCED SODIUM: Use low-sodium soy sauce.
Diabetic Exchanges: 1½ vegetable; ½ fat

STIR-FRIED BOK CHOY

Bok choy is the vegetable with the big white stalks and dark green leaves—not the bigger, lighter-leafed Chinese cabbage. Baby bok choy is also available in many markets; this is a small head with light green stems and dark leaves. You can use any of these in this recipe.

3 tablespoons water

2 tablespoons mirin or dry sherry

2 teaspoons soy sauce

2 teaspoons cornstarch

1 teaspoon sugar

2 teaspoons vegetable oil

10 cups lightly packed bok choy, cut into bite-size pieces

2 cloves garlic, minced

1   In a small bowl, stir together the water, mirin, soy sauce, cornstarch, and sugar.

2   In a nonstick wok or large nonstick skillet, heat the oil over high heat. Add the bok choy and garlic. Cook, stirring, until tender-crisp, about 5 minutes. Stir in the soy sauce mixture and cook, stirring, until sauce has thickened, about 1 minute.

SERVES: 4

Diabetic Exchanges: ¼ other carbohydrate; ¾ vegetable; ½ fat

REDUCED SODIUM: Use low-sodium soy sauce.

Diabetic Exchanges: ¼ other carbohydrate; ¾ vegetable; ½ fat

SAUTÉED BROCCOLI
with BELL PEPPERS

This is a very simple way to prepare broccoli. I like to use the stems as well as the florets. If the stems are "woody," peel them, then slice thin.

2 teaspoons olive oil

3 cups broccoli florets (and stems, if desired)

1 cup sliced red bell pepper

2 cloves garlic, sliced paper thin

3 tablespoons chicken or vegetable broth

1 tablespoon balsamic vinegar

Salt to taste

In a large nonstick skillet, heat the oil over high heat. Add the broccoli, bell pepper, and garlic. Cook, stirring, 5 minutes or until vegetables are tender-crisp. Add the broth and vinegar. Cook, stirring, until liquid evaporates, about 2 minutes. Add salt, if using.

SERVES: 4

Diabetic Exchanges: 1 vegetable; ½ fat

BROCCOLI SOUFFLÉ

This lovely side dish is a perfect "go with" for simple entrées such a Lemon Sole with White Wine (page 147) or grilled fish or chicken. You can bake this in any 1½-quart ovenproof baking dish.

1 tablespoon butter, divided

3 tablespoons grated Parmesan cheese, divided

1 cup vegetable broth, divided

3 cups chopped broccoli florets

⅓ cup sliced leek

¼ teaspoon dried tarragon

⅛ teaspoon dried thyme

1 tablespoon flour

4 egg whites

1 Preheat oven to 350°F. Using 1 teaspoon of the butter, grease a 1½-quart soufflé dish. Dust with 1 tablespoon of the Parmesan cheese.

2 In a 1-quart saucepan, bring ⅔ cup broth to a boil. Add the broccoli, leek, tarragon, and thyme, reduce heat, and simmer, covered, 20 minutes or until the vegetables are well cooked and most of the broth has evaporated.

3 Place the broccoli in a food processor container. Cover and process until finely chopped.

4 In the same saucepan, melt the remaining 2 teaspoons butter over medium heat. Stir in the flour until absorbed. Add the remaining ⅓ cup broth and the chopped vegetables. Cook, stirring, until mixture comes to a boil; let cool.

5 In a large bowl, beat egg whites until stiff. Fold in the broccoli mixture. Turn into prepared dish, top with remaining Parmesan cheese, and bake 25 minutes.

6 Serve immediately.

SERVES: 4

Diabetic Exchanges: 1 very lean meat; ¾ vegetable; ½ fat

REDUCED SODIUM: Use low-sodium broth and Parmesan cheese and unsalted butter.

Diabetic Exchanges: 1 very lean meat; ¾ vegetable; ½ fat

BROCCOLI RABE
with SHIITAKE MUSHROOMS

Broccoli rabe is not to everyone's taste. It definitely has a bitter edge which this preparation tames somewhat. The end result is very pleasing.

⅓ cup chicken broth

1 tablespoon mirin or dry sherry

2 teaspoons soy sauce

1 teaspoon black bean garlic sauce (available in Asian markets or the Asian section of your supermarket)

1 teaspoon cornstarch

2 teaspoons vegetable oil

4 cups chopped broccoli rabe

2 cups sliced shiitake mushrooms

2 cloves garlic, sliced paper thin

1   In a small bowl, combine the broth, mirin, soy sauce, black bean garlic sauce, and cornstarch.

2   In a nonstick wok or large nonstick skillet, heat the oil over high heat. Add the broccoli rabe, shiitake mushrooms, and garlic. Cook, stirring, until tender-crisp, about 5 minutes. Stir in the soy sauce mixture and cook, stirring, until sauce has thickened, about 1 minute.

SERVES: 4

Diabetic Exchanges: 1¼ vegetable; ¾ fat

REDUCED SODIUM: Use low-sodium broth and soy sauce. Reduce the black bean sauce to ½ teaspoon.

Diabetic Exchanges: 1¼ vegetable; ½ fat

BRUSSELS SPROUTS
with SESAME SEEDS

This is a very simple way to serve brussels sprouts. I like to use the sesame seeds that still have the hull because they are more flavorful than the hulled ones. You can find them in health food stores.

3 cups brussels sprouts

1½ teaspoons sesame seeds

1 teaspoon vegetable oil

2 cloves garlic, minced

¼ teaspoon ground pepper

Salt to taste

1   Trim the bottoms of the brussels sprouts and remove any yellowed leaves. Cut in half through the stems.

2   Cook the brussels sprouts in boiling water until tender, about 7 minutes or to desired doneness; drain.

3   In a dry nonstick skillet, toast the sesame seeds over medium heat, about 3 minutes, stirring constantly.

4   Add the oil and garlic to the skillet with the sesame seeds and cook, stirring, for 30 seconds. Add the brussels sprouts, pepper, and salt to the skillet. Cook, stirring, until brussels sprouts are heated through, about 2 to 3 minutes.

SERVES: 4
Diabetic Exchanges: ¾ vegetable; ¼ fat

PESTO CABBAGE

This is an unexpected flavor combination that resulted from a happy accident when I happened to be chopping some cabbage near some pesto sauce. You can make homemade pesto or use storebought.

> ¼ **cup water**
> 1 **tablespoon pesto sauce**
> 5 **cups shredded cabbage**
> ⅛ **teaspoon ground black pepper**
> **Salt to taste**

In a large nonstick skillet, heat the water and pesto sauce until boiling. Add the cabbage and cook, stirring, until cabbage is tender, about 4 minutes. Stir in the pepper and salt.

SERVES: 4
Diabetic Exchanges: 1¼ vegetable; ¼ fat

SAUTÉED GREEN *and* RED CABBAGE

The flavors in this dish are subtle with just a little kick from the pepper. You could add chopped apple or raisins when you sauté the vegetables if you want a "fancier" vegetable dish. You could also use only one type of cabbage, if you like.

1 tablespoon olive oil

2 cups shredded green cabbage

2 cups shredded red cabbage

½ cup chopped onion

2 tablespoons fresh lemon juice

¼ cup chopped fresh parsley

½ teaspoon ground black pepper

Salt to taste

In a large nonstick skillet, heat the oil over medium-high heat. Add the cabbages and onion and cook, stirring, until wilted, about 3 minutes. Stir in the lemon juice, parsley, pepper, and salt.

SERVES: 4
Diabetic Exchanges: 1½ vegetable; 1 fat

SWEET *and* SOUR RED CABBAGE

This is a subtle "sweet and sour." I like to serve this with any roast such as pork, turkey, or chicken.

2 teaspoons vegetable oil

4 cups shredded red cabbage

½ cup chopped onion

¼ cup apple juice

2 tablespoons fresh lemon juice

1 tablespoon firmly pressed brown sugar

⅛ teaspoon ground cloves

⅛ teaspoon ground black pepper

Salt to taste

1   In a large nonstick skillet, heat the oil over medium-high heat. Add the cabbage and onion. Cook, stirring, until slightly softened, about 4 minutes.

2   Stir in the apple juice, lemon juice, brown sugar, cloves, pepper, and salt. Cook, stirring, until all liquid has evaporated and cabbage is soft, about 4 minutes.

SERVES: 4

Diabetic Exchanges: ¼ other carbohydrate; ¼ fruit; 1¼ vegetable; ½ fat

ORANGE-GLAZED CARROTS *and* TURNIPS

Because carrots and orange juice are high in sugar, this is not an everyday dish. It's a perfect side dish for Thanksgiving. You might even try substituting it for candied yams. It's orange and tastes *almost* as good. For a sweeter dish use rutabaga (yellow turnip) instead of the white.

¼ cup orange juice

1 tablespoon dry sherry

1 tablespoon honey

2 teaspoons honey mustard

1 teaspoon grated orange rind

1 tablespoon vegetable oil

2 cups julienned carrots

2 cups julienned turnip

1 tablespoon minced fresh ginger

Salt to taste

1   In a small bowl, stir together the orange juice, sherry, honey, mustard, and orange rind.

2   In a large nonstick skillet, heat the oil over medium-high heat. Add the carrots, turnip, and ginger. Cook, stirring, until vegetables are tender-crisp, about 3 minutes. Stir in the orange mixture and cook, stirring, until vegetables are glazed. Add salt, if using.

SERVES: 4

Diabetic Exchanges: 1¾ vegetable; ¾ fat

CAULIFLOWER *with* PREISEL

This is a Viennese recipe my mom used when preparing cauliflower on special occasions. Of course she used butter instead of oil—and lots of it!

> **4 cups cauliflower florets**
> **2 teaspoons vegetable oil**
> **3 tablespoons plain dry bread crumbs**
> **⅛ teaspoon ground black pepper**
> **Salt to taste**

1   Cook the cauliflower in boiling water for 5 minutes. Drain well.

2   In a large nonstick skillet, heat the oil over medium-high heat. Add the bread crumbs and cook, stirring, until browned, about 3 minutes. Stir in the pepper and salt. Add the cauliflower to the skillet and cook, stirring, until heated through, about 2 minutes.

SERVES: 4

Diabetic Exchanges: ¼ bread; ¾ vegetable; ½ fat

SPICY GRILLED CAULIFLOWER

This is such an attractive way to serve cauliflower; the slices resemble fans. You will not be using the entire head of cauliflower—only the middle part. Use the leftover florets for another recipe. Vary the spiciness by using more or less Tabasco.

> **1 head cauliflower**
> **2 teaspoons olive oil**
> **1 teaspoon Old Bay Seasoning or Cajun Shake (page 70)**
> **½ teaspoon fresh lemon juice**
> **1 clove garlic, minced**
> **3 drops Tabasco**

1   Preheat grill or broiler.

2   Remove the leaves from the cauliflower head. Slice in half through the stem. Continue cutting through the stem to form four ½-inch thick pieces of cauliflower.

3   In a small bowl, combine the oil, seasoning, lemon juice, garlic, and Tabasco. Brush lightly on the slices of cauliflower.

4   Grill or broil 3 minutes per side until the cauliflower is tender-crisp, or to desired doneness.

SERVES: 4

Diabetic Exchanges: 1 vegetable; ½ fat

REDUCED SODIUM: Use Cajun Shake without salt.

Diabetic Exchanges: 1 vegetable; ½ fat

BRAISED CELERY *with* FENNEL

Such a simple yet delicious recipe. You can, of course, just make braised celery or braised fennel instead of the combination. You can freeze the leftover broth to use in other recipes.

> **2 teaspoons olive oil**
>
> **3 cups 1-inch celery chunks**
>
> **2 cups cubed fennel**
>
> **2 cloves garlic, minced**
>
> **1 cup chicken or vegetable broth**
>
> **1 tablespoon chopped fresh parsley**
>
> **⅛ teaspoon ground black pepper**
>
> **Salt to taste**

1   In a large nonstick skillet, heat the oil over high heat. Add the celery, fennel, and garlic; cook, stirring, until slightly softened, about 3 minutes.

2   Add the broth and parsley; bring to a boil. Reduce heat and simmer, covered, 20 minutes or until vegetables are soft. Drain (you may want to reserve the broth for other uses). Season with parsley, pepper, and salt.

SERVES: 4

Diabetic Exchanges: 1 vegetable; ½ fat

REDUCED SODIUM: Use low-sodium broth.

Diabetic Exchanges: 1 vegetable; ½ fat

SAUTÉED CELERY
with CARROTS *and* SNOW PEAS

Toss in a little tofu and serve over brown rice and you have a nice entrée. If you want to spice this up, substitute extra chili oil for some of the sesame oil.

> **2 teaspoons vegetable oil**
>
> **2 cups julienned celery**
>
> **1 cup julienned snow peas**
>
> **½ cup julienned carrot**
>
> **2 cloves garlic, cut into slivers**
>
> **2 teaspoons soy sauce**
>
> **1 teaspoon mirin or dry sherry**
>
> **1 teaspoon sesame oil**
>
> **¼ teaspoon chili oil (optional)**

In a medium nonstick skillet, heat the vegetable oil over medium-high heat. Add the celery, snow peas, carrot, and garlic. Cook, stirring, until vegetables are tender-crisp, about 4 minutes. Stir in the soy sauce, mirin, sesame oil, and chili oil, if using.

SERVES: 4

Diabetic Exchanges: ¼ bread; ¾ vegetable; ¾ fat

REDUCED SODIUM: Use low-sodium soy sauce.

Diabetic Exchanges: ¼ bread; ¾ vegetable; ¾ fat

SAUTÉED CORN *and* ZUCCHINI

I use canned corn for this recipe and, instead of the water, the liquid from the can. The zucchini and onion are cooked until very soft so that all the flavors blend. If you prefer your veggies crispier, you can sauté the veggies, add the corn, and cook just until the corn is heated through.

> **1 teaspoon olive oil**
> **1 cup diced zucchini**
> **⅓ cup chopped onion**
> **⅓ cup chopped green bell pepper**
> **1 cup cooked corn kernels (fresh, canned, or frozen)**
> **2 tablespoons water or liquid from corn**
> **¼ teaspoon chili powder**
> **¼ teaspoon ground black pepper**
> **Salt to taste**

1   In a medium nonstick skillet, heat the oil over medium-high heat. Add the zucchini, onion, and bell pepper. Cook, stirring, until slightly softened, about 3 minutes.

2   Add the corn, water, chili powder, pepper, and salt. Cover and simmer 10 minutes.

SERVES: 4

Diabetic Exchanges: ¾ bread; ½ vegetable; ¼ fat

REDUCED SODIUM: Use fresh corn kernels instead of canned.

Diabetic Exchanges: ¾ bread; ½ vegetable; ¼ fat

Stuffed Eggplant

I use two very small eggplants, but you can use one ¾- to 1-pound eggplant for this recipe instead. The amount of pepper called for makes for a slightly spicy filling—use less for a tamer result.

> **2 small eggplants (about 6 to 7 ounces each)**
>
> **1 tablespoon olive oil**
>
> **1 cup chopped portobello mushrooms**
>
> **½ cup chopped onion**
>
> **2 cloves garlic, minced**
>
> **½ cup chopped tomato**
>
> **2 tablespoons chopped fresh parsley**
>
> **1 tablespoon plain dry bread crumbs**
>
> **1 tablespoon grated Parmesan cheese**
>
> **¼ teaspoon ground pepper**
>
> **Salt to taste**

1   Preheat oven to 350°F.

2   Cut the eggplants in half lengthwise. Scoop out the flesh, leaving a ¼-inch-thick eggplant shell; chop the scooped flesh. Place the shells on a baking pan and bake 15 minutes.

3   While the shells are baking, in a medium nonstick skillet, heat the oil over medium-high heat. Add the chopped eggplant, mushroom, onion, and garlic. Cook, stirring, until vegetables are slightly softened, about 4 minutes. Stir in the tomato. Cook, stirring, 1 minute longer. Add the parsley, bread crumbs, Parmesan cheese, pepper, and salt.

4   Spoon mixture into the eggplant shells. Return to the oven. Bake 15 to 20 minutes or until filling is heated through.

SERVES: 4

Diabetic Exchanges: ¼ bread; 1¾ vegetable; ¾ fat

GRILLED EGGPLANT PARMESAN

I prepare this recipe a lot. I think the taste is so delicious that I don't miss all the fat or the breading. In fact, I often use this as an entrée by doubling the portion size.

1 teaspoon olive oil

2 tablespoons chicken or vegetable broth

½ teaspoon dried oregano

1 clove garlic, minced

8 slices eggplant (½ inch thick)

1 cup marinara sauce, divided

1 cup shredded mozzarella cheese (4 ounces), divided

2 tablespoons grated Parmesan cheese, divided

1   Preheat broiler. Grease an 8-inch-square baking dish with olive oil.

2   In a small bowl, stir together the broth, oregano, and garlic.

3   Pierce the eggplant slices all over with a fork. Brush the eggplant slices on both sides with the broth mixture. Place on a baking sheet lined with greased aluminum foil. Cook 6 inches from the heat, 3 to 4 minutes per side or until browned on each side.

4   Reduce oven temperature to 350°F. Place 4 of the eggplant slices in the greased baking pan. Top each with 2 tablespoons sauce and 2 tablespoons of mozzarella cheese. Sprinkle 1 tablespoon of the Parmesan cheese over the 4 slices. Place the remaining ingredients on top in the same order. Bake 20 minutes or until cheese has melted and eggplant is hot.

SERVES: 8
Diabetic Exchanges: ¼ bread; ½ lean meat; 1 vegetable; ½ fat

REDUCED FAT/SATURATED FAT/CHOLESTEROL: Use low-fat mozzarella cheese and fat-free Parmesan cheese.
Diabetic Exchanges: ¼ bread; ½ lean meat; 1 vegetable; ½ fat

REDUCED SODIUM: Use low-sodium sauce, mozzarella, and Parmesan cheese.
Diabetic Exchanges: ¼ bread; ½ lean meat; 1 vegetable; ¼ fat

GREEK VEGETABLE STEW

This is closely related to ratatouille but with the Greek additions of cinnamon and green beans.

> **1 tablespoon olive oil**
>
> **1 cup sliced onion**
>
> **½ cup diced green bell pepper**
>
> **2 cloves garlic, minced**
>
> **3 cups cubed eggplant (1½-inch pieces)**
>
> **1 cup sliced zucchini (½ inch thick)**
>
> **½ cup vegetable broth**
>
> **¼ cup chopped fresh parsley**
>
> **1 tablespoon tomato paste**
>
> **½ teaspoon dried oregano**
>
> **½ teaspoon sugar**
>
> **¼ teaspoon ground cinnamon**
>
> **⅛ teaspoon ground black pepper**
>
> **Salt to taste**
>
> **2 cups green beans cut into 2-inch pieces**

1 In a 3-quart nonstick saucepan, heat the oil over medium-high heat. Add the onion, bell pepper, and garlic. Cook, stirring, until slightly softened, about 2 minutes. Add the eggplant and zucchini; cook, stirring, until slightly cooked, about 5 minutes.

2 Stir in the broth, parsley, tomato paste, oregano, sugar, cinnamon, pepper, and salt. Bring to a boil. Add the green beans, reduce heat, and simmer, covered, 30 minutes or until all the vegetables are soft.

SERVES: 6
Diabetic Exchanges: 1¾ vegetable; ½ fat

REDUCED SODIUM: Use low-sodium broth and tomato paste.
Diabetic Exchanges: 1¾ vegetable; ½ fat

GRILLED FENNEL *and* RED ONION *with* ORANGE MARINADE

You can use an all-fruit or sugar-free marmalade, but I have given the nutritional information using regular marmalade. If you do not have anise seed, you can use fennel seed or just omit it; the recipe will be fine anyway.

> **1 large or 2 small fennel**
> **1 medium red onion**
> **2 tablespoons orange juice**
> **1 tablespoon orange marmalade**
> **1 tablespoon sherry**
> **1 teaspoon fennel fronds**
> **¼ teaspoon orange rind**
> **¼ teaspoon anise seed**
> **1 clove garlic, minced**

1 Cut off the fennel stalks and fronds, reserving top of the fronds for the marinade and discarding the rest. Cut the fennel bulb into 8 wedges, keeping the root intact so the wedges hold together. Cut the red onion into 8 wedges as well.

2 In a 9-inch-square baking pan, combine the orange juice, marmalade, sherry, fennel fronds, orange rind, anise seed, and garlic.

3 Place the fennel and onion in the baking dish with the orange mixture. Let stand 20 minutes or longer in the refrigerator, turning once.

4 Preheat broiler. Place the vegetables with the marinade 6 inches from the heat. Broil 6 to 7 minutes per side or until vegetables have browned.

SERVES: 4

Diabetic Exchanges: ¼ other carbohydrate; 1½ vegetable

GREEN BEANS *à la* GRECQUE

I usually order these when I eat at my local Greek diner. This is one of those times when I like my green beans well cooked and less crunchy. If you want your green beans really soft, you may want to add a little extra water and cook them a little longer. If you don't have fennel seed you can use anise seed or nothing at all.

> **2 teaspoons olive oil**
>
> **3 cups green beans cut into 1½-inch pieces**
>
> **½ cup chopped onion**
>
> **One 8-ounce can tomato sauce**
>
> **½ cup water**
>
> **½ teaspoon dried oregano**
>
> **¼ teaspoon fennel seed**
>
> **⅛ teaspoon ground black pepper**
>
> **Salt to taste**

1 In a 2-quart nonstick saucepan, heat the oil over medium-high heat. Add the green beans and onion, and cook, stirring, until onion is slightly softened, about 3 minutes.

2 Add the tomato sauce, water, oregano, fennel seed, black pepper, and salt. Bring to a boil. Reduce heat and simmer, covered, 30 minutes.

SERVES: 4

Diabetic Exchanges: 2½ vegetable; ½ fat

REDUCED SODIUM: Use low-sodium tomato sauce.

Diabetic Exchanges: ¼ other carbohydrate; 1½ vegetable; ½ fat

GREEN BEANS *with* MUSHROOMS *and* DILL

This has become one of my favorite ways to prepare green beans. It's easy and a wonderful combination of flavors. Don't worry if the lemon turns the beans off color. For a more dramatic presentation, leave the green beans whole.

2 teaspoons olive oil

2½ cups green beans cut into 2-inch pieces

1½ cups sliced mushrooms (¼ inch thick)

2 cloves garlic, minced

2 tablespoons snipped fresh dill or ½ teaspoon dried dillweed

1½ teaspoons fresh lemon juice

1 teaspoon Dijon mustard

Salt to taste

1   In a large nonstick skillet, heat the oil over medium-high heat. Add the green beans, mushrooms, and garlic. Cook, stirring, until green beans are tender, about 5 minutes.

2   Stir in the dill, lemon juice, mustard, and salt until heated through.

SERVES: 4

Diabetic Exchanges: 1¼ vegetable; ½ fat

SHERRIED GREEN BEANS *and* JICAMA

This is a wonderful combination. Don't be distressed if (as with the lemon juice in the previous recipe) the green beans turn slightly off color when you add the lime juice.

2 teaspoons olive oil

2 cups green beans cut into 2-inch pieces

2 cups julienned jicama

1 tablespoon sherry

1 tablespoon fresh lime juice

Salt to taste

1   In a large nonstick skillet, heat the oil over medium-high heat. Add the green beans and jicama. Cook, stirring, until green beans turn bright green and jicama is slightly softened, about 4 minutes.

2   Add the sherry, lime juice, and salt. Cook, stirring, 1 minute longer.

SERVES: 4

Diabetic Exchanges: 2 vegetable; ½ fat

SOUTHERN-STYLE COLLARDS *and* KALE

Most but not all of the liquid should be cooked away by the time the greens are done. Check your saucepan about 5 minutes before the end of the cooking time to make sure the liquid has not all cooked away. If so, add a little water. Use less red pepper flakes or ½ teaspoon ground black pepper for a milder version.

> **2 teaspoons olive oil**
> **½ cup finely chopped onion**
> **2 cloves garlic, minced**
> **3 cups loosely packed chopped collard greens**
> **3 cups loosely packed chopped kale**
> **1 cup chicken or vegetable broth**
> **1 cup water**
> **1 teaspoon sugar**
> **¼ teaspoon red pepper flakes**
> **Salt to taste**

1   In a 3-quart nonstick pot, heat the oil over medium-high heat. Add the onion and garlic, and cook, stirring, 2 minutes or until onion is slightly softened.

2   Add the collards, kale, broth, water, sugar, pepper, and salt. Bring to a boil. Reduce heat and simmer, covered, 25 minutes or until vegetables are very tender.

SERVES: 4
Diabetic Exchanges: 1¾ vegetable; ½ fat

REDUCED SODIUM: Use low-sodium broth.
Diabetic Exchanges: 1¾ vegetable; ½ fat

BRAISED GREENS *and* CAULIFLOWER

Use just one or any combination of greens you like: collard greens, Swiss chard, beet greens, kale.

2 teaspoons olive oil

1 cup chopped onion

2 cloves garlic, minced

4 cups chopped fresh greens, well rinsed and dried

¾ cup chicken or vegetable broth

1 cup water

¼ teaspoon ground black pepper

5 cups cauliflower florets

Salt to taste

1   In a 4-quart nonstick pot, heat the oil over medium-high heat. Add the onion and garlic, and cook, stirring, until slightly softened, about 2 minutes. Add the greens and cook, stirring, until wilted, about 4 minutes.

2   Add the broth, water, and pepper. Bring to a boil. Reduce heat and simmer, uncovered, 20 minutes.

3   Increase the heat to medium. Add the cauliflower and salt, if using, and cook, covered, 5 to 7 minutes or until cauliflower is tender.

SERVES: 6
Diabetic Exchanges: 1½ vegetable; ½ fat

REDUCED SODIUM: Substitute low-sodium chicken broth for the regular.
Diabetic Exchanges: 1½ vegetable; ¼ fat

ETHIOPIAN KALE

Ethiopian cuisine is one of my favorites. The interesting thing is that the spices are not too complicated—but very well balanced. These greens are a good example. Use collards or other greens in this recipe if you like. This dish is perfect with any simple roast or grilled meat and also with any curry.

> **2 cups water**
>
> **6 cups lightly packed, torn kale leaves**
>
> **1 cup chopped red onion**
>
> **2 teaspoons olive oil**
>
> **1 tablespoon minced ginger**
>
> **4 cloves garlic, minced**
>
> **¼ teaspoon red pepper flakes**
>
> **Salt to taste**

In a 2-quart saucepan, bring the water to a boil over medium-high heat. Add the kale, onion, oil, ginger, garlic, pepper, and salt. Return to the boil, then reduce heat and simmer, uncovered, 25 minutes.

SERVES: 4

Diabetic Exchanges: 2 vegetable; ½ fat

SAUTÉED PORTOBELLO MUSHROOMS *with* VEGETABLES

If you don't have portobello mushrooms, use shiitake or cremini mushrooms. If none of those is available, white mushrooms are okay too.

2 teaspoons olive oil

1 cup sliced celery

½ cup sliced leek (white and light green parts)

½ cup chopped red bell pepper

2 cloves garlic, minced

3 cups chopped portobello mushrooms

⅛ teaspoon ground black pepper

Salt to taste

1 In a large nonstick skillet, heat the oil over medium-high heat. Add the celery, leek, red pepper, and garlic. Cook, stirring, until vegetables are tender-crisp, about 4 minutes.

2 Add the mushrooms. Cook, stirring, until cooked, about 3 minutes. Stir in the pepper and salt.

SERVES: 4

Diabetic Exchanges: 1½ vegetable; ½ fat

WHITE *and* SHIITAKE MUSHROOMS

This is more a condiment than a vegetable. It would be great served with any simple meat entrée like grilled chicken or steak.

>**1 tablespoon olive oil**
>
>**3 cups sliced white mushrooms**
>
>**1 tablespoon minced shallot**
>
>**2 cups sliced shiitake mushrooms**
>
>**2 tablespoons chopped fresh parsley**
>
>**1 tablespoon Madeira**
>
>**⅛ teaspoon ground black pepper**
>
>**Salt to taste**

1   In a medium nonstick skillet heat the oil over medium-high heat. Add the mushooms and shallot. Cook, stirring, 3 minutes, until mushrooms are slightly softened.

2   Add the parsley and Madeira. Cook, stirring, 1 minute or until the Madeira is absorbed. Season with pepper and salt.

SERVES: 4

Diabetic Exchanges: 1 vegetable; ½ fat

OKRA *with* TOMATOES

This is a wonderful summer dish when tomatoes are at their peak. Okra has had a bad rap—as long as you don't overcook it, it doesn't become slimey.

> **1 tablespoon olive oil**
> **½ cup chopped green bell pepper**
> **2 cloves garlic, minced**
> **2 cups sliced okra (½ inch thick)**
> **2 cups ripe tomato wedges**
> **¼ teaspoon ground black pepper**
> **Salt to taste**

1 In a large nonstick skillet, heat the oil over medium-high heat. Add the green pepper and garlic, and cook, stirring, 1 minute.

2 Add the okra and cook, stirring, 1 minute. Add the tomatoes and cook, stirring, 2 minutes or until the tomatoes are heated through. Season with pepper and salt.

SERVES: 4

Diabetic Exchanges: 1¾ vegetable; ¾ fat

REDUCED FAT: Use only 1 teaspoon olive oil.

Diabetic Exchanges: 1¾ vegetable; ¼ fat

SAUTÉED SNOW PEAS
with MUSHROOMS

The unusual thing about this recipe is that it uses balsamic vinegar for flavoring instead of the expected soy sauce.

2 teaspoons olive oil

1 tablespoon minced shallot

1½ cups snow peas, halved crosswise

1 ½ cups sliced mushrooms

½ cup sliced water chestnuts

1 tablespoon balsamic vinegar

1 teaspoon sesame oil

Salt to taste

1   In a large nonstick skillet, heat the oil over medium-high heat. Add the shallot and cook, stirring, 30 seconds. Add the snow peas and mushrooms, and cook, stirring, until slightly softened, about 4 minutes.

2   Stir in the water chestnuts, vinegar, oil, and salt. Cook, stirring, until heated through, about 1 minute.

SERVES: 4

Diabetic Exchanges: ¼ bread; ¾ vegetable; ¾ fat

SAUTÉED SNOW PEAS
with GRAPE TOMATOES

If you prefer your vegetables tame, omit the pepper flakes. If you don't have grape tomatoes, cherry tomatoes make an excellent substitute. If the cherry tomatoes are on the large side, cut them in half.

> 2 teaspoons vegetable oil
>
> 2 cups snow peas, cut into bite-size pieces (about ⅓ pound)
>
> 1½ cups grape tomatoes
>
> 2 cloves garlic, minced
>
> ½ teaspoon dried mint, crushed
>
> ⅛ teaspoon crushed red pepper
>
> 2 tablespoons chopped fresh parsley
>
> Salt to taste

1   Heat the oil in a large nonstick skillet over medium-high heat. Add the snow peas, tomatoes, garlic, mint, and pepper. Cook, stirring, until almost tender-crisp, about 2 minutes.

2   Add the parsley and salt. Cook, stirring, 1 minute longer.

SERVES: 6
Diabetic Exchanges: ¼ bread; ½ vegetable; ¼ fat

CREAMED SPINACH

This is one of my favorite vegetable dishes. Although I call for either milk or broth, you can also use some of each. Some people like to put a pinch of ground nutmeg in their creamed spinach. The portions for this recipe are small.

> **2 teaspoons butter**
>
> **1 tablespoon all-purpose flour**
>
> **⅔ cup milk or chicken broth**
>
> **1 package frozen chopped spinach, thawed and squeezed dry**
>
> **1 clove garlic, minced**
>
> **⅛ teaspoon ground black pepper**
>
> **Salt to taste**

1   In a 1-quart nonstick saucepan, melt the butter over medium-high heat. Stir in the flour until absorbed.

2   Add the milk and stir until mixture comes to a boil. Stir in spinach, garlic, pepper, and salt. Cook, stirring, until mixture is heated through.

SERVES: 4
Diabetic Exchanges: ½ bread; 2 vegetable; ½ milk; 2¼ fat

REDUCED FAT/SATURATED FAT/PROTEIN/CHOLESTEROL/SODIUM: Use low-sodium chicken broth, chopped fresh spinach cooked without salt, and unsalted butter.
Diabetic Exchanges: ½ bread; ¼ lean meat; 2½ vegetable; ¾ fat

Vegetable Stir-Fry

This recipe requires a lot of julienning, which is cutting into matchstick-size pieces. I recommend using a mandoline (not the musical instrument, but a wonderful slicing machine—which I believe is French in origin) or your food processor for the zucchini, yellow squash, and carrot. If your processor doesn't have a julienning blade, just slice the vegetables using the thin slicing blade. (Don't bother to julienne—just use them sliced.) The baby corn you'll have to julienne by hand as any machine will just make a mush of it.

> **1 tablespoon vegetable oil**
>
> **3 cups julienned zucchini**
>
> **2 cups julienned yellow squash**
>
> **½ cup julienned carrot**
>
> **⅓ cup thinly sliced leek (white and light green parts only)**
>
> **½ cup julienned (canned) baby corn**
>
> **2 tablespoons mirin or dry sherry**
>
> **1 tablespoon soy sauce**

1 In a large nonstick skillet, heat the oil over high heat. Add the zucchini, squash, carrot, and leek. Cook, stirring, until vegetables are tender-crisp, about 4 minutes.

2 Add the baby corn, mirin, and soy sauce. Cook, stirring, until heated through, about 1 minute.

SERVES: 6

Diabetic Exchanges: ¾ bread; ½ vegetable; 1 fat

REDUCED SODIUM: Use light soy sauce, omit baby corn.
Diabetic Exchanges: ¼ bread; ½ vegetable; 1 fat

SAUTÉED ZUCCHINI
with TOMATOES *and* RAISINS

The sweet-and-sour element to this dish makes it a perfect accompaniment for simple entrées, such as grilled chicken, pork roast, or broiled fish.

2 teaspoons olive oil

3 cups zucchini cut into ¾-inch cubes

½ cup chopped onion

1 cup diced tomato

2 tablespoons vegetable broth or water

1 tablespoon dark raisins

2 teaspoons balsamic vinegar

½ teaspoon ground ginger

⅛ teaspoon ground black pepper

Salt to taste

In a large nonstick skillet, heat the oil over medium-high heat. Add the zucchini and onion, and cook, stirring, until slightly softened, about 4 minutes. Stir in the tomato, broth, raisins, vinegar, ginger, pepper, and salt. Cook, stirring, until soft, about 5 minutes.

SERVES: 4

Diabetic Exchanges: ¼ bread; ¾ vegetable; ½ fat

SAUTÉ *of* JULIENNED ZUCCHINI *and* SNOW PEAS

I brought this dish to a potluck supper and everyone loved it. Substitute some yellow squash for some of the zucchini for a more colorful dish. Make sure you use only the yellow part of the lemon rind (zest), and not the bitter white part (pith).

2 teaspoons fresh lemon juice

2 teaspoons soy sauce

¼ teaspoon grated lemon zest

2 teaspoons vegetable oil

2 cups julienned zucchini

1½ cups julienned snow peas

½ cup julienned red bell pepper

½ cup julienned leek

¼ teaspoon curry powder

⅓ cup chopped walnuts

Salt to taste

1   In a small bowl, stir together the lemon juice, soy sauce, and lemon zest.

2   In a large nonstick skillet, heat the oil over medium-high heat. Add the zucchini, snow peas, red bell pepper, and leek. Cook, stirring, until tender-crisp, 4 minutes. Stir in the curry powder until absorbed.

3   Add the lemon juice mixture and cook, stirring, 1 minute.

4   Stir in the walnuts and salt.

SERVES: 4

Diabetic Exchanges: ½ bread; ¼ lean meat; ½ vegetable; 1½ fat

REDUCED SODIUM: Use low-sodium soy sauce.

Diabetic Exchanges: ½ bread; ¼ lean meat; ½ vegetable; 1½ fat

YELLOW SQUASH
with STEWED TOMATOES

If you have ever tasted canned zucchini and tomatoes, you will be thrilled with this fresh version. It tastes even better! Of course, you can substitute zucchini for the yellow squash.

> **1 teaspoon olive oil**
> **½ cup chopped onion**
> **⅓ cup finely chopped green bell pepper**
> **One 14- to 15-ounce can whole peeled tomatoes, undrained**
> **3 cups sliced yellow squash**
> **1 teaspoon sugar**
> **¼ teaspoon dried basil**
> **¼ teaspoon ground black pepper**
> **Salt to taste**

1   In a 2-quart nonstick saucepan, heat the oil over medium-high heat. Add the onion and green pepper and cook, stirring, until slightly softened, about 2 minutes.

2   Add the tomatoes with canning liquid, breaking them up with the back of a spoon. Add the squash, sugar, basil, pepper, and salt. Bring to a boil. Reduce heat and simmer, uncovered, 20 minutes.

SERVES: 4

Diabetic Exchanges: 2½ vegetable; ¼ fat

REDUCED SODIUM: Use reduced-sodium tomatoes.

Diabetic Exchanges: 2¾ vegetable; ¼ fat

YELLOW SQUASH *with* RED PEPPERS *and* FRESH HERBS

I never ate squash (or eggplant or fish) growing up. They just weren't in my mom's Hungarian cooking vocabulary. I think it's common for food prejudices to pass from one generation to the next. Fortunately I overcame this one. If you don't have fresh herbs on hand, you can use dried herbs and have a wonderful dish, too.

> **2 teaspoons olive oil**
>
> **3 cups sliced yellow squash**
>
> **1 cup sliced red bell pepper**
>
> **¾ cup sliced onion**
>
> **1 clove garlic, minced**
>
> **1 tablespoon chopped fresh basil or ½ teaspoon dried basil**
>
> **1 teaspoon chopped fresh rosemary or ¼ teaspoon dried rosemary**
>
> **½ teaspoon fresh thyme leaves or ⅛ teaspoon dried thyme**
>
> **⅛ teaspoon ground black pepper**
>
> **Salt to taste**

In a large nonstick skillet, heat the oil over medium-high heat. Add the squash, pepper, onion, garlic, basil, rosemary, thyme, and black pepper. Cook, stirring, 5 minutes or until vegetables are tender-crisp. Season with salt, if desired.

SERVES: 4
Diabetic Exchanges: 1½ vegetable; ½ fat

Yellow Squash Ratatouille

People frequently ask me how I come up with ideas for recipes. This one is a very typical inspiration. I saw some beautiful vegetables in the market and just brought them home. Then I had to figure out what to do with them. With the exception of the yellow squash, they were typical ratatouille vegetables, so instead of using zucchini and green bell peppers (which I didn't have in my refrigerator) I used yellow squash and red bell peppers. This is every bit as good as the greener version—perhaps even a little sweeter.

> 1½ **tablespoons olive oil**
>
> 4 **cups cubed eggplant (1½-inch pieces)**
>
> 2 **cups cubed yellow squash (1½-inch pieces)**
>
> 1½ **cups cubed red bell pepper (1-inch pieces)**
>
> 1 **cup red onion wedges**
>
> 2 **cloves garlic, minced**
>
> 3 **cups tomato wedges**
>
> ¼ **cup chopped fresh parsley**
>
> ¼ **cup chopped fresh basil**
>
> 2 **tablespoons red wine or water**
>
> ½ **teaspoon dried rosemary**
>
> ½ **teaspoon sugar**
>
> ¼ **teaspoon ground black pepper**
>
> ⅛ **teaspoon dried thyme**
>
> **Salt to taste**

1   In a large nonstick skillet, heat the oil over medium-high heat. Add the eggplant, squash, bell pepper, onion, and garlic. Cook, stirring, until the vegetables are slightly softened, about 5 minutes.

2   Add the tomatoes, parsley, basil, wine, rosemary, sugar, pepper, thyme, and salt. Reduce heat to medium. Cook, stirring occasionally, for 20 minutes or until the mixture is cooked through.

SERVES: 6

Diabetic Exchanges: 2½ vegetable; ¾ fat

BABY PATTYPAN SQUASH *with* BASIL

Pattypan squash look a little like flying saucers. They come in yellow and green. If you can't find them, you can prepare this dish with any sliced summer squash.

> **1 tablespoon olive oil**
>
> **2 cups baby pattypan squash, cut in half horizontally**
>
> **2 cloves garlic, sliced paper thin**
>
> **⅛ teaspoon dried rosemary, crumbled**
>
> **2 tablespoons chopped fresh basil**
>
> **⅛ teaspoon ground black pepper**
>
> **Salt to taste**

1   In a medium nonstick skillet, heat the oil over medium-high heat. Add the squash, garlic, and rosemary, and cook, stirring, until tender-crisp, about 5 minutes.

2   Add the basil, pepper, and salt. Cook, stirring, 1 minute.

SERVES: 4

Diabetic Exchanges: ¼ bread; ¾ fat

SPAGHETTI SQUASH *with* MIXED VEGETABLES

Spaghetti squash is a great low-carbohydrate substitute for pasta. You can use any combination of vegetables—cauliflower, carrots, yellow squash, bell peppers, etc.—not just the ones listed here, but do include the tomatoes as they add to the dish's character. Top with grated Parmesan cheese, if you like, and serve this as an entrée or side dish.

> **1 medium spaghetti squash (2 pounds)**
> **1 tablespoon olive oil**
> **1 cup broccoli florets**
> **1 cup sliced zucchini**
> **1 cup sliced mushrooms**
> **½ cup sliced onion**
> **½ cup sliced red bell pepper**
> **2 cloves garlic, minced**
> **1½ cups tomato wedges**
> **½ cup vegetable broth**
> **¼ cup chopped fresh parsley**
> **½ teaspoon dried basil**

1   Pierce the squash all over with a fork. Bake at 375°F for 45 minutes. Cut in half and discard seeds. Pull out the flesh with a fork so that it forms spaghetti-like strands. You should have 2 cups spaghetti squash.

2   While the squash is baking, in a large nonstick skillet heat the oil over medium-high heat. Add the broccoli, zucchini, mushrooms, onion, pepper, and garlic, and cook, stirring, until vegetables are tender, about 5 minutes. Add the tomato wedges, broth, parsley, and basil and cook, stirring, 3 minutes or until the tomatoes are slightly softened.

3   Add the spaghetti squash and cook, stirring, until heated through, about 3 minutes.

SERVES: 6
Diabetic Exchanges: 1¾ vegetable; ½ fat

GINGER BUTTERNUT SQUASH *and* YELLOW TURNIP PURÉE

This is an excellent substitute for mashed sweet potatoes at Thanksgiving—or anytime. I make it in the microwave, but if you don't have one, you can steam the vegetables until very soft.

> **2 cups cubed yellow turnip (rutabaga)**
> **2 cups cubed butternut squash**
> **1 tablespoon honey**
> **¼ teaspoon grated orange rind**
> **⅛ teaspoon ground cardamon**
> **Salt to taste**

1   Put the turnip in a large microwave-safe bowl; cover lightly with wax paper and microwave (650 watt) at high heat 5 minutes. Add the squash, cover, and microwave at high, 12 minutes, stirring occasionally.

2   Place the turnip, squash, honey, orange rind, cardamom, and salt in a food processor container fitted with a steel blade. Cover and process until smooth

SERVES: 4

Diabetic Exchanges: ¼ other carbohydrate; 2¼ vegetable

SUGAR SNAPS *with* CARROTS

For an exotic look use black sesame seeds, found in Asian markets or the Asian section of your local supermarket. Cut the carrot sticks the same length as the sugar snaps. This recipe does not make a very large yield but that's because these are slightly starchy vegetables and should be eaten sparingly. For a really quick preparation, buy a bag of peeled baby carrots and just cut them in half lengthwise.

> **1 cup carrot sticks (¼ inch thick)**
>
> **2 teaspoons vegetable oil**
>
> **1 cup sugar snaps**
>
> **1½ teaspoons sesame seeds**
>
> **Salt to taste**

1   Blanch the carrots for 1 minute in boiling water; drain.

2   In a medium nonstick skillet, heat the oil over medium-high heat. Add the sugar snaps, carrots, and sesame seeds. Cook, stirring, 2 minutes or until vegetables are tender-crisp. Season with salt.

SERVES: 4

Diabetic Exchanges: ¼ bread; ½ vegetable; ½ fat

BAKED HERB-STUFFED TOMATOES

If you don't have fresh herbs, or are in a hurry, you can just use flavored bread crumbs. If you're not worried about a little extra fat (not to mention cholesterol), a tablespoon or two of grated Parmesan cheese makes these even better.

> **2 medium tomatoes**
> **¼ cup plain dry bread crumbs**
> **2 tablespoons chopped fresh parsley**
> **2 tablespoons chopped fresh basil**
> **1 clove garlic, minced**
> **⅛ teaspoon dried thyme**
> **⅛ teaspoon ground black pepper**
> **Salt to taste**

1   Preheat oven to 350°F.

2   Cut tomatoes in half horizontally and scoop out the insides. Chop the pulp. In a medium bowl combine the pulp, bread crumbs, parsley, basil, garlic, thyme, pepper, and salt. Put a quarter of the filling into each shell.

3   Bake 25 minutes or until tomatoes are cooked through.

SERVES: 4

Diabetic Exchanges: ¼ bread; ¾ vegetable

SAUTÉED TOMATOES *with* BASIL

I love this combination both as a salad and as a cooked side dish. It is really essential to have perfect ingredients when used raw as a salad, but for the cooked version, you can use less than perfect tomatoes.

2 teaspoons olive oil

3 cups tomato wedges

2 cloves garlic, minced

2 tablespoons chopped fresh basil

⅛ teaspoon ground black pepper

Salt to taste

In a large nonstick skillet, heat the oil over medium-high heat. Add the tomatoes and garlic; cook, stirring, until tomatoes are cooked, about 6 minutes. Stir in the basil, pepper, and salt.

SERVES: 4

Diabetic Exchanges: 1¼ vegetable; ½ fat

Starches

Starches (starchy vegetables, grains, bread, and pasta/noodles) are complex carbohydrates. That means that unlike simple carbohydrates (such as sugar, syrups, and other "empty calories"), complex carbohydrates usually contain lots of valuable nutrients, especially B vitamins and fiber.

When choosing grains, bread, and pasta/noodles it's best to go with whole grain products, since many of the nutrients are found in the hull and germ of the grain and these are the parts that are removed to make white flour, white rice, pearled barley, etc.

Just how much starch to include in your daily intake is a subject you should discuss with your physician or diabetic educator.

GARLIC MASHED POTATOES

If you'd like the garlic flavor to be subtle, use only the 4 cloves of garlic that get cooked, omitting the 2 raw cloves of garlic.

> **4 cups water**
> **4 cups peeled, cubed potatoes**
> **4 whole cloves garlic, peeled**
> **6 tablespoons milk**
> **¼ cup chicken or vegetable broth**
> **2 teaspoons butter**
> **2 cloves garlic, minced**
> **Salt to taste**

1   In a 2-quart saucepan, bring water to a boil over high heat. Add the potatoes and 4 whole cloves garlic, and return to the boil. Reduce heat and simmer, uncovered, 20 minutes or until potatoes are tender. Drain the potatoes and garlic.

2   Return the potatoes and garlic to the pot; add the milk, broth, butter, minced garlic, and salt. Using a fork (or for smoother potatoes an electric mixer) mash the potatoes to desired smoothness.

SERVES: 6

Diabetic Exchanges: 1 bread; ½ fat

REDUCED FAT/SATURATED FAT/CHOLESTEROL: Use skim milk and omit the butter.

Diabetic Exchanges: 1 bread

REDUCED PROTEIN: Use ⅔ cup vegetable broth instead of the milk and chicken broth.

Diabetic Exchanges: 1 bread; ¼ fat

GRILLED POTATOES
with OLIVE OIL *and* THYME

I've cooked these in the broiler, baked them in the oven (45 minutes at 400°F), cooked them on my George Foreman indoor grill, but never on a real grill because I live in an apartment and don't have an outdoor grill to grill on. No matter what the cooking method, these are always a real hit—the only complaint is there are never enough. You can use any type of potato for this recipe, although I like Idaho baking potatoes myself.

> **1 large baking potato (12 ounces)**
>
> **1 tablespoon olive oil**
>
> **¼ teaspoon paprika**
>
> **¼ teaspoon dried thyme**
>
> **1 clove garlic, minced**
>
> **⅛ teaspoon ground black pepper**
>
> **Salt to taste**

1   Preheat grill, oven, or broiler.

2   Peel or thoroughly scrub the potato; cut into ¼-inch-thick slices. In a saucepan, cook the potato in boiling water for 5 minutes over medium-high heat; drain thoroughly.

3   In a medium bowl, stir together the oil, paprika, thyme, garlic, and black pepper. Brush potatoes on both sides with the oil mixture.

4   Cook on grill about 5 to 6 minutes per side or until tender when pierced with a fork. Season with salt, if desired.

SERVES: 4
Diabetic Exchanges: 1 bread; ¾ fat

TWICE-BAKED POTATOES

This makes a good lunch along with either a cup of soup or a salad. Otherwise, if you are serving these as a side dish, consider serving them with a mildly flavored dish so that the subtle flavors of the potatoes don't get lost. Also, you can skip restuffing the potato skins and just serve the mixture as mashed potatoes.

> **2 medium baking potatoes**
> **¼ cup chicken or vegetable broth**
> **¼ cup plain yogurt**
> **2 tablespoons thinly sliced scallion (green part only)**
> **1 tablespoon snipped fresh dill**
> **¼ teaspoon ground black pepper**
> **Salt to taste**

1 Preheat oven to 350°F. Rinse the potatoes thoroughly and prick with a fork to vent.

2 Bake the potatoes 60 minutes or until soft. Cut the potatoes in half lengthwise. Scoop out the flesh into a medium bowl, saving the potato skins. Using a fork or electric mixer, combine the potatoes, broth, yogurt, scallion, dill, pepper, and salt. Place a quarter of the filling mixture in each of the potato shells.

3 Return to oven and bake 20 minutes or until tops are browned.

SERVES: 4
Diabetic Exchanges: 1 bread; ¼ fat

HERBED ORZO

I think orzo is one of the most fun pastas to eat, and this is one of the easiest ways to prepare it. You can use this recipe on any pasta shape. Start with 5 ounces of dry pasta and the nutritional information will be the same as this. If you have fresh basil on hand, use 2 tablespoons chopped instead of the dried.

> ¾ **cup dry orzo**
> ¼ **cup chopped fresh parsley**
> **1 tablespoon olive oil**
> **2 cloves garlic, minced**
> ½ **teaspoon dried basil**
> ¼ **teaspoon ground black pepper**
> **Salt to taste**

1   Cook the orzo in boiling salted water 10 minutes or until al dente; drain.

2   Stir in the parsley, oil, garlic, basil, pepper, and salt.

SERVES: 4

Diabetic Exchanges: 1½ bread; ¾ fat

CAJUN BARLEY

You can adjust the heat to your own taste by using more or less Cajun seasoning. This version is only mildly spicy. I used the Cajun Shake in this recipe, but you can substitute any Cajun seasoning you have on hand. If you don't have either, you can improvise using minced garlic, lots of pepper, and a pinch of cumin, paprika, and oregano.

> **2 teaspoons vegetable oil**
> **¾ cup chopped onion**
> **½ cup chopped green bell pepper**
> **1½ teaspoons Cajun Shake (page 70) or Cajun seasoning**
> **One 14- to 15-ounce can diced tomatoes, undrained**
> **1¼ cups chicken or vegetable broth**
> **1 bay leaf**
> **¾ cup pearled barley**
> **1 cup sliced okra**
> **Salt to taste**

1   In a 2-quart nonstick saucepan, heat the oil over medium-high heat. Add the onion and green pepper; cook, stirring, until slightly softened, about 2 minutes. Stir in the Cajun seasoning, then the tomatoes with canning liquid. Add the broth and bay leaf and bring to a boil.

2   Stir in the barley and return to the boil. Reduce heat and simmer, covered, 20 minutes.

3   Stir in the okra; cover and simmer 15 minutes longer. Discard bay leaf. Stir in salt, if desired.

SERVES: 8
Diabetic Exchanges: 1 bread; 1 vegetable; ¼ fat

REDUCED SODIUM: Use low-sodium tomatoes and broth. Use Cajun spice without salt.
Diabetic Exchanges: 1 bread; 1 vegetable; ¼ fat

BARLEY *with* MUSHROOMS *and* ZUCCHINI

Add an extra ¼ cup of broth or water for a slightly creamier consistency.

> **2 teaspoons olive oil**
> **2 cups sliced mushrooms**
> **1 cup chopped onion**
> **2 cloves garlic, minced**
> **1¾ cups chicken or vegetable broth**
> **¾ cup pearled barley**
> **1½ cups chopped zucchini**
> **¼ cup chopped fresh parsley**
> **¼ teaspoon ground pepper**
> **Salt to taste**

1   In a 2-quart nonstick saucepan, heat the oil over medium-high heat. Add the mushrooms, onion, and garlic; cook, stirring, until softened, about 2 minutes. Add the broth and bring to a boil.

2   Stir in the barley and return to the boil. Reduce heat and simmer, covered, 30 minutes.

3   Stir in the zucchini and parsley; cover and simmer 7 minutes longer. Stir in pepper and salt, if desired.

SERVES: 6

Diabetic Exchanges: 1¾ bread; ½ vegetable; ¾ fat

REDUCED SODIUM: Use low-sodium broth.

Diabetic Exchanges: 1¾ bread; ½ vegetable; ½ fat

BULGUR *with* BASIL *and* SUN-DRIED TOMATOES

Bulgur is cracked wheat that has been cooked, then dried. Because it's precooked, the cooking time is relatively short. Pignoli are also called pine nuts. You can toast the pignoli by cooking them in a dry skillet, over medium heat, stirring constantly, about 3 minutes or until they start to brown and smell nutty. Be careful not to overcook them.

> **1 teaspoon olive oil**
> **½ cup chopped onion**
> **1 cup water**
> **½ cup medium bulgur**
> **2 tablespoons chopped fresh basil or ½ teaspoon dried basil**
> **2 tablespoons chopped oil-marinated sun-dried tomatoes**
> **1 tablespoon toasted pignoli**
> **Salt to taste**

1   In a 1½-quart nonstick saucepan, heat the oil over medium-high heat. Add the onion and cook, stirring, until slightly softened, about 2 minutes. Add the water and bring to a boil.

2   Add the bulgur and return to the boil. Reduce heat and simmer 20 minutes, covered. Stir in the basil, sun-dried tomatoes, pignoli, and salt.

SERVES: 4

Diabetic Exchanges: ¾ bread; ½ vegetable; ½ fat

BULGUR *with* RED PEPPER *and* PEAS

Like couscous, bulgur is a great grain to keep around the house for those last-minute occasions when you've prepared the salad and main dish and haven't given much thought to the starch. The bulgur in this recipe is slightly al dente; for softer bulgur, add ¼ cup more water and cook 5 minutes longer.

1 teaspoon olive oil

¾ cup chopped red bell pepper

½ cup chopped onion

1 cup chicken or vegetable broth

½ cup medium bulgur

¼ cup frozen peas

2 tablespoons chopped fresh parsley

¼ teaspoon ground black pepper

Salt to taste

1   In a 2-quart nonstick saucepan, heat the oil over medium-high heat. Add the bell pepper and onion; cook, stirring, until slightly softened, about 2 minutes.

2   Add the broth and bring to a boil. Add the bulgur, peas, parsley, and pepper; return to the boil. Reduce heat and simmer, covered, 15 minutes or until all the liquid has been absorbed. Season with salt if using.

SERVES: 4

Diabetic Exchanges: ½ bread; ¾ vegetable; ¼ fat

REDUCED SODIUM: Use low-sodium broth.

Diabetic Exchanges: ½ bread; ¾ vegetable; ¼ fat

KASHA *with* MUSHROOMS *and* WALNUTS

Kasha is roasted buckwheat, a grain with a very distinctive flavor. It is usually prepared with bowtie pasta in Eastern European recipes, but, I figure, why serve two carbs in one recipe? I call for medium or large grain kasha in this recipe. I think if you use fine-grain, the end result will be too mushy and if you use whole kasha it will be too coarse.

> **1 egg white**
> **½ cup medium or large-grain kasha**
> **2 teaspoons vegetable oil**
> **1 cup chopped portobello mushrooms**
> **1 cup chopped onion**
> **1 cup chicken or vegetable broth**
> **¼ teaspoon ground black pepper**
> **Salt to taste**
> **⅓ cup chopped walnuts**

1   In a medium bowl, beat egg white and stir in kasha. In a dry 2-quart nonstick saucepan, cook mixture until the beaten egg has dried onto the kasha; remove from pan. Add vegetable oil, mushrooms, and onion to the saucepan. Cook, stirring, until slightly softened, about 2 minutes.

2   Add broth, pepper, and salt; bring to a boil. Stir in the reserved kasha and return to the boil. Cover and simmer 10 to 12 minutes or until liquid is absorbed. Let stand 5 minutes longer. Stir in walnuts.

SERVES: 4

Diabetic Exchanges: ¼ bread; ½ very lean meat; 1 vegetable; 1¾ fat

REDUCED SODIUM: Use low-sodium broth.

Diabetic Exchanges: ¼ bread; ½ very lean meat; 1 vegetable; 1½ fat

Brown Rice Pilaf

The rice in this dish is a tiny bit al dente. If you want your rice softer, add about ¼ cup more water and cook 5 minutes longer. The subtle flavor of this pilaf makes it a good choice to serve with entrées that have a lot of punch such as a curry, or that have a flavorful sauce such as Coq au Vin.

> **2 teaspoons olive oil**
> **½ cup chopped onion**
> **½ cup chopped celery**
> **½ cup chopped green bell pepper**
> **1 cup chicken or vegetable broth**
> **½ cup water**
> **¾ cup long-grain brown rice**
> **¼ teaspoon ground black pepper**
> **¼ cup chopped fresh parsley**
> **Salt to taste**

1 In a 2-quart nonstick saucepan, heat the oil over medium-high heat. Add the onion, celery, and bell pepper. Cook, stirring, until slightly softened, about 3 minutes.

2 Add the broth and water and bring to a boil. Add the brown rice and pepper; return to the boil. Reduce heat and simmer, covered, 45 minutes or until all the liquid has been absorbed. Stir in parsley and season with salt if using.

SERVES: 6

Diabetic Exchanges: 1¼ bread; ½ vegetable; ½ fat

REDUCED SODIUM: Use low-sodium broth.

Diabetic Exchanges: 1¼ bread; ½ vegetable; ¼ fat

Brown Rice *with* Chopped Nuts

I prefer to use short-grain brown rice (found in health-food stores) rather than long-grain in this recipe. It has a nicer texture and flavor than its long-grain cousin.

> **1½ teaspoons vegetable oil**
> **½ cup chopped onion**
> **1½ cups cooked brown rice**
> **¼ cup finely chopped pecans**
> **2 tablespoons chopped walnuts**
> **⅛ teaspoon ground allspice**
> **⅛ teaspoon ground nutmeg**
> **⅛ teaspoon ground black pepper**
> **Salt to taste**

In a large nonstick skillet, heat the oil over medium-high heat. Add the onion and cook, stirring, until slightly softened. Stir in the brown rice, pecans, walnuts, allspice, nutmeg, pepper, and salt. Cook, stirring, until heated through, about 2 minutes.

SERVES: 4

Diabetic Exchanges: 1 bread; ¼ vegetable; 1¾ fat

VEGETABLE FRIED RICE

You can use any variety of vegetables you have on hand. I've used frozen mixed vegetables instead of the peas. You can also make this into a low-protein entrée by stirring in 1 cup of diced cooked meat (pork, chicken, beef, shrimp) or tofu when you add the rice.

> **1 tablespoon soy sauce**
> **1 tablespoon mirin or dry sherry**
> **2 teaspoons vegetable oil**
> **1 cup chopped onion**
> **⅓ cup chopped snow peas**
> **⅓ cup fresh or frozen peas**
> **¼ cup julienned carrot**
> **1 tablespoon minced ginger**
> **2 cloves garlic, minced**
> **2 cups bean sprouts**
> **2 cups cooked white or brown rice**
> **½ teaspoon sesame oil**

1   In a small bowl, stir together the soy sauce and mirin.

2   In a nonstick wok or large nonstick skillet, heat the oil over high heat. Add the onion, snow peas, peas, carrot, ginger, and garlic. Cook, stirring, until tender-crisp, about 2 minutes. Stir in the bean sprouts and cook until wilted, about 1 minute. Add the rice. Cook, stirring, until heated through, about 2 minutes. Add the soy sauce mixture and cook, stirring, until completely combined with rice mixture. Stir in sesame oil.

SERVES: 4
Diabetic Exchanges: 1 bread; 1 vegetable; ½ fat

REDUCED SODIUM: Use low-sodium soy sauce.
Diabetic Exchanges: 1 bread; 1 vegetable; ½ fat

WILD RICE *and* VEGETABLE MEDLEY

This is a real showcase dish. Wild rice is native to America and is a grass, not a true grain. To this day much wild rice is still harvested by canoe (which is why it's so expensive).

1 cup water

½ cup wild rice

1 tablespoon olive oil

½ cup chopped red bell pepper

½ cup chopped asparagus

½ cup chopped zucchini

½ cup chopped yellow squash

⅓ cup chopped leek (white and light green parts)

2 cloves garlic, minced

¼ cup chopped fresh parsley

½ teaspoon curry powder

⅛ teaspoon ground black pepper

Salt to taste

1   In a 1-quart saucepan, bring the water to a boil. Stir in the wild rice. Return to the boil, reduce heat, and simmer, covered, 40 to 50 minutes or until wild rice is tender and water is absorbed.

2   In a large nonstick skillet, heat the oil over medium-high heat. Add the red bell pepper, asparagus, zucchini, squash, leek, and garlic. Cook, stirring, until the vegetables are tender-crisp, about 4 minutes.

3   Add the wild rice, parsley, curry powder, pepper, and salt. Cook, stirring, until heated through, about 2 minutes.

SERVES: 4

Diabetic Exchanges: 1 bread; ½ vegetable; ¾ fat

DILLY WHEAT BERRIES *with* VEGETABLES

Wheat berries are also known as whole-grain wheat—which is exactly what they are. The only thing done to the wheat is the chaff is removed. Wheat berries still have the hull, germ, and endosperm. When finely ground, wheat berries become whole-wheat flour. I call for cooked cauliflower, since I don't think that simple sautéing will cook it enough. Take as many liberties as you like with this recipe—substitute zucchini, green beans, carrots, or any vegetable you like for the cauliflower. You can also substitute any cooked whole grain for the wheat berries.

> **1¼ cups water**
>
> **½ cup wheat berries**
>
> **1½ teaspoons olive oil**
>
> **½ cup chopped onion**
>
> **½ cup diced celery**
>
> **½ cup chopped green bell pepper**
>
> **2 cloves garlic, minced**
>
> **1 cup cooked cauliflower florets (steamed, boiled, or microwaved)**
>
> **3 tablespoons snipped fresh dill**
>
> **¼ teaspoon ground black pepper**
>
> **Salt to taste**

1 In a 1½-quart saucepan, bring the water to a boil over high heat. Add the wheat berries and return to the boil. Reduce heat and simmer, covered, 1½ to 2 hours or until the liquid is absorbed.

2 In a large nonstick skillet, heat the oil over medium-high heat. Add the onion, celery, green pepper, and garlic. Cook, stirring, until vegetables are slightly softened, about 3 minutes.

3 Add the wheat berries, cauliflower, dill, pepper, and salt. Cook, stirring, until heated through, about 2 minutes.

SERVES: 4

Diabetic Exchanges: 1 bread; 1 vegetable; ¼ fat

WOODLAND MUSHROOMS *with* WHEAT BERRIES

The flavors of this dish are best described as "woodsy." Taste the interesting combination of sweet wine, salty soy sauce, acidic vinegar, and musky mushrooms in this dish and you will see what I mean.

1 tablespoon olive oil

4 cups coarsely chopped mushrooms (use any combination of white, portobello, shiitake, or other interesting mushroom)

2 cloves garlic, minced

1½ cups cooked wheat berries

¼ cup cooked fresh or frozen peas

3 tablespoons thinly sliced scallion

1 tablespoon Marsala

2 teaspoons balsamic vinegar

1 teaspoon soy sauce

¼ teaspoon ground black pepper

Salt to taste

In a large nonstick skillet, heat the oil over medium-high heat. Add the mushrooms and garlic, and cook, stirring, until softened, about 4 minutes. Add the wheat berries, peas, scallion, Marsala, balsamic vinegar, soy sauce, pepper, and salt. Cook, stirring, until heated through, about 2 minutes.

SERVES: 4

Diabetic Exchanges: 1 bread; 1 vegetable; ¾ fat

WHOLE WHEAT COUSCOUS PILAF

This is a perfect last-minute dish. It takes only about 10 minutes to make, and you can keep all the ingredients on hand for whenever you need a quick starch. Oh, and yes, it tastes great and goes well with any entrée. Use whole wheat couscous for its added nutrients and lower glycemic rating than regular couscous.

1 teaspoon olive oil

⅓ cup finely chopped onion

1⅔ cups chicken or vegetable broth

1 cup whole wheat couscous

⅓ cup chopped fresh parsley or 1 tablespoon dried parsley

⅛ teaspoon ground black pepper

Salt to taste

1   In a 2-quart nonstick saucepan, heat the oil over medium-high heat. Add the onion and cook, stirring, until slightly softened, about 2 minutes.

2   Add the broth and bring to a boil. Stir in the couscous and return to the boil. Reduce heat and simmer, covered, 2 minutes or until broth is absorbed. Stir in the parsley, pepper, and salt.

SERVES: 6

Diabetic Exchanges: 1¾ bread; ¼ vegetable; ¼ fat

REDUCED SODIUM: Substitute low-sodium chicken broth for the vegetable broth.

Diabetic Exchanges: 1¾ bread; ¼ vegetable

COUSCOUS *with* ZUCCHINI *and* SCALLION

Be sure to store your grains someplace cool and dark. Before you use any grain that you've had around the house for a long time, give it a sniff. If it smells stale, discard it.

1 teaspoon olive oil

½ cup thinly sliced zucchini

1 cup chicken or vegetable broth

½ cup water

¾ cup couscous

¼ cup frozen peas

3 tablespoons thinly sliced scallion

2 tablespoons chopped fresh parsley

1 tablespoon snipped fresh dill

2 teaspoons chopped fresh mint

⅛ teaspoon ground black pepper

Salt to taste

1   In a 2-quart nonstick saucepan, heat the oil over medium-high heat. Add the zucchini and cook, stirring, until slightly softened, about 2 minutes.

2   Add the broth and water and bring to a boil. Stir in the couscous and peas and return to the boil. Reduce heat and simmer, covered, 3 minutes or until broth is absorbed. Stir in the scallion, parsley, dill, mint, pepper, and salt.

SERVES: 5
Diabetic Exchanges: 1¾ bread; ¼ fat

REDUCED SODIUM: Use low-sodium broth.
Diabetic Exchanges: 1¾ bread; ¼ fat

POLENTA

During my years as a vegetarian, polenta served with sautéed escarole was one of my favorite meals. I usually use the instant or prepared polenta rather than starting from scratch, which is time-consuming and tiring. But if you cannot find the easier versions, this one is quite delicious. You can just spoon the polenta onto a plate to serve, or you can place it into a greased container, let stand 5 minutes, turn onto a serving plate, then slice and serve. If you're not worried about cholesterol, total fat, or saturated fat, it's really delicious served with a pat of butter.

4 cups water, divided
1¼ cups yellow cornmeal
Salt to taste

1   In a 3-quart saucepan, bring 2 cups water to a boil over high heat.

2   In a jar with a tight lid, combine the remaining 2 cups water and the cornmeal. Shake until totally combined. Add the cornmeal mixture to the boiling water, stirring furiously until completely combined.

3   Reduce heat so mixture is just simmering and cook, stirring constantly, until polenta pulls away from the side of the pot as it is stirred, about 25 minutes. Stir in salt if using.

SERVES: 6
Diabetic Exchanges: 1¼ bread

QUINOA *with* SUGAR SNAPS

The proper pronunciation of quinoa is *KEEN-wa*. Quinoa has a substance in its seed covering that is a natural insecticide, which makes it taste slightly bitter. However, with adequate rinsing the flavor becomes very mild. Unlike most grains, which have a starchy "mouthfeel," quinoa is light and fluffy. If you can't find sugar snaps, snow peas or plain peas would be fine.

>   **½ cup quinoa**
>   **1½ teaspoons olive oil**
>   **½ cup chopped onion**
>   **1 clove garlic, minced**
>   **1 teaspoon curry powder**
>   **l cup chicken or vegetable broth**
>   **¾ cup chopped sugar snaps**
>   **1 tablespoon chopped cilantro leaves (fresh coriander)**
>   **⅛ teaspoon ground black pepper**
>   **Salt to taste**

1   Rinse the quinoa thoroughly.

2   In a 2-quart noonstick saucepan, heat the oil over medium-high heat. Add the onion and garlic and cook, stirring, until slightly softened, about 2 minutes. Stir in the curry powder until absorbed. Add the quinoa and cook, stirring, until coated with curry mixture, about 1 minute. Add the broth and bring to a boil. Reduce heat and simmer, covered, 12 minutes. Stir in the sugar snaps, cilantro, pepper, and salt. Simmer, covered, 3 to 5 minutes longer or until quinoa has cooked through.

SERVES: 4
Diabetic Exchanges: 1 bread; 1¼ vegetable; ½ fat

REDUCED SODIUM: Use low-sodium broth.
Diabetic Exchanges: 1 bread; 1¼ vegetable; ¼ fat

LENTIL PURÉE

Okay, okay—so the truth of the matter is this was intended to be a lentil soup and it failed—but it does make a delicious purée!

1½ cups water

¾ cup chicken or vegetable broth

½ cup baby lentils

½ cup chopped celery

2 tablespoons red wine

2 cloves garlic, minced

1 bay leaf

¼ teaspoon oregano

⅛ teaspoon ground black pepper

2 tablespoons chopped fresh parsley

Salt to taste

1   In a 2-quart saucepan, bring the water and broth to a boil. Add the lentils, celery, wine, garlic, bay leaf, oregano, and black pepper. Return to the boil; reduce heat and simmer, uncovered, 30 minutes. Add the parsley and simmer 10 minutes longer. Discard bay leaf; season with salt.

2   Place the mixture in a blender or food processor container fitted with a steel blade. Cover and blend until puréed, pushing down the ingredients with a spoon when necessary.

SERVES: 4

Diabetic Exchanges: 1 bread; ¼ fat

REDUCED SODIUM: Use low-sodium broth.

Diabetic Exchanges: 1 bread; ¼ fat

CURRIED LENTILS

Serve this with rice as a vegetarian entrée, or add some cooked chicken pieces 10 minutes before the end of the cooking time. As a side dish this curry will pep up any grilled, broiled, or baked chicken or fish. Keep an eye on the lentils toward the end of the cooking time; you may need to stir in a bit of water to make sure they don't stick to the bottom of the pot.

> **1 tablespoon vegetable oil**
> **¾ cup chopped onion**
> **2 cloves garlic, minced**
> **2 teaspoons curry powder**
> **½ teaspoon ground turmeric**
> **½ teaspoon ground cumin**
> **½ teaspoon ground cinnamon**
> **⅛ teaspoon ground cloves**
> **1¼ cups chicken or vegetable broth**
> **¼ cup apple juice**
> **½ cup lentils**
> **½ cup finely chopped carrot**
> **Salt to taste**

1   In a 1½-quart nonstick saucepan, heat the oil over medium-high heat. Add the onion and garlic; cook, stirring, until slightly softened, about 2 minutes. Stir in the curry powder, turmeric, cumin, cinnamon, and cloves until absorbed. Stir in the broth and apple juice; bring to a boil.

2   Add the lentils and carrot; return to the boil. Reduce heat and simmer, uncovered, 30 minutes or until the lentils are softened and the water has been absorbed. Season with salt, if using.

SERVES: 4

Diabetic Exchanges: 1 bread; ¼ very lean meat; 1 vegetable; 1 fat

REDUCED SODIUM: Use low-sodium broth.

Diabetic Exchanges: 1 bread; 1 vegetable; ¾ fat

Salads

Salads are a delicious way of adding vegetables to your diet. They also add a crisp and crunchy texture to a meal. Try to eat salad at both lunch and dinner. Feel free to add a little cheese, cooked chicken, fish, or meat to a salad to make it into an entrée.

Most of the salads in this chapter use vinaigrettes. That's because vinaigrettes tend to be less fatty than creamy dressings.

TRICOLORE SALADE

This is the salad I usually order when I go out to dinner in an Italian restaurant. But there's no need to go to a restaurant when you can make it just as well at home.

3 cups arugula torn into bite-size pieces

1 cup radicchio torn into bite-size pieces

1 cup Belgian endive cut into 1-inch pieces

1 tablespoon olive oil

2 teaspoons red wine vinegar

1 teaspoon Dijon mustard

1 teaspoon minced shallot

Freshly ground black pepper

Salt to taste

1 In a large bowl, combine the arugula, radicchio, and endive.

2 In a small bowl combine the oil, vinegar, mustard, shallot, pepper and salt. Pour over salad and toss to combine.

SERVES: 4

Diabetic Exchanges: ½ vegetable; ¾ fat

SPINACH *and* MUSHROOM SALAD

I originally thought this salad would serve six, but everyone tends to like it so much—it only serves four.

10 cups spinach

2 cups sliced mushrooms

½ cup sliced red onion

1½ tablespoons olive oil

2 tablespoons fresh lemon juice

1 teaspoon Dijon mustard

½ clove garlic, minced

¼ teaspoon dried oregano

⅛ teaspoon ground black pepper

Salt to taste

1   Rinse the spinach well and remove coarse stems; spin dry (if you don't have a salad spinner, dry with paper towels).

2   In a large bowl, combine the spinach, mushrooms, and onion.

3   In a small bowl, stir together the oil, lemon juice, mustard, garlic, oregano, pepper, and salt. Pour over salad and toss.

SERVES: 4

Diabetic Exchanges: 1½ vegetable; 1 fat

WATERCRESS *and* ENDIVE *with* BLUE CHEESE DRESSING

I use a plain Danish blue for this recipe, but if you have Roquefort or Stilton that would be even better. This salad also makes a lovely appetizer.

> **4 cups watercress, coarse stems removed**
> **2 cups Belgian endive cut into 1-inch pieces**
> **2 tablespoons crumbled blue cheese**
> **1 tablespoon mayonnaise**
> **⅛ teaspoon Worcestershire sauce**
> **Pinch ground red pepper**
> **3 tablespoons buttermilk**

1   In a large bowl, combine the watercress and endive.

2   In a small bowl, combine the blue cheese, mayonnaise, Worcestershire sauce, and pepper. Stir in the buttermilk. Pour over salad or serve on the side.

SERVES: 4
Diabetic Exchanges: ½ vegetable; ¾ fat

REDUCED FAT/CHOLESTEROL: Use a purchased fat-free blue cheese dressing instead of the one here.
Diabetic Exchanges: ¾ other carbohydrate; ¼ vegetable

WATERCRESS *and* PEAR SALAD *with* WALNUTS

I was able to find the pear-infused vinegar in my local supermarket. If you can't find it, any balsamic vinegar will do. For even richer flavor, toast the walnuts (bake at 350° for 7 to 10 minutes).

> **1 tablespoon olive oil**
>
> **2 teaspoons pear-infused or plain balsamic vinegar**
>
> **1 teaspoon minced shallot**
>
> **1 teaspoon Dijon mustard**
>
> **1 bunch watercress (5 ounces), rinsed**
>
> **½ ripe pear, thinly sliced**
>
> **2 tablespoons chopped walnuts**

1   In a small bowl, using a whisk combine the oil, vinegar, shallot, and mustard.

2   In a large bowl, toss the watercress, pears, and walnuts with the dressing.

SERVES: 4

Diabetic Exchanges: ¼ fruit; ¼ vegetable; 1 fat

ARUGULA *and* CUCUMBER *with* PARMESAN DRESSING

I've become very partial to grape tomatoes, but if they are not available in your area, cherry tomatoes will be just fine.

1 bunch arugula, rinsed

½ cup sliced cucumber

⅓ cup halved grape or cherry tomatoes

¼ cup thinly sliced red onion

⅓ cup yogurt

2 tablespoons grated Parmesan cheese

2 teaspoons mayonnaise

⅛ teaspoon ground pepper

1 In a large bowl, combine the arugula, cucumber, tomatoes, and onion.

2 In a small bowl, stir together the yogurt, Parmesan cheese, mayonnaise, and pepper. Pour over salad and toss to combine.

SERVES: 4

Diabetic Exchanges: ½ vegetable; ½ fat

REDUCED FAT: Use fat-free yogurt and mayonnaise.

Diabetic Exchanges: ½ vegetable

ARUGULA *and* FENNEL SALAD
with AVOCADO

This spectacular salad is a wonderful way to start a meal or, what's better, end it. You won't even want dessert. Save any extra grapefruit juice for breakfast the next day.

1 medium grapefruit

1 bunch arugula

1 cup very thinly sliced fennel

½ cup diced avocado

1 tablespoon fresh lemon juice

2 teaspoons balsamic vinegar

2 teaspoons olive oil

1 teaspoon honey mustard

Salt to taste

1   Using a sharp paring knife, slice the rind and pith from the top and bottom of the grapefruit. Remove the remaining rind and white pith. Cut the segments from the membrane, cutting toward the center alongside the membrane over a bowl. Squeeze any remaining juice from the membranes into the bowl and reserve.

2   Thoroughly rinse the arugula and remove large stems. Arrange the arugula on each of 4 salad plates. Top each with a quarter of the fennel slices and grapefruit segments, and sprinkle with a quarter of the avocado.

3   In a small bowl, stir together 1 tablespoon of the reserved grapefruit juice, the lemon juice, balsamic vinegar, oil, mustard, and salt to taste. Drizzle over each of the salads.

SERVES: 4

Diabetic Exchanges: ½ fruit; ½ vegetable; 1 fat

REDUCED FAT: Omit the avocado.

Diabetic Exchanges: ¼ fruit; ½ vegetable; ½ fat

WARM MEDLEY *of* WHITE *and* WILD MUSHROOMS *on* MESCLUN

I was torn as to where to place this recipe in the book. Should it be in the appetizer or salad chapter, as it is excellent in either spot. It is very light and a perfect starter for a hearty stew or starchy entrée. On the other hand it is a salad!

1 tablespoon olive oil, divided

1 tablespoon plus 1 teaspoon balsamic vinegar, divided

½ teaspoon Dijon mustard

Salt to taste

1 cup sliced white (cultivated) mushrooms

1 cup sliced assorted wild mushrooms

2 teaspoons minced shallots

4 cups lightly packed mesclun

1   In a small bowl, stir together 1½ teaspoons of the olive oil, 1 tablespoon of the balsamic vinegar, the mustard, and salt, and set aside.

2   In a medium skillet, heat the remaining 1½ teaspoons oil over medium-high heat. Add all of the mushrooms and the shallots. Cook, stirring, until softened, about 3 minutes. Stir in the remaining 1 teaspoon balsamic vinegar and salt.

3   In a large bowl, toss the mesclun with the dressing. Divide the mesclun among 4 plates, each topped with a quarter of the mushroom mixture.

SERVES: 4

Diabetic Exchanges: 1 vegetable; ¾ fat

CHOPPED PARSLEY SALAD

One day I was at the local farmers market and bought the largest bunch of parsley I've ever seen. It was much more than I could ever use for just a normal week of recipe testing, so I made parsley salad. The nice thing about parsley salad is that you can dress it in advance—it doesn't have to be a last-minute affair. Be warned that the dressing is very tart. You may want to start with 1½ tablespoons of lemon juice and increase from there.

2 cups chopped fresh curly parsley

½ cup finely chopped cucumber

⅓ cup finely chopped celery

¼ cup finely chopped red bell pepper

¼ cup thinly sliced scallion (green and white parts)

2 tablespoons fresh lemon juice

1 tablespoon apple juice

1 tablespoon olive oil

⅛ teaspoon ground black pepper

Salt to taste

1   In a large bowl, combine the parsley, cucumber, celery, red pepper, and scallion.

2   Add the lemon juice, apple juice, oil, pepper, and salt. Toss to combine.

SERVES: 4

Diabetic Exchanges: 1 vegetable; ¾ fat

MARINATED TOMATO SALAD

Dress this salad at least two hours in advance to let the flavors mingle. You can add other vegetables to this salad, such as celery, cucumbers, or bell peppers.

3 cups tomato wedges

1 tablespoon olive oil

2 teaspoons red wine vinegar

1 clove garlic, minced

¼ teaspoon Italian seasoning (or some combination of dried basil, oregano, and thyme)

⅛ teaspoon ground pepper

Salt to taste

In a medium bowl, combine the tomatoes, oil, vinegar, garlic, Italian seasoning, pepper, and salt. Let stand at least 2 hours to marinate.

SERVES: 4

Diabetic Exchanges: ¾ vegetable; ½ fat

CHOPPED TOMATO and CUCUMBER SALAD

This is really a salsa that is wonderful served with grilled fish or chicken in the summer when tomatoes are at their peak. You can omit the jalapeños if you don't like spicy foods.

1½ cups chopped tomatoes

1½ cups peeled and chopped cucumbers

¼ cup sliced scallions

2 tablespoons chopped cilantro leaves (fresh coriander)

1 tablespoon seeded and minced jalapeño pepper, or to taste (optional)

1 tablespoon fresh lime juice

2 teaspoons olive oil

1 clove garlic, minced

Salt to taste

In a large bowl, combine the tomatoes, cucumbers, scallions, cilantro, optional jalapeño pepper, lime juice, oil, garlic, and salt. Toss to combine.

SERVES: 4

Diabetic Exchanges: 1 vegetable; ½ fat

Sliced Cucumber Salad

I peel, then cut my cucumbers in half lengthwise and scoop out the seeds before slicing. This is especially compatible with hearty stews.

3 cups thinly sliced cucumbers
½ cup thinly sliced red bell pepper
¼ cup thinly sliced red onion
1 tablespoon distilled white vinegar
1½ teaspoons olive oil
¼ teaspoon sugar
¼ teaspoon dried dillweed
⅛ teaspoon ground black pepper
Salt to taste

In a medium bowl, combine all the ingredients. Let stand at least 15 minutes before serving.

SERVES: 4
Diabetic Exchanges: ¾ vegetable; ¼ fat

SPICY CUCUMBER YOGURT SALAD

This salad is similar to an Indian raita and as such goes well with any kind of curry. I omit the ground red pepper when serving it with spicy foods.

3 cups thinly sliced cucumbers

½ cup plain yogurt

2 tablespoons chopped fresh parsley

2 tablespoons thinly sliced scallion

1 teaspoon chopped fresh mint

1 clove garlic, minced

⅛ teaspoon ground red pepper

Salt to taste

Put all the ingredients into a large bowl. Toss until combined.

SERVES: 4

Diabetic Exchanges: ½ vegetable; ¼ fat

ISRAELI SALAD

This salad—or one like it—is served daily in Israel at both breakfast and dinner, hence the name. On my kibbutz, we put a plate of fresh vegetables on each table and people would dice their vegetables of choice. I don't recall whether or not the salads were dressed, but one element that I didn't include is dill pickle—which was a popular salad item. Dice the vegetables into pieces ¼ inch or smaller.

> 1½ **cups finely diced cucumbers**
> ¾ **cup finely diced red bell pepper**
> ½ **cup finely diced tomato**
> ½ **cup chopped fresh parsley**
> ⅓ **cup finely diced onion**
> 1 **tablespoon plus 1 teaspoon distilled white vinegar**
> 2 **teaspoons vegetable oil**
> ⅛ **teaspoon ground black pepper**
> **Salt to taste**

In a medium bowl, combine all the ingredients. Let stand at least 20 minutes before serving.

SERVES: 6
Diabetic Exchanges: ¾ vegetable; ¼ fat

STRING BEAN *and* TOMATO SALAD *with* BLACK OLIVES

When grape tomatoes first came on the market they were so amazingly sweet that I would eat them for dessert. But as they have become increasingly available, they seem to have become less sweet and more like regular cherry tomatoes, so use whichever you can easily find.

> **2 cups green beans**
> **12 grape or cherry tomatoes, halved**
> **8 medium pitted black olives, halved**
> **¼ cup chopped fresh parsley**
> **1 tablespoon olive oil**
> **2 teaspoons wine vinegar**
> **1 teaspoon Dijon mustard**
> **1 teaspoon minced shallot**
> **⅛ teaspoon ground black pepper**
> **Salt to taste**

1   Cook the green beans in boiling water until bright green. Drain and rinse until cool.

2   In a large bowl, combine the green beans, tomatoes, olives, and parsley.

3   In a small bowl, combine the oil, vinegar, mustard, shallot, pepper, and salt. Pour over salad and toss to combine.

SERVES: 4
Diabetic Exchanges: 1½ vegetable; ¾ fat

REDUCED SODIUM: Omit the olives.
Diabetic Exchanges: 1½ vegetable; ¾ fat

GREEN BEAN *and* RED ONION SALAD

This is a wonderful salad with a Greek pedigree. Instead of cooking the green beans in boiling water, you can also blanch them by wrapping in wet paper towels and microwaving for a minute or until the green beans turn bright green.

> ¼ **cup walnuts**
> **3 cups whole green beans**
> ½ **cup thinly sliced red onion**
> ¼ **cup crumbled feta cheese**
> **1 tablespoon olive oil**
> **1 tablespoon fresh lemon juice**
> **1 teaspoon red wine vinegar**
> ⅛ **teaspoon ground black pepper**
> **Salt to taste**

1   Toast the walnuts by placing in a 350°F oven for 7 to 10 minutes or until the walnuts are lightly browned and give off a nutty aroma. Let cool and coarsely chop.

2   Cook the green beans in boiling water until bright green. Drain and rinse until cool.

3   In a large bowl, combine the green beans, onion, feta cheese, and walnuts. Add the olive oil, lemon juice, vinegar, pepper, and salt. Toss to combine.

SERVES: 6

Diabetic Exchanges: ¼ very lean meat; 1 vegetable; 1¼ fat

REDUCED FAT/PROTEIN/SODIUM: Omit feta cheese.

Diabetic Exchanges: ¼ very lean meat; 1 vegetable; 1 fat

Salads

ROASTED RED PEPPER *and* ZUCCHINI SALAD

You can prepare this salad with most leftover cooked vegetables instead of the zucchini. It's good with broccoli, or cauliflower, yellow squash, fennel, etc.

> **2 cups sliced zucchini or other vegetables**
> **½ cup roasted red pepper strips (page 26)**
> **1 tablespoon snipped fresh dill**
> **2 teaspoons red wine vinegar**
> **2 teaspoons balsamic vinegar**
> **2 teaspoons olive oil**
> **1 teaspoon Dijon mustard**
> **1 clove garlic, minced**
> **⅛ teaspoon ground pepper**
> **Salt to taste**

1   Cook the zucchini in boiling water 2 minutes or until just cooked. Drain and cool.

2   In a medium bowl, combine the zucchini, pepper strips, and dill.

3   In a small bowl, stir together both the vinegars, oil, mustard, garlic, pepper, and salt. Pour over salad and toss to combine.

SERVES: 4
Diabetic Exchanges: ½ vegetable; ½ fat

THE ULTIMATE DIABETES COOKBOOK

ASPARAGUS SALAD

Whether you choose thick or thin asparagus spears, make sure that they are fresh and not wrinkled. To prepare asparagus, hold the middle of the spear in one hand and the bottom in the other, then bend the asparagus until it snaps. Discard the bottom part.

> **2 cups asparagus cut into 2-inch pieces**
>
> **½ cup thinly sliced orange or red bell pepper**
>
> **2 tablespoons chopped walnuts**
>
> **2 tablespoons chopped fresh parsley**
>
> **2 teaspoons red wine vinegar**
>
> **2 teaspoons balsamic vinegar**
>
> **2 teaspoons olive oil**
>
> **1 teaspoon orange juice**
>
> **1 teaspoon Dijon mustard**
>
> **⅛ teaspoon grated orange rind**
>
> **1 clove garlic, minced**
>
> **Salt to taste**

1   Wrap the asparagus in wet paper towels, then microwave them on high power 1 to 2 minutes or until bright green. Cool.

2   In a medium bowl, combine the asparagus, bell pepper, walnuts, and parsley.

3   In a small bowl, combine the red wine and balsamic vinegars, oil, orange juice, mustard, orange rind, garlic, and salt. Pour over salad and toss to combine.

SERVES: 4
Diabetic Exchanges: 1 vegetable; 1 fat

TARRAGON BROCCOLI
and CAULIFLOWER SALAD

If you are not a tarragon fan, some chopped fresh dill would make a lovely substitute.

2 cups broccoli florets

2 cups cauliflower florets

2 tablespoons sliced scallion (white and green parts)

1½ tablespoons olive oil

1 tablespoon fresh lemon juice

2 teaspoons cider vinegar

1 teaspoon Dijon mustard

1 teaspoon fresh chopped tarragon or ½ teaspoon dried tarragon, crumbled

⅛ teaspoon ground pepper

Salt to taste

1   In a 3-quart pot of boiling water, cook the broccoli and cauliflower, over medium-high heat, until just tender, about 3 minutes. Drain and chill.

2   In a large bowl, combine the broccoli, cauliflower, and scallion.

3   In a small bowl, combine the oil, lemon juice, vinegar, mustard, tarragon, ground pepper, and salt. Pour over salad and toss to combine.

SERVES: 4

Diabetic Exchanges: 1 vegetable; 1 fat

CHUNKY MEDITERRANEAN SALAD

This salad is very versatile. You can serve it as an appetizer for eight, a side salad for six, or add extra cheese to make it a luncheon salad for four.

2 cups celery cut into 1-inch pieces

1 cup cubed (peeled) cucumber

l cup cubed red or orange bell pepper (¾-inch pieces)

⅓ cup crumbled feta cheese

1 tablespoon snipped fresh dill

1 tablespoon red wine vinegar

1½ teaspoons olive oil

½ teaspoon capers, chopped

¼ teaspoon dried oregano

1 clove garlic, minced

⅛ teaspoon ground black pepper

Salt to taste

1   In a large bowl, combine the celery, cucumber, bell pepper, feta cheese, and dill.

2   In a small bowl, combine the vinegar, oil, capers, oregano, garlic, and pepper. Pour over the salad and toss to combine. Season with salt, if desired.

SERVES: 6

Diabetic Exchanges: ¼ lean meat; ¾ vegetable; ½ fat

REDUCED FAT/SATURATED FAT/PROTEIN/SODIUM: Omit the feta cheese.

Diabetic Exchanges: ¾ vegetable; ¼ fat

SESAME SNOW PEA SALAD

The orange bell peppers make this salad look really dramatic. If you can't find them—or if they're extremely expensive—substitute red or yellow peppers. If you can't find any other bright pepper use julienned carrots—I'm going for color here, not necessarily the flavor of the bell peppers.

3 cups snow peas

½ cup sliced orange bell pepper

⅓ cup sliced baby corn (canned)

⅓ cup sliced scallions (green and white parts)

1 tablespoon cider vinegar

1½ teaspoons sesame seeds

1 teaspoon sesame oil

1 teaspoon vegetable oil

½ teaspoon soy sauce

½ teaspoon sugar

½ teaspoon minced fresh ginger

¼ teaspoon chili (hot sesame) oil

Salt to taste

1   Cook the snow peas in boiling water 1 to 2 minutes or until bright green. Drain and cool.

2   In a large bowl, toss together the snow peas, bell pepper, baby corn, and scallion.

3   In a small bowl, stir together the cider vinegar, sesame seeds, sesame oil, vegetable oil, soy sauce, sugar, ginger, chili oil, and salt. Pour over the salad and toss to combine.

SERVES: 6

Diabetic Exchanges: 1½ vegetable; ¼ fat

LOW: calorie, fat, saturated fat, protein, fiber, cholesterol, calcium, iron, magnesium, phosphorus, sodium

RADISH SALAD

I slice the radishes with the thin blade of my food processor. It makes this a very easy, quick dish. The dressing is watery, but the flavor is delicate and delicious. An excellent side dish for a sandwich or simple grilled or broiled chicken.

> ¼ cup buttermilk
> 2 tablespoons snipped fresh dill
> 1 tablespoon mayonnaise
> Salt to taste
> 4 cups thinly sliced radishes
> ¼ cup thinly sliced scallion (green and white parts)

1   In a small bowl, stir together the buttermilk, mayonnaise, dill, and salt.

2   In a medium bowl, combine the radish slices and scallion. Add the dressing and toss to combine.

SERVES: 6
Diabetic Exchanges: ¾ vegetable; ½ fat

REDUCED FAT: Use fat-free mayonnaise.
Diabetic Exchanges: ¾ vegetable

Salads

CURRIED COLESLAW

I think the peanuts add a nice surprise to the slaw, but you can leave them out.

4 cups shredded cabbage

½ cup shredded carrot

3 tablespoons thinly sliced scallion (white and dark green parts)

2 tablespoons chopped peanuts

⅓ cup plain yogurt

1 tablespoon mayonnaise

1 tablespoon chopped cilantro leaves (fresh coriander)

½ teaspoon curry powder

⅛ teaspoon ground black pepper

Salt to taste

1   In a large bowl, combine the cabbage, carrot, scallion, and peanuts.

2   In a small bowl, stir together the yogurt, mayonnaise, cilantro, curry powder, pepper, and salt. Pour over the cabbage and toss to combine.

SERVES: 4

Diabetic Exchanges: ¼ lean meat; 1¼ vegetable; 1 fat

REDUCED FAT/SATURATED FAT/PROTEIN/FIBER: Omit peanuts; use fat-free mayonnaise and yogurt.

Diabetic Exchanges: 1¼ vegetable

CELERIAC SLAW

Celeriac, also called celery root, is a vegetable with a consistency similar to parsnip. In fact, if you can't find celeriac you can substitute parsnip. This is a very lightly dressed salad that goes well with most entrées—roasts, stews, grilled meat, or fish—or can be served as an appetizer.

> **3 cups coarsely shredded celeriac (celery root)**
>
> **⅓ cup coarsely shredded carrot**
>
> **3 tablespoons chopped fresh parsley**
>
> **2 tablespoons thinly sliced scallion (green and white parts)**
>
> **3 tablespoons plain yogurt**
>
> **1 tablespoon mayonnaise**
>
> **1½ teaspoons honey mustard**
>
> **1 teaspoon distilled white vinegar**
>
> **¼ teaspoon ground black pepper**
>
> **Salt to taste**

1   In a large bowl, toss together the celeriac, carrot, parsley, and scallion.

2   In a small bowl, stir together the yogurt, mayonnaise, mustard, vinegar, pepper, and salt. Pour over salad and toss to combine.

SERVES: 4

Diabetic Exchanges: 2¼ vegetable; ¾ fat

REDUCED FAT: Use fat-free yogurt and mayonnaise.

Diabetic Exchanges: ¼ other carbohydrate; 2¼ vegetable

HIGH: **fiber, potassium**

LOW: **saturated fat, protein, cholesterol, calcium, iron, phosphorus, sodium**

SHREDDED KOHLRABI *and* JICAMA SLAW

I remember kohlrabi from my youth only as a "free food" for dieters—that alone was enough to assure me that it had to be something horrible. I've since become a fan of this underrated vegetable. Jicama is a Mexican root vegetable with a sweet flavor and a crunchy texture. The peel is tough on both these vegetables, so be sure to remove it before shredding. This salad is light and crunchy and a perfect foil for any hearty dish.

> **3 cups peeled and coarsely shredded kohlrabi**
>
> **l cup peeled and coarsely shredded jicama**
>
> **l tablespoon chopped cilantro leaves (fresh coriander)**
>
> **2 tablespoons cider vinegar**
>
> **1 tablespoon vegetable oil**
>
> **1 tablespoon orange juice**
>
> **½ teaspoon dry mustard**
>
> **¼ teaspoon sugar**
>
> **Salt to taste**

1   In a large bowl, combine the kohlrabi, jicama, and cilantro.

2   In a small bowl, stir together the vinegar, oil, orange juice, mustard, sugar, and salt. Pour over salad and toss to combine.

SERVES: 4

Diabetic Exchanges: 1¾ vegetable; ¾ fat

FENNEL FETA SALAD

Try to select fennel with the feathery fronds—this will assure that the fennel is fresh. If all the fronds have been cut off, and especially if the bulb looks a little wrinkled, hold this salad for another day—or use celery instead of the fennel. If you can find fresh fennel, but without the fronds, you can substitute fresh dill for them.

> **4 cups very thinly sliced fresh fennel**
> **½ cup thinly sliced red onion**
> **¼ cup crumbled feta cheese**
> **2 tablespoons chopped kalamata olives**
> **2 tablespoons chopped fresh parsley**
> **2 tablespoons fresh lemon juice**
> **1 tablespoon fennel fronds**
> **1 tablespoon olive oil**
> **1 teaspoon Dijon mustard**
> **⅛ teaspoon ground black pepper**

In a large bowl, combine the fennel, onion, feta, olives, parsley, lemon juice, fennel fronds, oil, mustard, and pepper. Toss to combine.

SERVES: 6

Diabetic Exchanges: 1 vegetable; 1 fat

REDUCED FAT/SATURATED FAT/PROTEIN/SODIUM: Omit the olives and cheese.

Diabetic Exchanges: 1 vegetable; ½ fat

CHICKPEA LEEK SALAD

It's important that you use only the light green part of the leek. The white part is too sharp, and the dark green part is too tough. Grate the rind of the orange first, then using a sharp knife remove the rest of the rind and all the white pith before dicing the orange into ¼-inch pieces. If you don't have white wine vinegar, substitute cider vinegar.

> **1½ cups sliced leeks (⅛ inch thick)**
>
> **1 cup cooked chickpeas (from dry or canned, drained)**
>
> **½ cup finely diced orange**
>
> **1 tablespoon chopped cilantro leaves (fresh coriander)**
>
> **1 tablespoon olive oil**
>
> **1 tablespoon white wine vinegar**
>
> **½ teaspoon grated orange rind**
>
> **Salt to taste**

1   In a medium bowl, combine the leeks, chickpeas, orange, cilantro, oil, vinegar, orange rind, and salt.

2   Toss to combine. Let stand at least 1 hour before serving.

SERVES: 6

Diabetic Exchanges: ¾ bread; ¼ very lean protein; ¼ fruit; 1 vegetable; ¾ fat

REDUCED SODIUM: Use home-cooked beans prepared without salt.

Diabetic Exchanges: ¾ bread; ¼ very lean protein; ¼ fruit; 1 vegetable; ¾ fat

ORIENTAL COUSCOUS SALAD

Use only fresh bean sprouts for this salad; canned ones are not acceptable. If you can't find fresh sprouts, try using coarsely shredded kohlrabi or daikon radish instead.

⅔ cup water

6 tablespoons whole wheat couscous

½ cup fresh mung bean sprouts

½ cup chopped snow peas

¼ cup chopped water chestnuts

3 tablespoons thinly sliced scallion

1½ tablespoons mirin or dry sherry

1 tablespoon soy sauce

2 teaspoons vegetable oil

1½ teaspoons rice or cider vinegar

½ teaspoon sugar

¼ to ½ teaspoon chili (hot sesame) oil

1 clove garlic, minced

1   In a 1-quart pot, bring the water to a boil over medium-high heat. Add the couscous and cook, covered, 3 minutes. Fluff with a fork and let cool.

2   In a large bowl, stir together the couscous, sprouts, snow peas, water chestnuts, and scallion.

3   In a small bowl, stir together the mirin, soy sauce, oil, vinegar, sugar, chili oil, and garlic. Pour over salad and toss to combine.

SERVES: 4

Diabetic Exchanges: 1 bread; ¼ vegetable; 1 fat

REDUCED SODIUM: Use low-sodium soy sauce; use chopped daikon radishes instead of the water chestnuts.

Diabetic Exchanges: 1 bread; ¼ vegetable; 1 fat

MOROCCAN COUSCOUS, CHICKPEA, *and* CARROT SALAD

Couscous, especially whole wheat, has a shorter shelf life than most whole grains. Make sure yours is fresh. You can vary this recipe by using shredded zucchini, yellow squash, jicama, daikon radish, or rutabaga instead of the carrot. To add an interesting flavor, try stirring in 1 teaspoon finely crushed coriander seeds.

⅔ **cup water**

6 tablespoons whole wheat couscous

¾ **cup cooked chickpeas (from dry or canned, drained)**

½ **cup shredded carrot**

¼ **cup chopped fresh parsley**

3 tablespoons chopped scallion

2 tablespoons fresh lemon juice

1 tablespoon olive oil

½ **teaspoon ground turmeric**

⅛ **teaspoon ground red pepper**

Salt to taste

1   In a 1-quart pot, bring the water to a boil over medium-high heat. Add the couscous and cook, covered, 3 minutes. Fluff with a fork and let cool.

2   In a large bowl, combine the couscous, chickpeas, carrot, parsley, and scallion.

3   In a small bowl, combine the lemon juice, oil, turmeric, red pepper, and salt. Pour over salad and toss to coat.

SERVES: 6

Diabetic Exchanges: 2 bread; ¼ vegetable; ½ fat

REDUCED SODIUM: Use chickpeas cooked from dry without salt (not canned).

Diabetic Exchanges: 2 bread; ¼ vegetable; ½ fat

TABOULI

I added some chopped fresh basil and chopped walnuts to this salad to make an ordinary tabouli extraordinary. For a plain tabouli, omit the walnuts and basil. Add crumbled feta cheese and it becomes a small meal.

> **1 cup water**
> **½ cup bulgur**
> **¾ cup finely chopped tomato**
> **½ cup finely chopped cucumber**
> **½ cup chopped walnuts**
> **½ cup chopped fresh parsley**
> **¼ cup thinly sliced scallion (green and white parts)**
> **3 tablespoons chopped fresh mint or 2 teaspoons dried mint**
> **2 tablespoons chopped fresh basil or 1 teaspoon dried basil**
> **2½ tablespoons fresh lemon juice**
> **2 tablespoons olive oil**
> **¼ teaspoon ground black pepper**
> **Salt to taste**

1   In a 1½-quart saucepan, bring the water to a boil. Add the bulgur. Cover and cook 20 minutes or until the liquid has been absorbed. Let cool.

2   In a large bowl, combine the bulgur, tomato, cucumber, walnuts, parsley, scallion, mint, basil, lemon juice, olive oil, pepper, and salt. Toss to combine.

SERVES: 6
Diabetic Exchanges: ½ bread; ½ vegetable; 2 fat

REDUCED FAT/SATURATED FAT: Omit the walnuts and reduce oil to 1 tablespoon.
Diabetic Exchanges: ½ bread; ½ vegetable; ½ fat

GRILLED VEGETABLE *and* MIXED RICE SALAD

You do not have to cook up three different kinds of rice (although I really do). You can just use one or two types of rice, or you can buy one of those fancy rice mixes (Lundgren Farms makes many interesting ones) from a health-food store. (To learn how to cook wild rice, see page 261; brown rice is on page 258—white rice directions are on the box.) This is a great way to use up any leftover vegetables you have on hand.

> ½ **cup cooked white rice**
>
> ½ **cup cooked brown rice**
>
> ½ **cup cooked wild rice**
>
> 1 **cup diced grilled eggplant**
>
> ¾ **cup chopped grilled zucchini and/or yellow squash**
>
> ⅓ **cup chopped roasted red bell pepper**
>
> ¼ **cup thinly sliced scallion (white and green parts)**
>
> 2 **tablespoons chopped fresh parsley**
>
> 1 **tablespoon olive oil**
>
> 1 **tablespoon red wine vinegar**
>
> 1 **tablespoon fresh lemon juice**
>
> ¼ **teaspoon ground black pepper**
>
> **Salt to taste**

1   In a large bowl, combine the white, brown, and wild rices: toss to combine. Add eggplant, squash, red pepper, scallion, and parsley.

2   Add the oil, vinegar, lemon juice, pepper, and salt. Toss to combine.

SERVES: 6

Diabetic Exchanges: ¾ bread; ½ vegetable; ½ fat

ORIENTAL CHICKEN SALAD

If you are serving this salad to nondiabetics, crispy Chinese noodles would be a nice topping. The mustard I use in the dressing is the spicy kind you get at a Chinese restaurant. I save the packets I get when I order food in. You can also look for it in the Asian section of your supermarket. If you don't have rice vinegar, substitute 1 tablespoon cider vinegar. You can substitute shredded romaine lettuce for the Chinese cabbage (or bok choy, if you like) if more convenient.

> **1½ cups cooked cubed chicken**
> **½ cup chopped water chestnuts**
> **¼ cup cooked peas (use fresh or frozen—not canned)**
> **3 tablespoons sliced scallion**
> **1½ tablespoons rice vinegar**
> **1 tablespoon vegetable oil**
> **2 teaspoons soy sauce**
> **1 teaspoon Chinese mustard**
> **½ teaspoon sesame oil**
> **¼ teaspoon ground ginger**
> **¼ teaspoon honey**
> **2 cups shredded Chinese cabbage**

1   In a medium bowl, combine the chicken, water chestnuts, peas, and scallion.

2   In a small bowl, stir together the vinegar, oil, soy sauce, mustard, sesame oil, ginger, and honey. Pour over the chicken salad and toss to combine. Serve over shredded cabbage.

SERVES: 4
Diabetic Exchanges: 2½ very lean meat; ¾ vegetable; 1 fat

REDUCED PROTEIN: Substitute one 15-ounce cake firm tofu, cubed, for the chicken.
Diabetic Exchanges: 1¼ bread; ½ very lean meat; ¾ vegetable; ¾ fat

REDUCED SODIUM: Use low-sodium soy sauce.
Diabetic Exchanges: 2½ very low protein; ¾ vegetable; 1 fat

SHRIMP *and* CUCUMBER SALAD

This is a lovely dish for an elegant lunch or summer supper. Serve on a bed of lettuce, if desired.

1¼ pounds shrimp

⅓ cup plain yogurt

1 tablespoon mayonnaise

1 tablespoon finely chopped scallion (white and green parts)

1 tablespoon finely chopped fresh parsley

½ clove garlic, minced

¼ teaspoon dried tarragon

4 cups peeled, sliced cucumbers

1   Cook the shrimp in boiling water until no longer translucent, 3 to 5 minutes, depending on the size of the shrimp. Drain the shrimp and place in a bowl of ice water to chill. Shell the shrimp and remove the vein in the back. Cut the shrimp in half, lengthwise. Place in refrigerator to chill.

2   In a medium bowl, combine the yogurt, mayonnaise, scallion, parsley, garlic, and tarragon.

3   In a large bowl, combine the cucumbers, shrimp, and dressing. Toss until combined.

SERVES: 4

Diabetic Exchanges: 4 very lean meat; ¾ vegetable; ¾ fat

REDUCED FAT/SATURATED FAT/CHOLESTEROL: Use fat-free yogurt and mayonnaise.
Diabetic Exchanges: 4 very lean meat; ¾ vegetable; ¼ fat

TUNA, AVOCADO, *and* TOMATO SALAD

This is a perfect lunch for a summer day when tomatoes are really worth eating! I was tempted to add some sliced black olives—and would have, had I had some the day I prepared this. If you do have some on hand, just toss them in—but don't forget they will increase the sodium and fat counts.

> **One 6½-ounce can tuna packed in water, drained thoroughly**
>
> **3 cups tomato wedges**
>
> **⅓ cup chopped green bell pepper**
>
> **⅓ cup diced avocado**
>
> **3 tablespoons thinly sliced scallion (white and green parts)**
>
> **2 tablespoons red wine vinegar**
>
> **1 tablespoon olive oil**
>
> **½ teaspoon white wine Worcestershire sauce**
>
> **⅛ teaspoon ground pepper**
>
> **Salt to taste**

1   In a large bowl, break up the tuna into bite-size pieces. Add the tomatoes, green pepper, avocado, and scallion.

2   Add the vinegar, oil, Worcestershire, pepper, and salt. Toss to combine.

SERVES: 4

Diabetic Exchanges: 1½ very lean meat; 1½ vegetable; 1 fat

REDUCED PROTEIN: Use a 3¼-ounce can of tuna and increase the tomato to 4 cups and avocado to ½ cup.

Diabetic Exchanges: ¾ very lean meat; 2 vegetable; 1¼ fat

REDUCED SODIUM: Use low-sodium tuna.

Diabetic Exchanges: ¾ very lean meat; 1½ vegetable; 1 fat

Breakfast and Brunch

Breakfast for a person with diabetes doesn't look all that much different from anyone else's. It's an important meal and it doesn't have to be repetitive. Of course, you must be sure that the breakfast you choose fits in with the plan that your physician or nutritionist has recommended for you.

Here are some simple suggestions:

■ Eggs—any style. Diabetics should not eat more than 4 whole eggs (meaning egg yolks, since you can have as many egg whites as you like) per week—and that includes the eggs used in baking or cooking. However, an occasional egg is still allowable, not to mention delicious.

■ Scrambled egg substitute (such as Egg Beaters) or egg whites with whole wheat toast.

■ Cottage cheese (low-fat or fat-free is preferable) on a slice of toast or with a piece of fruit

■ Unflavored yogurt (low-fat or fat-free is preferable) with a piece of fresh fruit and/or a sprinkling of wheat germ or Grape-Nuts

■ Hot cereal

■ Cold cereal

■ Peanut butter on a slice of bread or a rice cake

■ or any of the recipes in this chapter.

HIGH: **saturated fat, protein, cholesterol, calcium, phosphorus, sodium**
LOW: **fiber, iron,** *cholesterol*

CHEESE OMELET

I use a two-percent cheese such as American, Cheddar, or jalapeño Jack. You can also use part-skim mozzarella or any fat-free cheese.

> **2 eggs**
> **4 egg whites**
> **Salt to taste**
> **Ground black pepper to taste**
> **2 teaspoons butter**
> **2 slices low-fat cheese**

1   In a medium bowl, beat the eggs, egg whites, salt, and pepper until completely combined.

2   In a large nonstick skillet, melt the butter over medium-high heat. Add the egg mixture and cook, 2 to 4 minutes or until almost set. Turn over. Place cheese slices on top of eggs. Cook 1 minute covered, or until cheese is melted.

4   Slide omelet onto serving plate, folding the omelet to enclose the filling. Cut in half to serve.

SERVES: 2
Diabetic Exchanges: 1 very lean meat; 1½ lean meat; 1½ fat

REDUCED CHOLESTEROL: Omit the whole eggs and add 4 additional whites to the mixture. Or use ⅔ cup egg substitute (such as Egg Beaters or Egg Scramblers) for the eggs and egg whites.
Diabetic Exchanges (egg whites): 2 very lean meat; ¾ lean meat; 1 fat
Diabetic Exchanges (egg substitute): 1½ very lean meat; ¾ lean meat; 1¼ fat

Breakfast and Brunch

WESTERN OMELET *for* TWO

You can make a vegetable omelet the same way—just omit the ham. Add ½ cup chopped vegetable (such as zucchini, broccoli, or spinach) when you add the green pepper.

> **2 eggs**
> **4 egg whites**
> **Salt to taste**
> **1 teaspoon vegetable oil**
> **½ cup chopped green pepper**
> **¼ cup chopped onion**
> **⅓ cup diced ham**
> **2 teaspoons butter**

1   In a medium bowl, beat the eggs, egg whites, and salt until completely combined.

2   In a medium nonstick skillet, heat the oil over medium-high heat. Add the green pepper and onion and cook, stirring, until slightly softened, about 4 minutes. Stir in the ham. Remove from skillet and set aside.

3   In a large nonstick skillet, melt the butter over medium-high heat. Add the egg mixture and cook, covered, 2 to 4 minutes or until desired doneness.

4   Slide omelet onto serving plate. Place ham mixture over half the omelet. Fold the omelet to enclose the filling. Cut in half to serve.

SERVES: 2

Diabetic Exchange: 1 very lean meat; 1½ lean meat; ¾ vegetable; 2 fat

REDUCED CHOLESTEROL: Omit the whole eggs and add 4 additional whites to the mixture. Or use ⅔ cup egg substitute (such as Egg Beaters or Egg Scramblers) for the eggs and egg whites.
Diabetic Exchanges (egg whites): 2 very lean meat; ½ lean meat; ¾ vegetable; 1½ fat
Diabetic Exchanges (egg substitute): 1½ very lean meat; ½ lean meat; ¾ vegetable; 1¾ fat

REDUCED SODIUM: Use unsalted butter; omit ham.
Diabetic Exchanges: 1 very lean meat; 1 lean meat; ¾ vegetable; 1½ fat

EGG WHITE FRITTATA *for* TWO

Turning this frittata is not easy. Instead of trying to turn the whole thing at once, you can cut the frittata into half or quarters and turn it one part at a time. Or you can just place the skillet under a preheated broiler until the egg whites are cooked. Or you can cover the skillet with a lid and cook the frittata until the top is done. You can choose any combination of your favorite vegetables and (occasionally) use 2 beaten whole eggs plus 2 egg whites instead of the egg whites, or use egg substitute—like Egg Beaters or Egg Scramblers—instead of the egg whites.

> **6 egg whites**
>
> **2 tablespoons chopped fresh parsley**
>
> **2 teaspoons snipped fresh chives**
>
> **⅛ teaspoon ground black pepper**
>
> **Salt to taste**
>
> **2 teaspoons olive oil**
>
> **½ cup sliced mushrooms**
>
> **½ cup diced zucchini**
>
> **½ cup lightly packed, coarsely chopped fresh spinach**
>
> **⅓ cup chopped onion**
>
> **¼ teaspoon dried oregano**

1   In a medium bowl, beat the egg whites with the parsley, chives, pepper, and salt, and set aside.

2   In a medium skillet, heat the oil over medium-high heat. Add the mushrooms, zucchini, spinach, onion, and oregano. Cook, stirring, until vegetables are slightly softened, about 3 minutes. Stir in the egg whites and let cook, without further stirring, 2 minutes or until the egg is set on the bottom. Place a plate over the pan and turn the pan over. Slide the frittata back into the pan to finish cooking the bottom, about 1 to 2 minutes longer.

SERVES: 2

Diabetic Exchanges: 1½ very lean meat; 1 vegetable; 1 fat

EGGS FLORENTINE

I chop the spinach coarsely so that it retains its character. You can use one package of frozen whole leaf spinach, thawed and coarsely chopped, instead of fresh.

> 6 cups coarsely chopped spinach, thoroughly rinsed
>
> 6 cups water
>
> 1 tablespoon distilled white vinegar
>
> Salt
>
> 1 tablespoon butter
>
> 1½ tablespoons all-purpose flour
>
> ⅔ cup scalded milk
>
> ⅛ teaspoon ground pepper
>
> Pinch nutmeg
>
> 8 eggs

1   To a 4-quart nonstick saucepan, add the spinach with any water clinging to the leaves. Cook for 2 minutes or until the spinach is just wilted; drain.

2   To the same saucepan add the water, vinegar, and salt. Bring to a boil over high heat. (Keep at a simmer until you are ready to cook the eggs.)

3   In a 1-quart nonstick saucepan, melt the butter over medium heat. Remove from heat; stir in the flour until absorbed. Stir in the milk all at once, and continue to stir until all lumps are gone (if necessary mashing the lumps against the side of the pan). Over medium heat, cook, stirring, until mixture has thickened. Stir in the pepper, nutmeg, and salt to taste. Remove ¼ cup sauce from the pot and set aside. Stir the spinach into the remaining sauce.

3   Carefully crack and open each egg into a bowl. Slide eggs from bowl into the boiling water. Return to the boil and cook 2 minutes. Remove from water and drain well.

4   Divide the spinach sauce among 4 small plates; put 2 eggs on each plate, placing a dollop of the reserved sauce atop each egg.

SERVES: 4

Diabetic Exchanges: 1¾ lean meat; ¼ vegetable; ¼ milk; 2 fat

HUEVOS RANCHEROS

This is really a breakfast treat. I make the eggs in separate small skillets. If you have only one small skillet, you may want to make both eggs in a large skillet so they can cook at the same time and the first egg doesn't get cold while you are cooking the second one. As for the cheese, I like to use one- or two-percent-fat jalapeño Jack cheese but you can use American cheese or plain Jack cheese just as well—or eliminate the cheese completely, if you prefer.

> **Two 7-inch flour tortillas**
> **2 teaspoons butter, divided**
> **2 eggs**
> **2 egg whites, divided**
> **Salt to taste**
> **Pepper to taste**
> **2 slices cheese**
> **¼ cup salsa (homemade [page 24] or store-bought)**

1   Heat the tortillas in a 350°F oven for 5 minutes.

2   While the tortillas are heating, in each of 2 small nonstick skillets melt 1 teaspoon of butter over medium-high heat. To each skillet add 1 whole egg with the yolk unbroken and 1 egg white. Season with salt and pepper. Cook about 1 to 2 minutes or to desired doneness. (If you prefer eggs "over," turn them before topping with cheese. Place a slice of cheese over each egg portion.

3   Remove the tortillas from the oven and place one on each plate. Top each with one of the fried eggs, then put 2 tablespoons of salsa on each portion.

SERVES: 2

Diabetic Exchanges: 1½ bread; ½ very lean meat; 1½ lean meat; ½ vegetable; 1¾ fat

REDUCED FAT/CHOLESTEROL: Omit whole eggs, increase egg whites to 4. Use fat-free cheese.
Diabetic Exchanges: 1½ bread; 1 very lean meat; ¾ lean meat; ½ vegetable; 1¼ fat

Huevos *al* Nido (Eggs *in a* Nest)

These are very pretty and make a nice "company" breakfast or brunch (I'm a little too lazy to make these without any occasion). The eggs are in a tomato "nest" and the tomatoes are in aluminum foil "nests." If you prefer a less Mexican flavor, omit the chili powder and sprinkle the top of the eggs with grated Parmesan cheese instead of the Cheddar.

> **4 medium ripe tomatoes**
> **2 teaspoons vegetable oil**
> **¼ cup finely chopped onion**
> **¼ cup finely chopped green bell pepper**
> **¼ cup finely chopped mushroom**
> **1 clove garlic, minced**
> **1 tablespoon plain dry bread crumbs**
> **¼ teaspoon chili powder**
> **⅛ teaspoon ground black pepper**
> **Salt to taste**
> **4 eggs**
> **1-ounce slice low-fat Cheddar or American cheese, cut into quarters**

1   Preheat oven to 350°F.

2   Cut a thin slice off the top of each tomato so that you can scoop out the insides. Scoop out the inside of 1 tomato and chop; scoop out the remaining tomatoes and discard the pulp. Place each tomato on a 6-by-6-inch square of aluminum foil; wrap to close and bake 10 minutes or until heated through.

3   While the tomato shells are baking, in a medium nonstick skillet, heat the oil over medium-high heat. Add the onion, green pepper, mushroom, tomato pulp, and garlic. Cook, stirring, until vegetables are slightly softened, about 3 minutes. Stir in the bread crumbs, chili powder, pepper, and salt.

4   While the tomatoes are baking, poach (see page 308) the eggs in boiling salted water for 2 minutes. Drain.

5 Remove the tomato shells from the oven and turn oven setting to broil.

6 Open each foil packet and place a quarter of the vegetable mixture in each tomato shell; top each with 1 poached egg and a piece of cheese.

7 Place the tomatoes under broiler and cook about 1 minute or until cheese is melted.

SERVES: 4

Diabetic Exchanges: ¼ very lean meat; 1 lean meat; 1¾ vegetable; 1 fat

REDUCED CALORIE/FAT/SATURATED FAT/CHOLESTEROL: Poach only the egg whites.

Diabetic Exchanges: ¾ very lean meat; 1¾ vegetable; ½ fat

Breakfast and Brunch

CRUSTLESS VEGETABLE QUICHE

Who really needs a crust for a quiche? If you prefer, you can substitute 2 whole eggs or the egg substitute equivalent of 2 eggs for the 4 whites.

Olive oil and flour, for pie dish

1 cup cottage cheese

4 egg whites, beaten

2 tablespoons snipped fresh dill

1 tablespoon all-purpose flour

¼ teaspoon Worcestershire sauce

¼ teaspoon ground black pepper

Salt to taste

2 teaspoons olive oil

1½ cups sliced mushrooms

½ cup chopped asparagus

¼ cup chopped leek (white and light green parts)

¼ cup shredded carrot

2 cups bite-size spinach pieces

1   Preheat oven to 350°F. Thoroughly grease a 9-inch pie dish with olive oil and dust with flour.

2   Place the cottage cheese, egg whites, dill, flour, Worcestershire sauce, pepper, and salt in a food processor fitted with a steel blade. Process until smooth; set aside.

3   In a medium nonstick skillet, heat the oil over medium-high heat. Add the mushrooms, asparagus, leek, and carrot. Cook, stirring, until all the vegetables are slightly softened, about 3 minutes. Add the spinach and cook, stirring, until wilted, about 1 minute. Let cool completely.

4 Stir the cottage cheese mixture into the vegetable mixture. Pour into prepared pie dish.

5 Bake 40 minutes or until top is browned and knife inserted in center comes out clean. Run sharp knife around the edge of the pan to release the quiche.

SERVES: 6

Diabetic Exchanges: ¼ very lean meat; ¾ meat; ¾ vegetable; ½ fat

REDUCED FAT: Use one-percent cottage cheese.

Diabetic Exchanges: ¼ other carbohydrate; 1 very lean meat; ¾ vegetable; ½ fat

REDUCED SODIUM: Use low-sodium cottage cheese.

Diabetic Exchanges: ¼ very lean meat; ¾ meat; ¾ vegetable; ½ fat

Breakfast and Brunch

HIGH: **carbohydrate, fiber, cholesterol, sodium,** *protein*
LOW: *magnesium, phosphorus, cholesterol*

FRENCH TOAST

If you like your French toast "wet" inside, you need to dip the bread a little longer than the quick dip suggested here. In that case, the egg mixture will not make as many pieces of French toast.

> **2 eggs, lightly beaten**
> **⅓ cup milk**
> **1 tablespoon sugar**
> **½ teaspoon vanilla extract**
> **12 slices melba thin bread or 8 slices "lite" bread**
> **2 teaspoons butter**

1   In a shallow wide bowl, beat the eggs with the milk, sugar, and vanilla extract.

2   Quickly dip both sides of the bread slices in the egg mixture.

3   In a large nonstick skillet, melt the butter over medium-high heat. Place as many slices of bread as will fit in the pan in a single layer. Cook until browned on bottom, about 1 to 2 minutes; turn and cook the second side until browned, about 1 to 2 minutes longer.

SERVES: 4
Diabetic Exchanges: 1¾ bread; ¼ other carbohydrate; ½ lean meat; ¾ fat

REDUCED CHOLESTEROL: Substitute 4 egg whites or ⅔ cup egg substitute such as Egg Scramblers or Egg Beaters for the eggs. Use skim milk.
Diabetic Exchanges (egg whites): 1¾ bread; ¼ other carbohydrate; ⅕ very lean meat; ½ fat
Diabetic Exchanges (egg substitute): 1¾ bread; ¼ other carbohydrate; ¾ very lean meat; 1¼ fat

THE ULTIMATE DIABETES COOKBOOK

Cottage Cheese Pancakes

These are not exactly like regular pancakes—they are less cakey and moister. But they are tasty and satisfy that desire for pancakes. If you like using artificial sweetener, you can substitute one or two packets for the sugar. Serve them with reduced-calorie or sugar-free maple syrup or fresh fruit. But remember, if you use fruit, to count the extra carbohydrates.

> ½ **cup cottage cheese**
> 2 **egg whites**
> 1 **teaspoon vanilla extract**
> ⅓ **cup all-purpose flour**
> ⅓ **cup whole wheat flour**
> 1 **tablespoon sugar**
> 1 **teaspoon baking powder**
> 1 **teaspoon baking soda**
> **Salt to taste**
> ¾ **cup buttermilk**
> 2 **teaspoons butter, divided**

1 Into a food processor container fitted with a steel blade, put the cottage cheese, egg whites, and vanilla; cover and process until smooth.

2 In a medium bowl, combine both flours, the sugar, baking powder, baking soda, and salt. Stir in the cottage cheese mixture and buttermilk until combined but not smooth.

3 In a large nonstick skillet, melt 1 teaspoon of the butter over medium-high heat. Drop the batter (about 3 tablespoons per pancake) and spread to form 3-inch pancakes. Cook 3 minutes or until browned on bottom. Turn and cook top 2 minutes longer or until browned. Add remaining butter to skillet if necessary when cooking remaining pancakes.

SERVES: 4

Diabetic Exchanges: 1 bread; ¼ other carbohydrate; ¼ very lean meat; ½ lean meat; ¼ milk; ½ fat

REDUCED FAT: Use fat-free cottage cheese and skim milk.

Diabetic Exchanges: 1 bread; ¼ other carbohydrate; ¾ very lean meat; ¼ milk; ½ fat

BLUEBERRY BRAN MUFFINS

If you like really bran-filled bran muffins try these. They are really good for you!

2 cups unprocessed bran

1½ cups buttermilk

2 egg whites

2 tablespoons butter, melted

¾ cup all-purpose flour

⅓ cup sugar

2 teaspoons baking powder

1 teaspoon baking soda

Salt to taste

¾ cup fresh or frozen blueberries

1   Preheat oven to 400°F. Grease twenty-two 2-inch muffin cups with butter, oil, Pam, or shortening.

2   In a medium bowl, combine the bran with the buttermilk; let stand 5 minutes. Beat in egg whites and melted butter.

3   On wax paper, mix together flour, sugar, baking powder, baking soda, and salt. Stir into bran mixture. Fold in blueberries.

4   Spoon into prepared muffin cups. Bake 25 minutes or until golden brown.

5   Remove from oven to cool on wire rack, let stand 10 minutes. Run sharp knife around edge of muffin to loosen before removing from pan.

SERVES: 22

Diabetic Exchanges: ½ bread; ½ fruit; ¼ fat

REDUCED SODIUM: Use low-sodium baking powder and butter.

Diabetic Exchanges: ½ bread; ½ fruit; ¼ fat

PEACH MILK SHAKE

I don't recommend skipping breakfast. If you can't bear food in the morning, try this—it's pretty nutritious. You can use frozen fruit to thicken and chill the mixture. You can use blueberries, raspberries, or strawberries instead of the peaches—and soy milk for the regular milk. You can also toss in a tablespoon of bran flakes or wheat germ for a little extra fiber.

> **½ cup frozen unsweetened peach slices**
> **½ cup whole milk**
> **1 teaspoon honey, or to taste**
> **¼ teaspoon vanilla extract**

1   Place the peaches, milk, honey, and vanilla into a blender container.

2   Cover and process until smooth.

SERVES: 1

Diabetic Exchanges: ¼ other carbohydrate; ½ fruit; ½ milk; ¾ fat

REDUCED FAT/SATURATED FAT/CHOLESTEROL: Use skim milk instead of whole.

Diabetic Exchanges: ¼ other carbohydrate; ½ fruit; ½ milk

Desserts

As I said in the introduction to this book, I don't believe artificial sweeteners are good for you. Nor do they taste particularly good. If you must eat dessert, try fruit. If you must have something sweeter, eat something delicious but not too much of it—and not too often. "Sweets" are not an everyday, or even every-week, item for diabetics. If you prefer desserts with artificial sweeteners, consult books devoted to that subject.

BROWNIE BITES

These are regular brownies—just smaller. If you like really fudge-y brownies, bake them 5 to 10 minutes less.

6 tablespoons butter

1½ squares unsweetened chocolate

¾ cup sugar

2 eggs

1 teaspoon vanilla extract

⅓ cup all-purpose flour

1   Preheat oven to 350°F. Heavily grease and flour an 8-inch-square baking pan.

2   In a 1-quart saucepan, heat the butter and chocolate over medium-low heat until completely melted, about 4 minutes.

3   In a medium bowl, beat the sugar and eggs until light in color, about 3 minutes. Beat in the chocolate mixture and vanilla, then stir in the flour.

4   Pour into baking pan and bake 30 minutes. Let cool completely.

5   Cut into 20 squares.

SERVES: 20

Diabetic Exchanges: ½ other carbohydrate; ¼ lean meat; 1 fat

FLAN

This is one of my very favorite desserts (surpassed only by crème brûlée, perhaps). I love the cool slippery feel of the custard and the sweet syrupy aftertaste. This is best if made a day in advance, to let all the caramel melt before turning it out of the cups.

> ¼ **cup water**
>
> **2 tablespoons plus ¼ cup sugar, divided**
>
> **1¼ cups milk**
>
> **2 eggs**
>
> **2 teaspoons vanilla extract**

1   Preheat oven to 350°F. Grease four 6-ounce custard cups.

2   Pour the water into a small saucepan. Add 2 tablespoons of the sugar to the pot. Place over medium-high heat and bring to a boil, stirring, until the sugar dissolves. Boil 4 minutes, without stirring. Then cook, stirring constantly, until mixture is amber-colored, about 2 minutes. Pour into the 4 custard cups.

3   Add the milk and remaining sugar to the small saucepan. Heat until scalded (small bubbles will form around the edge of the pan). Remove from heat.

4   In a large bowl, beat the eggs. Gradually stir in the warm milk, then the vanilla. Pour into the custard cups with the sugar mixture on the bottom.

5   Place a 9-inch-square baking pan on the middle rack of the oven and add boiling water to a depth of ¼ inch. Put custard cup into water bath. Bake 35 minutes or until a knife inserted in the center comes out clean. Chill at least 3 hours.

6   To serve, run a thin knife around the sides of the custard cups. Invert flan onto individual dessert dishes or saucers.

SERVES: 4

Diabetic Exchanges: 1 other carbohydrate; ½ lean meat; ¼ milk; ¾ fat

REDUCED FAT/SATURATED FAT/CHOLESTEROL: Use skim milk and egg substitute to equal 2 eggs.
Diabetic Exchanges: 1 other carbohydrate; ½ very lean meat; ¼ lean meat; ¼ milk; ¼ fat

POST-HALLOWEEN CHOCOLATE PUDDING

What do you do with leftover Hershey Kisses or other chocolates? Make this chocolate pudding—so rich and smooth, it puts any commercial pudding to shame. I've made this recipe with both 2 and 3 tablespoons of sugar, and I'm torn as to which is better. I think if you like milk chocolate you may prefer 3 tablespoons; if you like semisweet chocolate, you may prefer 2.

> **3 tablespoons cornstarch**
> **2 or 3 tablespoons sugar**
> **2 tablespoons cocoa**
> **2 cups milk, divided**
> **½ cup (3 ounces) milk-chocolate pieces**

1   In a 1½-quart saucepan, stir together the cornstarch, sugar, and cocoa. Stir in ½ cup of the milk until all lumps are dissolved. Stir in the remaining milk.

2   Bring to a boil over medium heat, stirring constantly (and I mean that!), about 10 minutes. Remove from heat; stir in the chocolate pieces until melted.

3   Pour into 6 small bowls and cover with plastic wrap. Chill at least 2 hours.

SERVES: 6

Diabetic Exchanges: ¼ bread; 1 other carbohydrate; ¼ milk; 1¼ fat

REDUCED FAT: Use skim milk.

Diabetic Exchanges: ¼ bread; 1 other carbohydrate; ¼ milk; ¾ fat

CHOCOLATE MOUSSE TORTE

This is either a chocolate omelet or a torte. It's hard to describe exactly what it is. It makes a bitter-chocolate, almost omelet-like batter, which tastes like chocolate mousse if you lick the beaters. It bakes into a sort of torte. If you are serving company, drop a dollop of whipped cream on their servings.

> **½ cup semisweet chocolate chips**
> **2 eggs, separated**
> **1 egg white**
> **¼ cup confectioners sugar**
> **2 teaspoons butter**

1   Preheat oven to 325°F.

2   Melt the chocolate chips over low heat, or in a double boiler over simmering water, or in the micowave oven. Let cool.

3   Beat the 3 egg whites until foamy, gradually add the confectioners sugar, and beat until the mixture forms stiff peaks.

4   Stir the egg yolks into the melted chocolate, then fold into the egg white mixture.

5   In a 10-inch ovenproof skillet, melt the butter over low heat. Spread the chocolate mixture in the pan and cook 3 to 5 minutes or until cooked on the bottom.

6   Place the skillet in the oven, and bake 10 to 12 minutes or until a knife inserted in the center comes out clean.

7   Cut into 6 wedges.

SERVES: 6

Diabetic Exchanges: 1 other carbohydrate; ½ lean meat; 1 fat

DEYSEE (TIBETAN RICE DESSERT)

I first tasted this dessert in my local Tibetan restaurant. It's like rice pudding, but much much easier to make. You heat the rice, then stir in yogurt. There are lots of flavor variations you can try. You can stir in spices such as ground cardamom (my favorite), cinnamon, or nutmeg or vanilla extract or rosewater. You could also omit the raisins or substitute chopped pistachios.

> **1 cup cooked white rice**
>
> **2 tablespoons sugar, or to taste**
>
> **1 tablespoon raisins**
>
> **¾ cup yogurt**

1   In a medium microwave-safe bowl, stir together the rice, sugar, and raisins. Microwave on high 1 minute or until rice is hot.

2   Stir in the yogurt.

SERVES: 4

Diabetic Exchanges: ½ bread; ¼ other carbohydrate; ¼ milk; ½ fat

REDUCED FAT/SATURATED FAT/CHOLESTEROL: Use fat-free yogurt.

Diabetic Exchanges: ½ bread; ¼ other carbohydrate; ¼ milk

GINGER BREAD PUDDING

With flavors that remind you of Christmas and winter nights in front of the fireplace, this bread pudding is a real standout. Serve warm or chilled (I like it best warm), sliced or scooped out of the pan. I like to use very seedy whole-grain bread—my choice for this recipe is Arnold's Best Winter Wheat. The low-fat version is really almost as good.

> **Butter for preparing pan**
>
> **1 egg**
>
> **2 egg whites**
>
> **1½ cups milk**
>
> **¼ cup firmly packed dark brown sugar**
>
> **2 tablespoons molasses**
>
> **2 teaspoons vanilla extract**
>
> **1 teaspoon ground ginger**
>
> **1 teaspoon ground cinnamon**
>
> **Salt to taste**
>
> **4 cups whole-grain bread cubes (about 6 slices)**
>
> **1 cup peeled, chopped apple**
>
> **¼ cup raisins or dried currants**

1   Preheat oven to 350°F. Heavily butter a 9-by-5-by-3-inch loaf pan.

2   In a large bowl, beat the egg and egg whites until completely combined. Stir in the milk, brown sugar, molasses, vanilla, ginger, cinnamon, and salt. Add the bread, apple, and raisins. Let stand 20 minutes, stirring occasionally. Pour into loaf pan.

3   Bake 45 to 50 minutes or until a knife comes out clean when inserted in center. Let cool 5 minutes, then using a large spatula turn onto a serving plate. Turn the loaf over so the crusty part is up. Using a serrated knife, slice into 8 pieces.

SERVES: 8

Diabetic Exchanges: ¾ bread; ¾ other carbohydrate; ¼ very lean meat; ¼ fruit; ¼ milk; ½ fat

REDUCED FAT: Use 3 egg whites and eliminate the whole egg; use fat-free milk.

Diabetic Exchanges: ¾ bread; ¾ other carbohydrate; ¼ very lean meat; ¼ fruit; ¼ milk

CHOCOLATE CHIP COOKIES

Be careful that you stick to the serving size, which is two cookies, not four or six or eight! If need be, send any extras home with guests instead of leaving temptation in your kitchen.

⅓ **cup butter (5 tablespoons plus one teaspoon), softened**

⅓ **cup granulated sugar**

¼ **cup firmly packed brown sugar**

1 egg

1 teaspoon vanilla extract

1 cup all-purpose flour

½ **teaspoon baking soda**

Salt to taste

½ **cup chopped chocolate chips, or mini chocolate chips**

1   Preheat oven to 350°F. Grease 2 cookie sheets.

2   In a medium bowl, cream the butter with both sugars. Beat in the egg and vanilla. Beat in the flour, baking soda, and salt. Stir in the chocolate chips.

3   Drop batter by rounded teaspoonfuls 2 inches apart onto the prepared cookie sheets. Bake 9 minutes or until browned on bottom. Cool on wire rack.

SERVES: 21 (2 cookies per serving)
Diabetic Exchanges: ¼ bread; ½ other carbohydrate; ¾ fat

REDUCED CHOLESTEROL: Use 2 egg whites instead of 1 whole egg and substitute margarine for butter.
Diabetic Exchanges: ¼ bread; ½ other carbohydrate; ¾ fat

REDUCED SODIUM: Use unsalted butter.
Diabetic Exchanges: ¼ bread; ½ other carbohydrate; ¾ fat

PEANUT BUTTER COOKIES

You will have to dip your fork in flour each time you press a cookie. These cookies come out of the oven soft, then crisp as they cool.

> ½ cup all-purpose flour
>
> ½ teaspoon baking powder
>
> ¼ cup (4 tablespoons) butter, softened
>
> ¼ cup granulated sugar
>
> ¼ cup firmly packed light or dark brown sugar
>
> 6 tablespoons smooth peanut butter
>
> 1 egg white

1   Preheat oven to 350°F. Grease 2 baking sheets.

2   On a piece of wax paper, with a whisk mix together the flour and baking powder.

2   In a medium bowl, cream the butter with both sugars until fluffy. Beat in the peanut butter, then the egg white. Stir in the flour mixture.

3   Drop by rounded teaspoonful onto the prepared baking sheets. Press, with a fork dipped in flour, in each direction to flatten and form a crosshatch pattern. Bake 10 minutes or until browned.

4   Cool on baking sheet 1 minute, then cool completely on wire rack.

SERVES: 18 (2 cookies per serving)
Diabetic Exchanges: ¼ bread; ¼ other carbohydrate; ¾ fat

REDUCED SODIUM: Use unsalted butter, peanut butter, and baking powder.
Diabetic Exchanges: ¼ bread; ¼ other carbohydrate; ¾ fat

OATMEAL CURRANT CRISPIES

These are really crispy and oatmeal-ly cookies. I ate two, then gave my friend Robert the rest of the batch to take home. I knew I wouldn't be safe with them in the house. One minute after Robert left I found myself with an intense desire to go running after him yelling, "Give them back to me right now!"

¼ **cup all-purpose flour**

¼ **teaspoon ground cinnamon**

¼ **teaspoon baking powder**

Salt to taste

¼ **cup (4 tablespoons) butter, softened**

¼ **cup sugar**

¾ **cup old-fashioned rolled oats**

2 tablespoons currants or chopped dark raisins

1 tablespoon milk

1   Preheat oven to 350°F. Grease 2 baking sheets.

2   On a piece of wax paper, mix together the flour, cinnamon, baking powder, and salt; set aside.

3   In a medium bowl, beat the butter and sugar until light and fluffy. Beat in the oatmeal and currants, then the milk. Stir in the flour mixture.

4   Drop by rounded teaspoonful about 2 inches apart onto the prepared baking sheets. Flatten slightly with a fork.

5   Bake 10 to 12 minutes or until cookies are golden on bottom. Cool on baking sheet 2 minutes. Remove to wire rack to cool completely.

SERVES: 12 (2 cookies per serving)
Diabetic Exchanges: ¼ bread; ¼ other carbohydrate; ¾ fat

GINGER COOKIES

These are like gingersnaps, but not too spicy. Add extra ginger for a "snappier" cookie.

> ¼ cup (4 tablespoons) butter, softened
> ¼ cup firmly packed dark brown sugar
> 1 egg white
> 1 tablespoon molasses
> ½ cup all-purpose flour
> 1 teaspoon ground ginger
> ¼ teaspoon baking soda
> Salt to taste

1   Preheat oven to 350°F. Grease a cookie sheet.

2   In a medium bowl, cream the butter and sugar until light and fluffy. Beat in the egg white and molasses. Beat in the flour, ginger, baking soda, and salt.

3   Drop by level teaspoonsful onto the greased cookie sheets, leaving 2 inches between each cookie.

4   Bake 8 minutes or until browned. Cool on wire rack.

SERVES: 20 (2 cookies per serving)
Diabetic Exchanges: ¼ other carbohydrate; ½ fat

Tuilles

These delicate, thin, crispy cookies just about melt in your mouth. They are called *tuilles* (tiles) because they resemble a type of French roof tile. If you find it too much trouble to make the cookies curve, just serve them flat; they are just as delicious. You can also omit the sliced almonds to reduce the calories somewhat.

¼ cup (4 tablespoons) butter, softened
¼ cup sugar
2 egg whites
¼ cup sifted all-purpose flour
¼ teaspoon vanilla extract
¼ teaspoon almond extract
1 tablespoon sliced almonds

1   Preheat oven to 400°F. Grease 2 cookie sheets.

2   In a medium bowl, cream the butter and sugar. Beat in the egg whites, flour, vanilla and almond extracts. Stir in the almonds.

3   Drop batter by rounded teaspoonful 2 inches apart onto a cookie sheet, baking no more than 5 cookies at a time. With the back of a spoon, spread the batter thinly into ovals 2 inches long. Bake 4 to 6 minutes or until the edges of the cookies have browned. Immediately remove from the sheets and fold in half lengthwise so that the cookies are slightly curved like a roof tile. If cookies stick to the sheet when you try to lift them, return to oven for 1 minute and then try again. Drop the cookies on the second sheet while the first one bakes.

SERVES: 15 (2 cookies per serving)
Diabetic Exchanges: ½ other carbohydrate; ½ fat

MINI PAVLOVAS

These heavenly bites are so good it's hard to believe they're only 30 calories each. To make French-style pavlovas, use sliced strawberries; to make the national New Zealand dessert, use sliced kiwis. Since meringues are humidity sensitive, don't try to make these on a rainy day.

> ¼ **cup granulated sugar**
> ¼ **teaspoon cornstarch**
> ⅛ **teaspoon salt**
> **2 egg whites**
> ⅓ **cup heavy cream**
> **1 tablespoon confectioners sugar**
> ½ **cup sliced strawberries or kiwis**

1   Preheat oven to 200°F. Line 2 baking sheets with parchment paper or plain brown paper.

2   On a piece of wax paper combine the sugar, cornstarch, and salt. In a clean dry bowl, using clean beaters, beat the egg whites until foamy. Gradually beat in the sugar mixture and continue beating until stiff peaks form.

3   Drop the meringues by rounded tablespoonsful onto the prepared baking sheets. You should have 18. Create a "well" in each meringue using the back of a spoon. Bake 40 minutes or until crisp. Remove from baking sheets and cool on racks.

4   In a medium bowl, beat the cream with the confectioners sugar until stiff peaks form. Place a dollop of whipped cream in the "well" of each meringue. Top with 1 or 2 slices of fruit.

SERVES: 18
Diabetic Exchanges: ¼ other carbohydrate; ¼ fat

MAPLE-GLAZED BANANAS

It's quick, it's easy, it's delicious, it's not too obscenely calorific—what more could you want from a dessert? Well, if you're not too concerned about your sugar levels, you might want some vanilla ice cream.

> **2 large or 3 small bananas**
> **1 tablespoon butter**
> **2 tablespoons maple syrup**
> **1 teaspoon fresh lemon juice**
> **Pinch nutmeg**

1   Peel the bananas and cut in half lengthwise.

2   In a large nonstick skillet, melt the butter over medium heat. Add the bananas cut side up and cook until browned on bottom, about 1 to 2 minutes. Turn and cook until browned on top and softened throughout, about 1 to 2 minutes more. Timing may vary depending on ripeness of bananas.

3   Add the maple syrup, lemon juice, and nutmeg to the pan and cook until the bananas are glazed, about 1 to 2 minutes, turning the bananas once to coat.

SERVES: 4

Diabetic Exchanges: ½ other carbohydrate/sugar; 1½ fruit; ½ fat

CHOCOLATE-DIPPED STRAWBERRIES

You can dip the strawberries in advance and chill until serving time, but do this the same day as you are going to use them. Although I don't truly believe that one strawberry is a serving, I thought it would be easier to give the nutritional information per berry. You can do the math after you've eaten as many as you feel are a portion!

12 medium strawberries (preferably with stems)
1 square semisweet chocolate (1 ounce)
1 tablespoon heavy cream
1 teaspoon coffee, almond, or hazelnut flavored liqueur

1   Rinse the strawberries and place on paper towels to dry thoroughly. Grease a sheet of aluminum foil.

2   In a small saucepan over low heat, heat the chocolate with the cream and liqueur until melted. Dip the strawberries into the chocolate to cover the nonstem half of the strawberry with chocolate. Place on aluminum foil and let chill in the refrigerator until serving time.

SERVES: 12
Diabetic Exchanges: ¼ fruit; ¼ fat

Baked Apples

Use small Macintosh apples for this recipe—they're just the right amount of tart and they bake nicely.

4 small Macintosh apples

2 tablespoons packed brown sugar

¼ cup chopped walnuts

1 tablespoon currants or chopped raisins

1 tablespoon apricot jam

¼ teaspoon ground cinnamon

2 teaspoons butter

1   Preheat oven to 350°F.

2   Peel the top half of each apple. Remove the core, creating an upside-down cone that is 1-inch in diameter at the top, and leaving the bottom of the apple intact.

3   In a small bowl, stir together the sugar, nuts, currants, jam, and cinnamon. Place ¼ of the nut mixture into the core of each apple. Dot each with ½ teaspoon of the butter. Cover baking dish with aluminum foil.

4   Bake 40 minutes or until apples are tender. Serve warm or cold.

SERVES: 4

Diabetic Exchanges: ½ other carbohydrate; ¼ very lean meat; 1¼ fruit; 1¼ fat

APPLE BROWN BETTY

I use Macintosh apples because I like the tartness, but most apples will work—except Granny Smiths. For some reason Grannies never seem to soften adequately.

2 slices raisin or cinnamon bread, cut into cubes

1 tablespoon butter, melted

3 cups peeled thinly sliced apples

3 tablespoons firmly packed light brown sugar

2 tablespoons granulated sugar

2 tablespoons water

2 teaspoons fresh lemon juice

½ teaspoon ground cinnamon

⅛ teaspoon ground allspice

Salt to taste

1   Preheat oven to 350°F. Grease a 1-quart baking dish.

2   In a medium bowl, toss together the bread cubes and butter.

3   In a large bowl, toss together the apples, both sugars, water, lemon juice, cinnamon, allspice, and salt.

4   Place half of the bread cubes in the baking dish. Top with all of the apples (but not the juice in the bowl). Top with remaining bread cubes and pour juice from apples over the bread cubes.

5   Cover and bake 30 minutes. Uncover and bake 20 to 30 minutes longer or until bread cubes are browned.

SERVES: 4

Diabetic Exchanges: ½ bread; 1 other carbohydrate; ½ fruit; ½ fat

PEACH *and* BLUEBERRY COBBLER

You can make this cobbler with fresh or frozen fruit. If using frozen, measure it while frozen, then thaw before continuing with the recipe. For a really delicious treat, serve this slightly warmed with some vanilla ice cream on the side.

> **2 tablespoons sugar**
> **1 tablespoon cornstarch**
> **2 cups blueberries**
> **1 cup sliced peaches**

Biscuits
> **½ cup self-rising flour**
> **1 tablespoon sugar**
> **2 tablespoons butter**
> **¼ cup milk**

1   Preheat oven to 375°F.

2   In a 1½-quart baking dish, stir together the sugar and cornstarch. Add the fruit and toss to coat.

3   In a medium bowl, combine the flour and sugar. Cut in the butter until the mixture resembles coarse cornmeal. Stir in the milk until the mixture forms a dough. Turn onto floured board and knead 12 times. Pinch off pieces of dough about 1½ inches large and scatter over the top of the fruit.

4   Bake 30 minutes or until the biscuits are dark and the fruit mixture is bubbly.

SERVES: 6

Diabetic Exchanges: ½ bread; ¼ other carbohydrate; ½ fruit; ¾ fat

BERRIES *with* ZABAGLIONE

You can just eat the zabaglione by itself, but I find it too rich. I prefer to use it as a dollop for fruit. Use any berries you like. I particularly like sliced strawberries, but raspberries or blueberries or blackberries or some combination of them all are pretty good too.

2 cups berries

2 tablespoons Madeira

1 tablespoon sugar

1 egg yolk

1 Divide the berries among 4 small bowls.

2 In the top of a double boiler, stir together the Madeira and sugar. Stir in the yolk.

3 Place over simmering water and beat with an electric mixer until fluffy, about 2 minutes.

4 Spoon over berries.

SERVES: 4

Diabetic Exchanges: ¼ other carbohydrate; ½ fruit; ½ fat

RASPBERRY SOUFFLÉ

This soufflé is just like eating pink clouds. Serve the soufflé as soon as it comes out of the oven so it is still puffy when it reaches the table.

⅓ cup sugar plus additional sugar for the dish

1 cup fresh raspberries

1 tablespoon orange or raspberry liqueur

¾ teaspoon cornstarch

4 egg whites

¼ teaspoon cream of tartar

1   Preheat the oven to 400°F. Grease a 1½-quart soufflé dish and dust with sugar.

2   Place the raspberries in a blender container. Cover and blend until smooth. Put purée through strainer over a small saucepan, and discard seeds. Stir the ⅓ cup sugar and liqueur into the strained raspberry purée. Stir in the cornstarch. Cook over medium heat, stirring cornstarch until mixture comes to the boil. Cool completely.

3   In a clean bowl, beat the egg whites with the cream of tartar until stiff but not dry. Fold the purée into the egg whites. Pour into the prepared dish.

4   Bake 12 to 14 minutes or until soufflé has risen 1 or 2 inches above the edge of the dish.

SERVES: 4

Diabetic Exchanges: 1 other carbohydrate; ½ very lean meat; ¼ fruit; ¼ fat

POACHED PEARS

You can use white wine or cranberry juice or orange juice instead of the white grape juice, but do not use purple grape juice as its flavor is too strong for the pears, not to mention the color.

> **1 cup water**
> **¼ cup white grape juice**
> **2 tablespoons sugar**
> **1 tablespoon fresh lemon or lime juice**
> **2 ripe pears, peeled, halved, and cored**

1   In a 2-quart saucepan, combine the water, grape juice, sugar, and lemon juice; bring to a boil over medium-high heat. Add the pear halves and return to the boil.

2   Reduce heat and simmer, uncovered, 20 minutes or until cooked through. Cooking time will depend on ripeness of pears.

SERVES: 4
Diabetic Exchanges: ¼ other carbohydrate; 1 fruit

Fresh Fruit Salad

Needless to say, you can vary this fruit salad endlessly. Use any combination of fruits, use any fruity liqueur or none at all, and add sugar to taste. If you are making the fruit salad with bananas more than an hour before serving, stir everything together except the bananas, and then add the bananas just before serving.

> **1 cup sliced peaches**
> **1 cup sliced strawberries**
> **½ cup blueberries**
> **1 tablespoon orange liqueur or orange juice**
> **1 teaspoon grenadine**

Combine all the ingredients in a medium bowl.

SERVES: 4
Diabetic Exchanges: ¾ fruit; ¼ fat

Nutrient Analysis of Recipes and Variations for One Serving

RECIPE	CALORIES (kcal)	TOTAL FAT (g)	SATURATED FAT (g)	PROTEIN (g)	CARBOHYDRATES (g)	DIETARY FIBER (g)
Appetizers						
Black Bean Dip	63.98	2.64	0.31	2.70	7.31	2.73
Low Fat	44.09	0.39	0.01	2.70	7.32	2.73
Low Sodium	65.15	2.46	0.35	2.90	8.45	2.89
Baba Ghanouj	61.21	4.08	0.58	1.95	5.63	1.80
Low Fat	39.10	2.09	0.30	1.29	4.82	1.62
Cucumber Feta Dip	36.85	2.46	1.68	2.00	1.79	0.10
Low Fat	15.29	0.34	0.21	1.18	1.94	0.10
Low Sodium	14.91	0.69	0.43	0.82	1.45	0.10
Tomato Salsa	12.28	0.12	0.02	0.41	2.74	0.86
Low Sodium	10.89	0.13	0.02	0.42	2.47	0.55
Thyme Stuffed Mushrooms	47.41	2.64	0.31	1.68	5.11	0.56
Red Peppers with Fennel	62.60	4.59	0.63	1.25	5.28	1.86
Low Fat	40.63	2.39	0.31	0.74	4.98	1.76
Lemon Zucchini Ribbons	37.35	2.36	0.32	1.01	3.85	1.10
Low Sodium	36.99	2.38	0.33	0.91	3.89	1.14
Tomatoes and Mozzarella	205.96	15.74	8.58	10.72	4.35	0.73
Low Fat	37.75	0.21	0.03	4.85	4.04	0.97
Low Sodium	202.72	13.28	6.65	16.19	4.85	0.73
Low Protein	67.58	3.59	0.48	4.85	4.04	0.97
Roasted Asparagus with Stilton	101.79	6.62	2.56	4.90	5.56	2.43
Low Protein	62.71	3.38	0.46	2.51	5.52	2.44
White Beans with Beets	99.19	3.71	0.47	3.24	13.55	3.46
Low Sodium	102.83	3.69	0.46	4.10	14.33	4.38
Salmon and Smoked Salmon Pâté	63.47	3.64	0.83	6.92	0.49	0.04
Low Sodium	62.92	3.49	0.74	7.08	0.51	0.04
Shrimp with Rémoulade Sauce	73.48	3.86	0.86	8.19	1.42	0.25
Low Fat	48.77	0.80	0.27	8.41	1.76	0.25
Low Sodium	72.95	3.80	0.84	8.16	1.42	0.23
Curried Shrimp	64.84	2.75	0.52	8.00	1.76	0.19

CHOLESTEROL (mg)	CALCIUM (mg)	IRON (mg)	MAGNESIUM (mg)	PHOSPHORUS (mg)	POTASSIUM (mg)	SODIUM (mg)	WATER (g)
0	24.11	1.16	3.40	7.53	53.56	196.96	53.54
0	24.15	1.15	3.43	7.56	53.56	197.04	56.01
0	18.52	0.86	23.47	47.72	155.33	63.92	38.04
0	16.17	0.50	15.48	73.10	165.20	4.49	56.30
0	10.88	0.33	11.92	43.48	147.99	3.18	56.19
10.00	68.59	0.10	5.72	51.05	58.95	102.79	35.66
1.25	40.23	0.05	5.32	32.9	69.97	14.74	30.49
2.59	27.59	0.05	4.13	22.98	53.80	9.88	31.06
0	17.10	0.19	5.03	11.14	97.96	70.50	48.88
0	3.86	0.20	5.21	11.43	99.97	33.84	40.44
0	9.30	0.91	6.54	61.8	222.88	22.56	55.00
0	20.05	0.62	14.35	34.33	216.44	17.82	65.99
0	19.50	0.42	9.40	23.52	203.71	17.73	65.85
0	9.79	0.40	12.80	19.88	175.96	4.40	68.11
0	11.22	0.39	14.89	23.11	195.71	5.52	68.14
44.55	330.67	0.71	8.00	16.62	143.14	86.59	89.76
1.18	124.79	0.33	11.78	87.46	159.67	137.89	58.06
30.62	421.15	0.48	22.74	313.73	197.00	14.66	86.35
1.18	124.80	0.34	11.78	87.50	159.67	137.89	58.06
8.46	86.07	0.51	2.95	45.91	310.85	157.21	109.42
0	26.90	0.47	0.53	2.49	285.17	0.28	106.95
0	34.14	1.31	8.99	18.88	135.63	211.18	91.13
0	54.62	1.79	38.75	89.89	258.29	19.67	99.15
10.94	56.69	0.30	8.34	97.28	89.88	364.28	29.48
11.57	79.77	0.28	9.31	114.57	100.56	56.98	29.28
70.96	51.98	1.35	19.06	70.92	133.82	180.83	54.08
68.20	60.84	1.33	19.95	78.37	145.94	164.48	53.11
71.25	51.91	1.35	18.82	71.68	133.47	120.60	53.39
59.27	29.85	1.07	16.25	85.34	94.76	72.39	35.54

Nutrient Analysis of Recipes and Variations for One Serving

RECIPE	CALORIES (kcal)	TOTAL FAT (g)	SATURATED FAT (g)	PROTEIN (g)	CARBOHYDRATES (g)	DIETARY FIBER (g)
Low Fat	47.12	0.72	0.13	8.00	1.90	0.19
Scallops with Orange	74.13	2.30	1.38	9.64	3.09	0.07
Low Sodium	74.13	2.30	1.38	9.64	3.09	0.07
Low Cholesterol	77.35	2.72	0.35	9.64	3.09	0.07
Seared Tuna with Butter Beans	167.02	5.52	0.46	23.22	7.39	1.93
Low Sodium	181.50	5.65	0.49	23.73	8.01	2.53
Tuna with Black Olive Vinaigrette	182.12	9.34	0.46	21.08	2.94	0.15
Low Sodium	146.52	5.58	0.47	21.17	1.94	0.27
Orange Teriyaki Salmon	114.18	6.16	1.24	11.87	1.62	0.05
Low Sodium	114.18	6.16	1.24	11.62	1.87	0.05
Ginger Lamb with Watercress Salad	105.5	5.02	1.62	12.40	2.16	0.33
Low Cholesterol	8.82	1.89	0.35	13.71	2.16	0.33
Thai Beef Salad	140.42	4.77	1.91	14.05	11.43	2.22
Low Sodium	140.42	4.77	1.91	13.71	11.77	2.22
Low Protein	108.00	4.05	0.59	8.59	12.54	2.45

Soups

RECIPE	CALORIES (kcal)	TOTAL FAT (g)	SATURATED FAT (g)	PROTEIN (g)	CARBOHYDRATES (g)	DIETARY FIBER (g)
Chicken Broth	35.20	0.62	0.17	7.70	0	0
Vegetable Broth	30.80	0.17	0	0	6.86	0
Vegetable Tomato Soup	66.46	1.54	0.18	2.88	11.79	2.88
Low Sodium	59.12	1.77	0.39	2.62	9.89	2.42
Bourbon Street Soup	80.00	4.01	0.46	2.19	10.65	2.89
Vegetable Broth	76.00	3.41	0.26	2.39	11.25	2.89
Low Sodium	78.22	3.52	0.41	2.60	10.95	2.87
Zucchini Escarole Soup	83.21	5.45	1.10	2.33	7.37	2.33
Vegetable Broth	67.79	3.21	0.34	3.04	9.53	2.29
Low Sodium	76.29	3.62	0.92	3.89	8.52	2.33
Broccoli Fennel Velvet Soup	60.18	2.81	0.66	2.92	7.54	3.15
Chicken Broth	62.68	1.78	0.50	4.29	10.53	3.15
Low Sodium	69.41	2.11	0.98	4.97	9.72	3.15
Low Protein	60.18	2.81	0.66	2.92	7.54	3.15
Creamy Portobello Mushroom Soup	153.53	7.12	3.30	3.95	13.89	2.02
Low Fat	124.55	3.19	0.74	5.03	14.52	2.02
Low Sodium	136.41	4.64	2.18	5.24	14.66	2.02
Hungarian Cauliflower and Cabbage Soup	102.45	5.98	1.43	3.92	9.96	3.39
Vegetable Broth	94.96	4.85	1.04	4.32	11.16	3.39

THE ULTIMATE DIABETES COOKBOOK

CHOLESTEROL (mg)	CALCIUM (mg)	IRON (mg)	MAGNESIUM (mg)	PHOSPHORUS (mg)	POTASSIUM (mg)	SODIUM (mg)	WATER (g)
57.56	29.52	1.05	15.66	80.51	86.87	59.50	34.78
23.71	15.81	0.20	33.73	127.00	216.18	105.68	59.28
23.71	15.81	0.20	33.73	127.00	216.18	91.51	59.28
18.71	15.81	0.21	33.73	127.02	216.18	91.52	58.83
0	64.40	14.59	0.64	183.73	185.58	167.52	99.45
0	55.28	14.76	16.00	223.38	188.44	1.04	87.04
0	53.04	14.11	2.05	186.35	28.18	169.67	83.49
0	53.60	14.16	3.28	189.05	53.15	3.62	78.56
33.45	9.09	0.23	16.54	134.07	216.55	263.63	47.11
33.45	9.09	0.23	16.54	134.07	216.55	184.88	47.11
37.12	30.89	1.10	18.24	106.62	248.56	44.48	66.83
32.89	29.89	0.52	21.36	124.62	248.56	46.47	82.74
21.11	36.91	1.78	34.31	149.47	617.32	354.31	229.60
28.11	36.91	1.78	34.31	149.47	617.32	249.31	229.60
0	92.37	1.67	64.49	142.30	519.02	325.15	249.56
0	22.0	—	19.36	0.22	409.20	101.2	431.38
0	26.40	—	13.20	0.22	325.60	35.2	432.3
0	46.20	1.43	13.97	35.83	226.51	381.74	240.61
0.96	47.71	0.97	22.37	49.13	385.41	54.83	231.47
1	45.84	0.74	28.66	48.16	375.48	825.44	288.90
0	45.84	0.74	28.66	48.16	369.48	825.64	288.29
0.77	48.92	0.74	28.66	48.16	363.88	39.18	279.73
3.75	34.23	0.64	23.26	41.99	333.44	760.28	349.08
0	33.78	0.63	22.60	41.03	303.50	760.93	436.79
2.88	45.77	0.64	23.26	41.99	310.94	91.80	318.02
3.13	54.62	1.02	24.41	60.79	391.93	665.38	317.27
3.28	79.0	1.03	24.41	60.79	410.68	677.72	315.36
5.69	88.61	1.02	24.41	60.79	410.68	120.03	289.01
3.13	54.62	1.02	24.41	60.79	391.93	665.38	317.27
14.38	39.00	0.43	4.38	123.97	488.74	544.00	272.79
2.47	51.99	0.44	7.86	154.89	474.45	77.24	250.59
11.30	46.69	0.43	4.38	123.97	473.74	77.10	251.10
6.67	87.2	0.61	21.33	77.26	335.47	437.48	302.47
4.78	87.31	0.61	21.48	77.30	323.62	437.73	301.25

Nutrient Analysis of Recipes and Variations for One Serving

RECIPE	CALORIES (kcal)	TOTAL FAT (g)	SATURATED FAT (g)	PROTEIN (g)	CARBOHYDRATES (g)	DIETARY FIBER (g)
Low Fat	83.16	2.89	0.50	4.98	11.72	3.39
Low Sodium	98.76	5.00	1.34	4.76	10.58	3.39
Low Protein	63.85	2.68	0.20	3.05	9.45	3.39
Curried Cauliflower Soup with Scallion Raita	90.72	5.38	0.83	4.68	12.08	2.44
Vegetable Broth	91.68	4.06	0.85	4.56	12.13	3.37
Low Protein	86.49	1.39	0.15	8.37	10.76	2.45
Low Sodium	99.41	4.09	1.07	6.03	11.72	2.45
Snap Pea Soup with Rosemary	124.46	4.34	1.26	5.26	16.65	3.97
Vegetable Broth	106.96	1.71	0.39	6.14	19.28	3.97
Low Sodium	116.38	2.18	1.06	7.08	18.00	3.97
Red Pepper Bisque	146.99	7.14	1.36	4.42	17.44	2.06
Vegetable Broth	132.57	4.98	.62	5.17	19.69	2.06
Low Sodium	139.25	5.31	1.19	5.86	18.54	2.08
Creamy Kohlrabi and Potato Soup	107.25	3.17	0.98	3.72	17.37	3.63
Vegetable Broth	94.68	1.30	0.35	4.34	19.25	3.63
Low Sodium	92.07	1.14	0.51	4.49	17.62	3.36
Manhattan Clam Chowder	78.60	3.09	0.48	5.06	8.97	1.75
Low Sodium	114.7	3.62	0.61	10.02	11.73	2.29
Low Protein	61.74	2.86	0.36	1.83	9.18	1.99
Split Pea and Barley Soup	180.64	3.48	0.85	9.39	29.28	3.05
Vegetable Broth	164.42	1.08	0.05	10.19	31.68	3.05
Low Sodium	173.26	1.52	0.66	11.05	30.51	3.05
Lentil Kale Soup	208.34	2.83	0.62	13.68	34.81	12.20
Vegetable Broth	198.34	1.33	0.12	14.18	36.31	12.20
Low Sodium	203.73	1.60	0.50	14.72	35.58	12.20
Cuban Black Bean Soup	152.81	0.72	0.16	9.41	28.59	9.88
Tuscan White Bean Soup	172.01	3.70	0.49	3.37	31.30	3.96
Low Fat	152.12	1.45	0.19	3.37	31.30	3.96
Low Sodium	177.13	3.85	0.55	4.22	33.63	5.21
Low Protein	147.01	3.58	0.49	2.12	26.80	2.71
Mango Gazpacho	116.42	1.68	0.25	2.53	29.69	3.77
Gazpacho Variation	89.61	1.57	0.22	2.32	22.67	3.03
Chilled Yogurt Basil Soup	84.34	3.68	1.50	4.20	10.58	2.12
Low Sodium	77.08	2.69	1.54	4.47	10.22	2.12
Low Fat	64.46	0.70	0.26	4.85	12.11	2.12

THE ULTIMATE DIABETES COOKBOOK

CHOLESTEROL (mg)	CALCIUM (mg)	IRON (mg)	MAGNESIUM (mg)	PHOSPHORUS (mg)	POTASSIUM (mg)	SODIUM (mg)	WATER (g)
2.29	94.00	0.59	17.07	42.38	266.65	84.15	281.49
6.21	93.36	0.61	21.33	77.26	323.47	80.95	284.41
0	42.84	0.59	17.07	42.38	266.65	420.83	269.04
3.89	63.48	0.65	18.26	90.72	377.25	789.25	362.02
3.98	74.89	0.65	25.14	90.72	438.26	487.95	360.69
0.55	102.45	2.08	21.16	85.68	518.36	176.03	293.05
4.75	94.09	0.61	20.10	61.05	402.05	127.37	254.11
6.37	84.36	1.95	38.08	89.23	304.12	894.7	326.29
1.99	84.36	1.95	38.08	89.23	277.87	895.59	323.61
5.36	97.82	1.95	38.08	89.23	277.87	114.82	326.58
5.89	89.21	0.87	24.27	102.39	383.19	822.54	316.94
2.45	88.97	0.87	24.30	102.27	360.50	823.35	314.65
5.03	101.99	0.85	26.08	105.19	375.28	154.70	282.52
5.07	50.24	1.06	31.97	77.30	614.15	654.36	363.21
1.99	50.29	1.06	32.03	77.31	595.46	654.92	361.30
2.40	41.38	1.06	30.20	62.77	571.73	90.19	321.55
8.38	15.60	1.24	14.09	30.73	244.00	592.16	257.49
21.36	55.27	9.23	24.78	141.48	540.99	90.96	264.85
0	21.32	0.70	15.73	34.42	285.54	302.88	221.05
4.00	41.16	1.78	19.85	48.11	299.99	844.98	361.92
0	41.16	1.78	19.85	48.11	275.99	845.77	359.48
3.08	53.47	1.78	19.85	48.11	275.99	131.93	325.79
2.50	94.16	5.03	67.52	270.20	819.68	550.28	479.20
0	94.15	5.03	67.51	270.20	804.8	550.77	477.88
1.92	101.85	5.03	67.52	270.20	804.68	104.63	457.04
0	58.19	2.57	77.62	157.50	505.87	27.31	369.25
0	50.46	1.82	21.59	32.17	412.43	256.46	278.41
0	50.46	1.81	21.59	32.14	412.43	256.46	278.41
0	70.16	1.96	48.71	88.83	577.26	18.92	265.06
0	40.46	1.37	21.59	32.17	412.43	188.96	252.28
0	36.58	0.93	35.53	60.99	627.84	14.78	359.15
0	32.46	0.88	31.82	56.45	563.49	13.95	325.45
7.78	112.95	0.89	35.95	104.68	419.99	283.34	270.49
8.74	116.79	0.88	35.95	104.66	419.99	60.26	259.91
1.25	113.79	0.85	28.86	46.54	325.30	65.59	255.05

Nutrient Analysis of Recipes and Variations for One Serving

RECIPE	CALORIES (kcal)	TOTAL FAT (g)	SATURATED FAT (g)	PROTEIN (g)	CARBOHYDRATES (g)	DIETARY FIBER (g)
Cucumber Soup with Spicy Salsa	60.56	1.27	0.62	4.18	9.17	1.45
Vegetable Broth	58.10	1.17	.47	3.97	9.46	1.45
Low Sodium	68.17	1.48	0.77	4.95	9.70	1.38
Poultry						
Eggplant and Chicken Provençal	285.58	9.81	2.47	35.64	11.98	3.65
Low Protein	158.35	5.40	1.21	11.26	17.80	7.40
Mom's Roasted Chicken	373.24	16.07	4.42	49.78	5.02	1.23
Low Fat	336.48	11.70	3.23	50.21	5.02	1.23
Chicken Creole	329.51	11.98	2.62	40.35	12.45	2.92
Low Sodium	327.86	12.11	2.63	40.44	13.51	3.09
Low Protein Brown Rice	327.61	9.16	1.75	24.99	34.76	3.94
Chicken with 40 Cloves	228.10	7.80	2.18	33.90	2.68	0.17
Chicken Chasseur	272.11	10.33	2.38	36.06	7.57	1.12
Low Sodium/Protein	173.80	6.52	1.29	20.02	9.53	1.70
Chicken Gumbo	300.88	10.25	2.38	36.50	13.58	3.58
Low Sodium	299.17	10.38	2.40	36.59	14.68	3.75
Low Protein	297.42	7.17	1.44	21.32	35.89	4.60
Chicken Curry	248.89	10.19	2.36	34.21	3.04	0.53
Reduced Protein	172.82	6.69	1.33	19.78	9.11	3.60
Coq au Vin	298.56	11.48	2.47	36.11	6.61	0.98
Low Protein	226.66	8.90	1.49	20.63	12.21	2.86
Southern Style Chicken and Rice	408.33	9.44	2.32	36.58	40.90	1.49
Low Sodium	408.33	9.44	2.32	36.58	40.90	1.49
Low Protein	402.15	6.60	1.36	21.67	61.34	2.23
Barbecue Chicken	252.16	7.90	2.20	34.30	9.50	0.60
Low Sodium	252.37	7.90	2.20	34.28	9.56	0.57
Chicken Gai Yang	251.31	11.23	2.67	34.12	1.46	0.08
Low Sodium	251.18	11.23	2.67	34.02	1.57	0.09
Low Fat	193.52	4.07	1.15	35.54	1.46	0.08
Chicken with Fennel	242.23	8.00	1.16	34.86	6.91	2.67
Low Protein	193.34	7.39	0.97	22.30	10.08	4.02
Chicken with Mung Bean Sprouts	257.25	6.11	0.91	33.84	17.95	4.17
Low Sodium	255.71	5.70	0.87	33.81	15.58	4.17
Low Protein	234.57	11.30	1.49	18.58	20.04	4.59
Chicken with Roasted Pepper Sauce	161.89	4.43	0.86	26.8	2.39	0.64

CHOLESTEROL (mg)	CALCIUM (mg)	IRON (mg)	MAGNESIUM (mg)	PHOSPHORUS (mg)	POTASSIUM (mg)	SODIUM (mg)	WATER (g)
3.34	115.83	0.58	28.40	102.56	383.29	128.52	261.45
2.94	112.46	0.58	28.44	102.41	383.07	283.20	269.92
4.18	140.81	0.44	31.81	121.04	412.48	104.67	295.80
104.36	38.60	2.23	55.53	283.73	622.42	101.69	230.61
26.93	42.47	1.83	53.46	148.62	647.14	58.02	256.90
148.49	36.32	2.67	51.96	360.11	528.21	137.45	158.07
152.35	37.31	2.63	54.66	379.73	545.57	138.99	161.07
116.41	61.88	2.67	48.17	310.27	723.41	314.40	278.43
116.41	75.25	2.63	60.08	329.12	784.65	143.91	277.06
63.08	61.46	2.36	75.97	282.95	639.62	270.73	301.78
103.36	30.90	1.49	33.63	254.54	323.44	94.36	88.39
104.36	28.88	2.38	44.51	310.95	591.68	163.64	176.66
50.68	22.98	2.19	33.08	234.67	619.53	60.03	182.02
104.36	85.36	2.67	66.68	295.42	716.47	286.53	286.15
104.36	99.20	2.63	79.01	314.94	779.89	109.96	284.73
50.68	85.34	2.35	94.81	269.69	633.31	242.82	324.38
104.36	25.45	1.45	34.66	256.54	341.29	94.67	127.39
51.88	47.85	1.82	39.58	188.97	434.02	64.66	171.59
104.36	31.44	2.58	44.67	316.81	571.14	100.36	159.03
51.88	42.11	2.49	49.26	243.99	741.34	66.59	223.99
102.01	51.91	3.09	49.85	313.08	403.59	576.62	192.45
102.01	51.49	3.09	49.79	313.08	403.39	97.09	192.45
50.68	62.64	3.32	44.15	229.20	319.98	745.44	244.48
104.36	36.46	1.90	51.43	260.80	503.31	269.01	119.84
104.36	36.23	1.89	51.13	260.34	498.08	123.67	119.85
104.36	21.55	1.41	32.65	248.56	311.91	170.82	85.19
104.36	21.78	1.43	33.11	250.02	314.31	138.59	85.03
96.39	22.51	1.23	34.10	262.80	311.77	161.25	84.06
82.22	70.56	1.83	66.38	345.06	695.78	222.93	178.03
49.33	85.64	1.74	57.90	255.68	731.28	208.70	174.86
66.60	52.25	2.95	78.85	343.23	648.59	617.98	332.15
66.41	54.81	2.95	78.85	343.23	643.60	351.45	332.15
0.83	149.27	3.96	122.58	293.19	500.82	554.90	324.60
66.60	17.11	1.39	34.05	230.03	350.69	244.78	153.10

Nutrient Analysis of Recipes and Variations for One Serving

RECIPE	CALORIES (kcal)	TOTAL FAT (g)	SATURATED FAT (g)	PROTEIN (g)	CARBOHYDRATES (g)	DIETARY FIBER (g)
Low Sodium	169.06	4.03	0.82	27.32	4.84	1.22
Low Protein (Squash)	141.37	4.13	0.77	14.73	12.40	2.81
Low Protein (Pasta)	121.22	3.82	0.69	14.64	7.03	1.13
Mexican Chicken with Orange Tomato Sauce	174.90	3.94	0.57	27.08	7.10	1.55
Low Carbohydrate	163.76	3.98	0.58	26.95	4.18	0.99
Chicken Breast with Wild Rice and Mushrooms	306.52	5.52	0.72	33.45	31.42	3.62
Low Protein	262.06	5.12	0.59	20.31	36.44	3.62
Chicken with Orange Mustard Sauce	184.48	4.72	0.81	26.52	5.87	0.13
Low Protein (butternut squash)	167.13	4.12	0.64	14.38	17.65	3.67
Low Protein (sweet potato)	224.62	4.31	0.68	14.98	29.59	3.09
Low Protein (parsnip)	194.69	4.31	0.67	14.53	23.32	2.89
Low Protein (carrot)	161.16	4.20	0.65	14.32	15.11	2.98
Chicken with Grapefruit Sauce	170.76	4.82	0.84	26.46	3.99	0.09
Low Protein	135.26	4.24	0.67	14.77	9.32	2.26
Chicken with Mustard Dill Sauce	181.10	6.14	1.49	27.62	2.54	0.13
Low Fat	164.97	4.02	0.70	27.80	3.49	0.13
Chicken Yakitori	141.72	2.64	0.75	23.99	2.80	0.04
Low Sodium	144.41	1.41	0.38	26.80	3.21	0.03
Low Protein	173.82	9.28	1.34	17.89	7.26	2.48
Chicken Kebab with Lemon	176.47	4.99	0.85	26.91	4.98	1.02
Low Protein	129.41	4.42	0.69	14.77	8.35	2.26
Chicken en Brochette with Orange Marmalade	252.00	1.88	0.48	34.00	27.00	1.50
Low Sodium/Protein	293.61	1.31	0.31	22.77	49.95	5.42
Stuffed Chicken Breast with Spinach and Feta	261.85	8.43	3.65	38.04	6.26	1.45
Low Sodium	212.35	4.43	0.86	35.38	5.49	1.45
Chicken Pot Pie	287.22	11.86	5.20	25.70	18.88	2.46
Low Sodium	284.00	11.25	4.70	26.13	19.01	2.46
Low Protein	247.36	10.93	4.45	16.39	21.90	4.00
Turkey Fajitas	230.02	7.58	1.23	6.22	35.07	3.65
Low Protein	265.28	9.97	1.54	9.88	35.91	3.82
Low Carbohydrate	138.55	7.81	0.64	4.04	15.66	4.07
Turkey Picadillo	269.47	11.06	2.76	23.15	20.97	3.51
Low Sodium	257.53	10.05	2.65	22.57	20.94	3.57

THE ULTIMATE DIABETES COOKBOOK

CHOLESTEROL (mg)	CALCIUM (mg)	IRON (mg)	MAGNESIUM (mg)	PHOSPHORUS (mg)	POTASSIUM (mg)	SODIUM (mg)	WATER (g)
66.41	23.11	1.12	38.08	235.89	400.51	93.09	170.60
33.72	43.43	1.51	35.22	140.59	387.46	235.82	216.09
33.72	13.50	1.17	23.42	134.47	213.81	208.45	84.78
65.77	29.59	1.16	42.62	243.28	501.46	79.86	177.58
65.77	17.22	1.23	41.72	243.95	490.33	81.88	169.39
65.77	27.43	2.61	81.69	404.00	723.78	83.07	257.03
0	24.99	3.60	49.94	181.74	434.61	169.93	209.09
65.77	19.58	0.95	36.34	231.09	354.95	88.63	101.90
32.89	61.02	1.25	55.79	152.31	573.95	55.72	149.36
32.89	32.57	1.11	30.07	145.59	407.84	64.48	131.29
32.89	46.53	1.11	49.02	188.48	578.41	61.49	137.96
32.89	36.54	1.00	34.49	159.90	514.43	85.12	142.91
65.77	18.65	0.92	36.36	229.68	354.66	74.57	127.75
32.89	32.95	1.36	33.62	147.10	365.35	45.05	143.20
69.75	59.09	1.01	36.36	262.99	356.80	190.78	117.04
66.40	59.53	0.99	32.68	233.88	309.33	193.56	114.61
62.65	14.19	0.80	22.02	170.80	197.33	514.89	58.16
65.77	15.50	0.85	32.13	224.84	295.21	376.48	83.79
0	729.14	11.16	62.04	204.57	258.00	475.15	94.33
65.77	24.93	1.06	37.52	241.23	388.48	106.87	137.62
32.89	30.52	1.03	38.24	155.27	445.80	72.43	178.37
82.22	48.00	1.34	41.52	285.83	498.00	196.00	184.00
49.33	61.02	1.46	32.16	186.34	705.57	134.55	266.17
98.90	192.13	2.87	79.49	376.18	611.64	397.20	197.52
82.22	99.69	2.75	75.89	312.99	600.05	187.95	187.17
75.75	44.99	2.09	41.87	238.74	540.45	395.98	217.30
75.99	50.17	2.09	42.51	240.33	538.81	116.12	203.67
46.54	47.62	2.53	40.45	200.39	599.15	345.34	239.97
2.30	82.47	2.26	25.50	95.40	265.21	318.56	140.34
0	125.81	2.95	54.84	157.70	312.03	320.72	134.89
4.25	42.38	1.29	25.73	70.55	404.17	168.96	258.69
89.59	44.97	2.91	47.62	238.69	734.68	339.28	316.10
89.59	45.35	2.72	54.02	249.92	880.23	136.93	307.96

Nutrient Analysis of Recipes and Variations for One Serving

RECIPE	CALORIES (kcal)	TOTAL FAT (g)	SATURATED FAT (g)	PROTEIN (g)	CARBOHYDRATES (g)	DIETARY FIBER (g)
Low Protein	177.04	4.10	0.54	5.40	33.66	6.58
Turkey Black Bean Chili	220.30	8.55	2.25	20.68	17.94	6.14
Low Sodium	240.00	8.82	2.32	21.91	19.47	6.45
Low Protein	180.75	4.82	0.51	7.04	34.42	10.84
Low Carbohydrate	277.96	12.82	3.38	27.27	14.16	4.71
Vegetable Stew with Turkey Meatballs	292.94	13.72	3.91	24.37	18.95	3.52
Low Sodium	276.80	13.85	3.93	23.53	16.28	2.76
Low Protein	243.67	8.61	2.25	15.01	28.96	5.69
Fish/Seafood						
Blackened Tuna	149.52	3.98	2.06	26.59	0.29	0.06
Low Sodium	147.47	3.83	2.02	26.51	0	0
Low Cholesterol	155.53	4.51	0.72	26.61	0.57	0.11
Cilantro Tuna Burgers	218.11	7.14	1.67	29.59	7.40	0.82
Low Protein	261.65	4.88	0.87	15.43	38.82	2.87
Pasta with Tuna Sauce	305.48	2.80	0.33	16.77	50.84	3.21
Low Sodium	302.08	3.28	0.50	21.47	47.26	3.59
Low Protein	266.99	2.71	0.28	9.04	52.19	3.41
Salmon with Cucumber Sauce	259.39	15.35	3.81	24.58	3.18	0.17
Low Fat	238.4	12.34	2.48	24.89	5.19	0.17
Low Carbohydrate	210.87	12.30	2.48	22.57	0.04	0
Salmon with Horseradish Sauce	242.43	14.16	3.24	23.60	1.76	0.12
Low Fat	226.54	12.33	2.48	23.74	2.92	0.12
Salmon with Black Sesame Seeds	280.47	16.63	3.25	28.88	2.22	0.33
Low Sodium	280.34	16.63	3.25	28.78	2.33	0.34
Asian Burgers	233.61	10.84	1.46	26.33	6.61	0.41
Low Sodium	233.89	10.87	1.46	26.08	6.86	0.41
Low Fat/Sodium	213.16	8.55	1.20	26.08	6.86	.41
Swordfish Kebabs	182.78	6.63	1.56	23.20	5.36	0.18
Low Fat	164.55	4.60	1.25	23.19	5.36	0.18
Low Sodium	182.78	6.63	1.56	22.95	5.61	0.18
Swordfish Puttanesca	182.11	6.53	1.44	23.76	4.71	0.99
Low Sodium	177.61	6.48	1.42	23.40	5.37	1.06
Low Protein	189.33	3.97	0.67	12.13	24.55	1.90
Halibut with Horseradish Crust	194.81	6.72	0.95	24.93	7.15	0.36
Halibut with Tomatoes	211.24	6.96	0.96	30.51	5.64	1.15

THE ULTIMATE DIABETES COOKBOOK

CHOLESTEROL (mg)	CALCIUM (mg)	IRON (mg)	MAGNESIUM (mg)	PHOSPHORUS (mg)	POTASSIUM (mg)	SODIUM (mg)	WATER (g)
0	37.05	2.15	47.91	89.11	516.86	236.10	287.55
74.66	80.52	3.12	35.41	181.61	694.76	708.15	231.58
74.66	48.84	3.11	68.30	246.12	704.74	138.23	196.00
0	126.76	3.31	38.98	67.55	847.87	949.91	352.65
111.98	90.77	3.33	53.12	272.41	772.13	672.23	270.04
97.20	97.98	3.76	51.06	230.46	747.82	364.43	291.04
97.20	92.75	3.04	62.87	249.31	754.32	208.10	287.40
48.60	115.18	3.42	52.87	759.01	791.47	319.94	393.85
58.80	19.00	0.83	56.77	217.41	511.78	189.76	81.14
58.53	19.39	0.83	56.70	216.59	504.75	41.96	81.25
51.03	18.14	0.84	56.70	216.63	518.21	278.96	80.58
43.09	45.40	2.11	68.15	311.67	420.39	137.20	119.44
10.77	54.68	2.96	57.18	170.66	380.47	107.02	192.73
9.21	48.69	2.35	41.9	149.64	254.94	401.58	104.08
8.51	83.75	4.03	67.28	179.67	593.11	38.09	187.13
0	62.79	1.80	49.16	124.62	474.15	224.47	168.99
74.76	83.45	0.50	40.55	319.07	520.94	153.08	139.29
68.02	83.96	0.46	34.02	267.36	437.68	160.81	135.99
66.91	14.05	0.42	32.24	264.91	414.44	67.15	82.54
71.22	49.33	0.46	36.52	291.97	469.15	140.33	109.87
67.46	49.45	0.44	33.26	266.07	428.11	145.58	108.70
83.63	43.47	0.76	39.91	331.50	535.81	191.75	99.52
83.63	43.70	0.78	40.37	332.96	538.21	159.52	99.35
62.37	40.67	1.60	39.87	244.27	631.55	367.73	104.50
62.37	40.67	1.60	39.87	244.27	631.55	288.98	104.50
62.37	40.67	1.60	39.87	244.27	631.55	288.91	104.50
44.23	9.60	1.01	32.77	303.49	359.80	345.70	104.86
44.23	9.60	1.01	32.77	303.49	359.80	345.58	104.86
44.23	9.60	1.01	32.77	303.49	359.80	266.95	104.86
45.36	28.58	1.67	35.26	309.62	377.82	365.58	173.09
44.23	34.17	1.55	42.09	319.14	525.51	156.35	170.27
15.88	30.46	1.41	27.45	148.60	181.79	298.24	162.12
36.29	78.87	1.62	99.18	271.92	544.02	209.76	92.88
45.36	78.91	1.92	130.48	341.49	877.15	87.98	204.21

Nutrient Analysis of Recipes and Variations for One Serving

RECIPE	CALORIES (kcal)	TOTAL FAT (g)	SATURATED FAT (g)	PROTEIN (g)	CARBOHYDRATES (g)	DIETARY FIBER (g)
Low Protein	96.19	4.67	1.02	3.21	12.62	3.98
Roasted Cod with Morrocan Flavors	134.65	4.32	0.63	20.76	2.55	0.57
Low Protein	123.52	8.30	1.16	9.11	5.71	0.99
Southwestern Chilean Sea Bass	160.31	3.44	0.53	25.83	3.18	0.78
Low Protein	125.93	7.25	1.03	9.13	6.34	1.21
Marlin with Strawberry Pepper Sauce	156.16	2.97	0.01	28.06	2.86	0.82
Mahi Mahi in Tomato Coulis	176.93	6.16	0.98	26.67	2.36	0.32
Low Protein	225.68	6.63	1.28	5.14	35.95	3.51
Caribbean Grouper	178.33	4.92	0.80	27.77	3.26	0.25
Monkfish Cozumel	137.89	4.29	0.73	17.54	7.30	1.65
Low Protein	165.22	3.03	0.47	8.74	27.69	9.14
Cajun Turbot	134.57	5.66	1.15	18.55	1.31	0.24
Low Sodium	135.98	5.62	1.16	18.35	0.79	0.17
Low Protein	180.99	11.58	1.64	17.12	5.86	2.68
Bluefish with Artichoke Hearts	192.71	8.50	1.32	20.75	7.87	1.71
Low Protein	149.96	7.30	3.17	7.07	16.12	4.86
Sea Bass with Leeks	201.53	6.39	1.06	27.26	6.28	0.44
Low Sodium	200.38	6.08	1.03	27.35	6.64	0.44
Broccoli-Stuffed Sole	157.86	4.80	1.90	21.69	6.73	2.59
Low Sodium	148.76	3.76	1.22	22.03	6.85	2.59
Low Protein	149.07	8.69	4.65	7.35	12.61	3.94
Lemon Sole with White Wine	161.52	6.86	4.32	21.40	0.23	0.03
Low Sodium	170.39	8.10	1.23	21.38	0.09	0
Low Saturated Fat	131.41	3.61	0.62	21.40	0.23	0.03
Salmon-Stuffed Flounder	200.91	7.85	1.40	28.20	1.12	0.28
Low Protein	105.48	6.64	1.11	7.94	3.68	1.41
Orange Orange Roughy	105.14	2.91	0.77	16.79	1.39	0.13
Red Rainbow Trout with Salsa	223.20	7.74	2.21	30.20	7.88	2.36
Sea Trout with Snow Peas	217.32	7.55	1.62	25.50	8.95	1.78
Citrus Red Snapper with Sesame	178.48	5.99	0.85	27.10	2.69	0.26
Cioppino	171.62	3.60	0.36	24.77	8.54	1.97
Low Sodium	169.97	3.73	0.38	24.86	9.60	2.14
Low Protein	218.72	3.38	0.33	16.76	28.87	2.91
Pan-Seared Cajun Shrimp	185.48	6.01	0.96	28.93	2.06	0.16
Low Sodium	183.07	5.97	0.96	28.85	1.63	.07
Low Protein/Sodium	205.78	5.26	0.81	20.60	18.58	1.55

THE ULTIMATE DIABETES COOKBOOK

CHOLESTEROL (mg)	CALCIUM (mg)	IRON (mg)	MAGNESIUM (mg)	PHOSPHORUS (mg)	POTASSIUM (mg)	SODIUM (mg)	WATER (g)
1.98	54.63	1.06	29.98	71.93	488.03	61.39	198.56
48.76	32.24	1.00	42.36	241.67	560.13	96.87	105.44
0	186.32	2.11	54.98	167.74	278.89	44.13	102.31
60.95	35.20	0.97	51.80	303.03	670.27	84.78	147.41
0	184.75	1.97	55.34	171.55	271.95	16.74	121.25
0	64.26	18.63	4.29	249.16	67.10	0.66	116.32
103.48	28.84	1.76	44.09	209.50	614.40	177.02	133.18
1.98	48.86	0.68	22.45	63.19	97.26	107.22	265.01
52.45	45.30	1.38	48.09	237.04	737.91	90.54	147.63
28.35	21.10	0.84	36.59	257.12	691.37	28.41	213.27
0	35.25	2.28	72.98	150.72	543.07	8.86	175.41
54.43	20.56	0.51	57.91	146.31	303.21	409.80	97.71
54.43	21.99	0.50	60.00	149.54	308.25	173.92	97.67
0	726.26	11.23	61.74	202.02	285.28	254.59	84.69
54.31	29.75	1.33	52.68	253.57	534.37	122.71	143.82
16.61	132.15	1.15	33.63	132.87	488.76	150.52	240.80
120.35	35.81	1.74	66.19	303.87	431.33	385.27	143.82
120.20	37.73	1.74	66.19	303.87	427.58	221.35	131.93
58.62	55.43	1.09	66.87	284.62	548.13	201.20	109.31
56.86	56.71	1.09	66.87	284.62	545.63	112.83	131.93
20.25	149.43	1.48	38.97	160.33	565.87	217.83	204.66
69.43	21.41	0.44	36.26	210.20	421.90	194.16	141.39
54.43	21.41	0.47	36.26	210.27	418.22	92.41	157.11
54.43	21.41	0.45	36.26	210.23	421.90	151.66	99.58
71.16	37.77	0.84	48.99	284.06	580.45	126.94	100.94
16.73	30.90	0.81	34.41	104.91	404.28	37.58	99.57
25.18	37.69	0.28	36.52	230.26	370.65	79.20	107.6
83.63	116.52	0.67	49.50	410.52	757.39	51.07	169.31
117.65	51.18	1.21	58.12	390.09	642.13	85.32	183.56
68.04	29.72	0.60	46.44	274.10	563.57	115.13	133.89
108.75	70.17	4.94	37.93	184.84	708.76	319.67	267.78
108.75	83.53	4.90	49.84	203.69	770.00	149.18	266.41
84.37	77.37	5.71	29.85	110.19	519.14	298.91	232.03
215.46	76.48	3.53	53.54	291.83	286.81	388.62	111.55
215.46	76.48	3.53	53.54	291.83	275.78	21.87	11.49
129.28	49.45	2.66	58.80	242.83	253.70	129.41	129.11

Nutrient Analysis of Recipes and Variations for One Serving

RECIPE	CALORIES (kcal)	TOTAL FAT (g)	SATURATED FAT (g)	PROTEIN (g)	CARBOHYDRATES (g)	DIETARY FIBER (g)
Shrimp with Brown Rice	281.15	5.63	0.72	18.97	37.40	3.11
Low Protein	346.75	7.02	0.74	11.37	60.39	9.39
Low Sodium	280.58	5.64	0.72	18.53	37.91	3.16
Garlic Scallops	142.58	5.20	2.78	19.26	3.81	0.09
Low Fat/Cholesterol/Sodium	149.19	5.94	0.78	19.21	3.81	0.09
Zuppa de Clams	613.03	8.98	0.92	99.85	26.92	1.51
Low Protein	810.43	9.92	1.06	106.53	66.60	3.33
Mussels in Saffron	147.46	4.45	0.74	14.30	9.08	0.62
Low Protein	246.10	3.54	0.56	10.84	39.18	2.13
Beef						
Mom's Pot Roast	422.02	20.70	6.21	48.38	8.83	2.16
Tenderloin Tips	356.39	28.60	10.62	20.66	1.18	0.06
Low Protein	237.54	16.26	5.58	12.06	9.91	2.62
Braised Beef with Red Wine	382.29	25.88	9.48	23.40	10.63	2.23
Low Protein	255.99	14.96	5.03	14.14	14.61	3.99
Mediterranean Beef Stew	378.68	25.59	9.44	28.09	8.25	1.93
Low Protein	197.33	5.55	0.70	8.75	30.40	8.41
Santa Fe Beef Stew	250.92	8.86	2.51	27.24	13.39	2.30
Low Sodium	252.05	9.13	2.53	27.52	15.12	2.76
Low Protein	249.74	3.15	0.36	12.25	43.63	9.68
Ropa Vieja	321.94	14.67	5.25	32.10	13.92	2.77
Low Sodium	322.47	14.63	5.25	30.99	13.66	2.55
Barbecue Beef	385.47	26.73	10.79	25.69	9.58	0.77
Low Protein	161.01	0.41	0.06	9.35	31.66	9.93
Herbed Meat Loaf	297.93	19.74	7.78	23.02	6.33	1.19
Low Sodium	297.93	19.75	7.78	23.01	6.33	1.23
Shepherd's Pie	275.64	13.49	5.40	17.33	20.92	2.75
Low Protein	234.52	10.31	3.92	15.24	20.34	3.16
Stuffed Green Peppers	180.03	3.29	1.17	20.54	19.40	2.70
Low Protein	201.18	5.45	3.09	8.18	31.75	4.24
Low Sodium	180.03	3.31	1.18	20.52	19.41	3.26
Veal						
Rosemary Veal Stew	272.90	7.13	1.33	31.95	20.07	5.62
Low Protein	240.19	5.76	0.70	18.18	29.57	8.12
Herbed Veal and Spinach Meat Loaf	257.59	10.21	4.08	31.47	8.23	0.89

THE ULTIMATE DIABETES COOKBOOK

CHOLESTEROL (mg)	CALCIUM (mg)	IRON (mg)	MAGNESIUM (mg)	PHOSPHORUS (mg)	POTASSIUM (mg)	SODIUM (mg)	WATER (g)
134.66	52.22	3.14	92.23	213.88	289.70	567.90	179.84
0.12	66.51	3.50	110.18	263.72	413.55	274.07	175.18
134.66	53.24	3.26	94.27	220.48	300.50	422.88	179.12
49.07	34.13	0.43	64.87	253.78	385.48	223.26	95.54
37.42	32.85	0.45	64.76	252.61	384.09	183.52	94.70
258.33	365.93	108.37	81.68	1333.7	2677.14	443.26	142.27
258.33	375.73	109.07	106.88	1409.3	2720.54	444.66	207.60
31.75	52.56	5.32	51.12	244.92	504.31	333.67	196.38
10.91	42.80	2.92	47.19	158.60	298.26	125.03	261.53
140.62	33.45	5.34	30.17	494.17	954.91	182.74	350.03
79.38	14.47	2.75	23.85	210.29	365.75	56.96	87.97
39.69	31.19	2.06	35.55	149.43	507.34	33.17	201.06
78.25	32.68	3.39	39.44	278.59	701.41	80.70	288.41
39.12	62.01	2.71	48.91	215.34	854.43	101.30	369.64
96.05	20.70	3.57	31.08	238.09	482.58	71.43	275.62
0	47.37	2.73	51.99	154.20	545.41	311.19	174.45
77.88	46.12	3.90	27.54	230.78	529.86	307.80	270.60
77.88	66.29	4.48	43.00	254.81	626.06	67.64	281.23
0	100.02	3.41	92.56	194.84	1026.26	261.11	290.46
73.13	34.23	3.84	48.06	304.80	883.25	473.23	277.33
73.13	29.96	3.70	42.69	294.90	715.25	126.03	278.48
93.9	26.48	3.14	34.62	254.63	547.27	233.37	218.63
0	69.58	3.31	60.29	168.99	649.63	161.91	139.85
78.25	22.51	2.88	33.47	179.05	521.04	315.00	125.57
78.25	22.51	2.88	33.47	179.05	521.04	90.46	125.57
53.62	31.86	2.15	37.46	171.24	625.35	334.05	161.02
39.12	28.12	2.29	39.14	169.96	593.12	189.15	258.70
45.00	39.26	2.73	21.15	43.84	358.17	531.13	120.37
14.83	153.72	2.22	43.82	164.41	582.25	690.88	247.30
45.00	29.26	2.55	21.15	43.84	358.97	82.30	257.32
119.07	94.99	2.54	47.71	334.64	1043.11	134.26	340.79
47.63	110.53	2.51	56.45	203.48	886.59	63.67	326.01
116.24	81.61	2.54	56.65	316.98	598.70	265.42	151.77

Nutrient Analysis of Recipes and Variations for One Serving

RECIPE	CALORIES (kcal)	TOTAL FAT (g)	SATURATED FAT (g)	PROTEIN (g)	CARBOHYDRATES (g)	DIETARY FIBER (g)
Veal with Peppers and Tomatoes	329.15	18.00	6.32	28.77	12.82	2.34
Low Sodium	327.90	17.93	6.32	28.65	12.64	2.34
Low Protein	308.45	9.30	3.25	17.17	37.61	1.45
Veal with Shiitake Mushrooms	183.88	6.73	1.62	23.80	3.94	0.30
Low Sodium	182.35	6.32	1.58	24.14	4.20	0.30
Low Protein	171.75	4.48	0.72	8.07	22.35	6.93
Lamb						
Braised Lamb and Green Beans	352.16	25.04	11.38	21.27	9.26	3.92
Low Protein	217.24	13.79	5.87	12.24	11.15	4.70
Leg of Lamb	252.51	8.78	3.12	40.00	0.98	0.21
Lamb and Chickpea Stew	414.55	22.70	9.49	24.91	28.82	7.83
Low Protein	268.81	11.57	4.79	13.97	29.36	8.10
Curried Lamb with Vegetables	336.63	20.29	6.98	24.03	15.80	5.42
Low Protein	209.15	7.54	0.73	7.73	30.80	9.17
Afghan Lamb with Spinach	319.91	20.02	7.97	22.59	12.84	2.88
Low Sodium	319.91	20.02	7.97	22.59	12.84	2.88
Low Protein	153.13	6.96	1.21	11.15	14.75	3.09
Shish Kebab	222.71	11.27	3.40	24.37	5.32	1.15
Low Protein	156.57	7.64	1.97	13.28	9.64	2.24
Lamb Tikka	210.19	8.72	3.61	29.74	1.78	0.57
Low Protein	94.20	4.96	0.95	8.46	6.19	1.29
Pork						
Spice-Crusted Pork	290.85	16.80	6.00	30.23	2.72	0.02
Pork with Herbs	249.43	14.59	5.34	27.07	0.65	0.17
Apple Pork Chops	292.96	16.10	4.86	21.43	15.20	1.67
Pork Chops with Leeks and Orange	213.62	8.09	2.06	26.84	6.84	0.28
Braised Pork Chops with Red Onion	292.53	11.22	2.79	36.50	8.31	1.26
Szekele Goulash	259.99	11.87	3.57	27.00	11.55	3.42
Low Sodium	259.99	11.84	3.57	26.99	11.56	3.42
Shredded Pork in Garlic Sauce	314.08	15.74	4.42	33.95	6.68	1.39
Low Sodium	313.31	15.53	4.40	33.87	7.06	1.39
Low Protein	136.26	8.17	0.97	8.24	8.60	1.60
Baked Ham	282.26	8.67	2.87	39.16	9.13	0.18
Vegetables						
Lemon Asparagus	56.91	2.75	2.00	2.46	5.37	2.46

THE ULTIMATE DIABETES COOKBOOK

CHOLESTEROL (mg)	CALCIUM (mg)	IRON (mg)	MAGNESIUM (mg)	PHOSPHORUS (mg)	POTASSIUM (mg)	SODIUM (mg)	WATER (g)
104.37	41.92	1.82	39.09	239.70	570.69	143.34	206.94
104.37	42.22	1.82	39.24	239.71	570.69	81.28	207.78
52.19	43.35	2.37	34.02	170.53	312.71	44.17	186.93
91.55	21.87	1.31	29.62	244.08	383.74	274.53	106.67
91.36	24.44	1.31	29.62	244.08	378.74	125.97	136.82
1.25	47.70	3.12	33.76	98.14	302.59	265.90	102.97
74.84	74.78	2.51	31.33	207.80	612.87	88.97	366.17
37.42	77.72	1.93	34.29	133.91	615.88	51.23	392.59
123.86	22.12	3.87	55.25	379.48	595.04	123.13	148.99
79.38	103.87	3.90	88.75	307.62	864.36	83.62	419.21
39.69	102.35	2.72	75.58	208.17	863.38	68.95	424.53
80.63	111.60	3.28	66.57	221.25	746.16	88.37	312.54
1.88	123.03	3.01	48.22	82.84	551.81	621.95	270.18
79.19	116.42	3.73	70.48	213.18	624.46	234.21	270.92
79.19	116.42	3.73	70.48	213.18	624.46	147.59	270.92
1.99	218.73	3.20	79.59	157.42	538.44	312.16	287.22
78.25	23.09	2.35	34.45	206.54	461.58	74.83	242.60
39.12	21.52	1.72	30.02	131.14	476.15	44.75	177.27
91.17	39.30	2.80	38.23	295.94	516.17	126.98	119.80
1.87	156.49	1.64	38.99	132.94	230.49	23.48	138.98
105.46	43.07	1.63	27.47	253.85	431.11	33.57	67.40
81.36	28.59	1.25	28.30	244.11	430.66	60.77	61.19
66.36	22.08	1.06	28.26	208.21	420.30	53.55	128.78
78.25	25.70	1.35	28.67	218.05	385.04	50.60	80.87
104.33	38.66	1.98	40.26	305.37	551.01	68.37	151.18
72.58	61.07	2.46	47.05	252.42	732.85	592.56	286.89
72.58	61.07	2.46	47.05	252.42	732.85	284.46	286.89
94.54	28.30	1.46	35.83	272.84	597.60	403.10	136.16
94.44	29.58	1.46	35.83	272.84	595.11	250.15	151.22
0.42	139.50	1.51	37.31	118.90	313.54	354.91	160.20
85.60	14.44	1.60	35.68	356.30	513.14	2107.23	110.19
7.50	24.79	0.44	0.34	0.34	287.54	21.31	56.18

Nutrient Analysis of Recipes and Variations for One Serving

RECIPE	CALORIES (kcal)	TOTAL FAT (g)	SATURATED FAT (g)	PROTEIN (g)	CARBOHYDRATES (g)	DIETARY FIBER (g)
Low Sodium	61.75	3.38	0.46	2.46	5.37	2.46
Mung Bean Sprouts	75.04	2.49	0.21	3.94	10.35	2.15
Low Sodium	75.04	2.49	0.21	3.69	10.6	2.15
Stir-Fried Bok Choy	60.94	2.68	0.21	3.14	6.34	1.76
Low Sodium	60.39	2.62	0.21	2.89	6.59	1.76
Broccoli with Peppers	47.56	2.68	0.39	1.95	5.34	2.04
Broccoli Soufflé	95.34	5.10	3.00	7.22	5.81	1.73
Low Sodium	84.81	3.52	2.12	8.38	6.23	1.73
Broccoli Rabe	71.08	2.74	0.26	3.86	7.99	0.37
Low Sodium	69.64	2.50	0.24	3.85	8.21	0.36
Brussels Sprouts with Sesame	36.25	1.87	0.13	1.53	4.76	1.24
Pesto Cabbage	47.19	2.08	0.51	2.30	6.29	2.67
Sautéed Cabbage	60.00	3.20	0.48	1.40	6.60	2.00
Sweet and Sour Red Cabbage	68.69	2.50	0.19	1.24	11.82	1.81
Orange-Glazed Carrots and Turnips	104.43	4.20	0.34	1.32	16.22	2.74
Cauliflower with Preisel	62.93	3.04	0.29	2.42	7.66	2.74
Spicy Grilled Cauliflower	46.52	2.48	0.33	1.98	5.52	2.45
Low Sodium	44.91	2.45	0.33	1.93	5.24	2.39
Braised Celery with Fennel	51.55	2.72	0.40	1.34	6.72	2.80
Low Sodium	50.97	2.56	0.38	1.47	6.82	2.80
Celery with Carrot and Snap Peas	67.66	3.68	0.38	2.14	6.89	2.39
Low Sodium	67.66	3.68	0.38	1.97	7.05	2.39
Sautéed Corn and Zucchini	64.02	1.53	0.22	1.70	12.92	1.97
Low Sodium	67.34	1.73	0.25	1.81	13.36	2.03
Stuffed Eggplant	86.51	4.11	0.76	2.75	11.00	3.23
Grilled Eggplant Parmesan	171.80	9.28	4.54	9.01	15.94	3.56
Low Sodium	137.37	5.32	3.20	10.24	14.19	4.48
Low Fat	80.52	3.49	1.62	5.07	8.00	1.78
Greek Vegetable Stew	65.45	2.54	0.34	1.91	9.98	3.51
Low Sodium	66.35	2.58	0.40	2.00	9.86	3.51
Grilled Fennel and Red Onion	57.36	0.24	0.01	1.54	13.25	3.28
Green Beans à la Grecque	71.81	2.41	0.32	2.08	11.28	4.33
Low Sodium	71.81	2.43	0.33	2.07	11.29	4.39
Green Beans with Mushrooms	54.12	2.49	0.33	2.07	6.46	2.99
Sherried Green Beans and Jicama	66.67	2.46	0.35	1.49	10.30	4.89
Collards and Kale	72.95	3.75	0.62	2.90	8.79	2.37

THE ULTIMATE DIABETES COOKBOOK

CHOLESTEROL (mg)	CALCIUM (mg)	IRON (mg)	MAGNESIUM (mg)	PHOSPHORUS (mg)	POTASSIUM (mg)	SODIUM (mg)	WATER (g)
0	24.79	0.45	0.34	0.38	287.54	0.06	110.63
0	22.80	1.11	24.23	62.19	186.09	238.29	115.69
0	22.80	1.11	24.23	62.19	186.09	159.54	115.69
0	184.59	1.44	34.13	65.97	447.57	344.80	188.31
0	184.59	1.44	34.13	65.97	447.57	266.05	188.20
0.23	31.49	0.64	15.99	41.83	224.19	62.88	73.51
11.71	83.83	0.76	21.40	74.45	247.76	411.50	131.95
9.66	100.57	0.77	21.88	82.02	241.27	100.55	131.95
0.42	30.02	0.97	0.62	3.18	10.48	272.03	152.36
0.32	31.14	0.97	0.51	2.91	7.01	140.85	152.36
0	20.52	0.65	9.70	28.41	157.91	120.42	41.64
1.25	80.12	0.79	18.81	39.77	285.03	50.22	118.06
0	45.00	0.67	15.00	32.00	220.00	13.00	102.62
0	44.24	0.51	14.42	38.30	215.39	10.18	102.62
0	43.92	0.59	23.66	58.02	379.92	31.47	109.51
0	27.01	0.63	11.06	38.48	148.93	58.19	90.52
0	22.30	0.44	14.48	42.99	298.85	148.21	89.42
0	22.30	0.44	14.48	42.99	291.49	29.71	88.38
0	58.08	0.74	17.25	45.17	429.05	157.09	118.42
0.24	59.02	0.74	17.25	45.17	427.17	101.38	129.73
0	43.39	1.01	17.72	41.94	296.04	207.89	99.75
0	43.38	1.01	17.72	41.94	296.04	155.39	99.75
0	10.20	0.47	18.87	50.41	217.42	201.46	100.39
0	8.46	0.46	21.75	60.00	214.55	72.11	76.86
1.01	37.14	0.73	19.04	46.74	390.46	80.82	139.90
23.97	201.69	0.97	41.63	178.26	597.98	579.71	99.03
15.54	229.75	0.94	39.12	201.67	564.91	19.14	102.63
8.24	117.47	0.448	20.79	82.50	300.09	304.56	99.84
0	36.18	0.70	16.73	31.45	332.43	109.32	148.64
0.32	37.46	0.70	16.73	31.45	332.43	15.80	148.64
0	53.30	0.75	19.23	56.28	430.60	49.76	116.2
0	56.91	0.99	14.40	26.82	463.23	372.23	178.56
0	56.91	0.99	14.40	26.82	463.23	8.40	178.57
0	40.33	0.76	4.24	42.90	312.61	33.45	100.52
0	32.74	1.09	21.60	33.11	262.88	4.52	112.39
1.25	113.71	0.98	21.89	39.76	315.16	277.61	85.70

Nutrient Analysis of Recipes and Variations for One Serving

RECIPE	CALORIES (kcal)	TOTAL FAT (g)	SATURATED FAT (g)	PROTEIN (g)	CARBOHYDRATES (g)	DIETARY FIBER (g)
Low Sodium	70.64	3.14	0.56	3.42	9.17	2.37
Braised Greens and Cauliflower	57.92	2.32	0.38	2.74	8.33	3.45
Low Sodium	56.76	2.02	0.35	3.00	8.52	3.45
Ethiopian Kale	65.67	2.75	0.37	2.50	9.62	2.86
Portobello Mushrooms with Vegetables	58.93	2.52	0.35	2.72	8.22	2.25
White and Shiitake Mushrooms	50.80	2.49	0.34	2.47	4.57	1.04
Okra with Tomatoes	72.50	3.76	0.52	2.03	9.68	2.96
Low Fat	52.61	1.51	0.21	2.03	9.68	2.96
Snow Peas with Mushrooms	74.22	3.67	0.52	2.98	8.32	2.35
Snow Peas with Tomatoes	63.77	2.62	0.36	2.90	8.11	2.66
Creamed Spinach	240.03	12.46	8.07	13.57	22.90	5.66
Low Sodium	144.00	5.85	3.22	11.34	17.67	7.93
Vegetable Stir-Fry	98.66	3.95	0.33	3.08	13.07	2.87
Low Sodium	83.35	3.77	0.30	2.36	9.76	2.47
Zucchini with Tomatoes and Raisins	60.97	2.60	0.36	1.88	9.06	2.15
Zucchini and Snow Peas	128.63	9.05	0.82	4.59	9.47	3.35
Low Sodium	128.63	9.05	0.82	4.43	9.63	3.35
Yellow Squash with Tomatoes	75.36	1.60	0.25	2.51	13.13	3.41
Low Sodium	73.47	1.75	0.27	2.61	14.34	3.61
Yellow Squash with Red Peppers	56.10	2.54	0.36	1.63	8.09	2.67
Ratatouille	91.39	4.01	0.56	2.13	13.23	3.74
Pattypan Squash with Basil	44.13	3.52	0.48	0.91	3.05	1.23
Spaghetti Squash with Vegetables	61.89	2.76	0.38	2.27	9.00	2.39
Butternut Squash with Turnip	72.80	0.21	0.03	1.56	18.24	4.14
Sugar Snaps with Carrots	52.67	2.89	0.19	1.70	5.76	1.89
Baked Herb-Stuffed Tomatoes	45.42	0.64	0.12	1.64	8.90	0.91
Sautéed Tomatoes with Basil	50.83	2.71	0.37	1.28	6.82	1.57

Starches

Garlic Mashed Potatoes	106.44	2.12	1.18	2.82	19.79	1.66
Low Fat	90.48	0.31	0.09	2.82	19.71	1.66
Low Protein	96.86	1.50	0.82	2.48	19.29	1.66
Grilled Potatoes	106.01	3.45	0.47	1.63	17.63	1.67
Twice-Baked Potatoes	80.06	0.82	0.40	2.08	16.47	1.58
Herbed Orzo	164.89	3.98	0.54	4.74	27.21	1.01
Cajun Barley	104.82	2.13	0.30	2.98	19.68	4.19
Low Sodium	102.44	1.75	0.27	3.27	19.70	4.15

THE ULTIMATE DIABETES COOKBOOK

CHOLESTEROL (mg)	CALCIUM (mg)	IRON (mg)	MAGNESIUM (mg)	PHOSPHORUS (mg)	POTASSIUM (mg)	SODIUM (mg)	WATER (g)
0.96	117.55	0.98	21.89	39.76	307.66	54.79	130.94
0.63	61.07	0.50	17.97	49.41	342.69	156.83	162.28
0.48	62.99	0.50	17.97	49.41	338.94	45.42	184.90
0	86.62	1.07	24.82	43.18	309.62	29.22	251.72
0	29.12	0.95	17.30	126.47	544.14	33.91	126.67
0	4.82	1.02	8.06	76.73	278.14	6.64	83.75
0	49.39	0.93	40.64	58.97	390.28	12.73	105.30
0	49.39	0.92	40.64	58.95	390.28	12.73	147.22
0	26.50	1.62	18.57	71.00	290.48	6.25	99.73
0	37.33	1.77	25.55	55.09	307.48	9.12	116.82
36.59	450.87	6.31	152.06	237.54	1073.34	381.02	407.18
15.26	281.35	7.70	226.43	132.10	1494.59	278.48	387.33
0	32.82	0.98	43.11	74.35	484.71	244.14	185.11
0	32.54	0.89	38.57	59.75	449.42	162.98	175.25
0	22.89	0.75	28.40	48.63	394.48	40.09	162.55
0	49.84	1.88	48.07	90.31	374.07	160.05	133.11
0	49.84	1.88	48.07	90.31	374.07	107.55	133.11
0	60.32	1.27	35.64	61.64	500.03	208.39	263.64
0	60.32	1.27	49.25	83.19	570.01	13.55	262.94
0	28.98	0.61	25.78	45.78	260.57	3.28	128.76
0	31.35	1.12	32.79	62.22	496.97	134.19	211.56
0	17.11	0.34	16.40	26.64	130.44	0.96	63.30
0	29.95	0.95	22.18	58.03	343.49	102.01	165.66
0	66.82	0.88	40.01	63.91	485.05	17.01	124.15
0	23.86	0.90	13.62	32.56	186.08	12.37	57.75
0	25.00	0.93	13.90	32.14	206.02	66.18	60.39
50.83	11.51	0.68	16.30	35.64	311.84	12.46	128.66
5.85	29.31	0.81	21.91	50.95	581.69	56.52	107.46
0.48	31.59	0.82	23.62	66.04	581.64	56.42	107.76
3.45	13.06	0.81	21.91	50.95	555.44	111.24	117.40
0	8.25	0.96	18.79	40.46	290.97	5.64	49.49
2.26	27.62	0.90	18.99	50.64	290.83	75.03	59.94
0	14.27	1.64	19.26	57.67	84.20	4.84	7.82
0.78	31.40	0.87	29.75	64.02	249.41	321.29	116.12
0.60	33.81	0.87	29.75	64.02	242.18	24.69	109.00

Nutrient Analysis of Recipes and Variations for One Serving

RECIPE	CALORIES (kcal)	TOTAL FAT (g)	SATURATED FAT (g)	PROTEIN (g)	CARBOHYDRATES (g)	DIETARY FIBER (g)
Barley with Mushrooms and Zucchini	190.97	4.47	0.82	6.46	33.51	7.23
Low Sodium	187.50	3.55	0.73	7.24	34.09	7.23
Bulgur with Basil	92.75	2.48	0.31	3.07	15.86	3.79
Bulgur with Red Pepper and Peas	53.81	1.54	0.18	2.11	9.19	2.23
Low Sodium	56.50	1.68	0.37	2.38	8.82	2.23
Kasha with Mushrooms and Walnuts	137.00	9.39	0.83	5.35	9.95	2.03
Low Sodium	134.70	8.78	0.77	5.87	10.34	2.03
Brown Rice Pilaf	116.41	2.92	0.52	2.42	20.33	1.53
Low Sodium	114.87	2.51	0.48	2.76	20.59	1.53
Brown Rice with Nuts	175.46	9.57	0.90	3.18	20.46	2.64
Vegetable Fried Rice	131.29	2.68	0.32	4.12	22.89	3.21
Low Sodium	131.29	2.68	0.32	3.95	23.06	3.21
Wild Rice with Vegetables	120.60	3.75	0.52	4.11	19.15	2.48
Wheat Berries with Vegetables	118.45	2.39	0.34	4.89	21.60	4.76
Mushrooms with Wheat Berries	153.38	4.00	0.55	7.41	24.09	4.31
Whole Wheat Couscous Pilaf	156.74	1.73	0.11	6.09	31.81	4.94
Low Sodium	159.72	1.88	0.32	6.39	31.40	4.94
Couscous with Zucchini	152.35	2.36	0.33	5.70	29.02	4.96
Low Sodium	150.50	1.86	0.29	6.11	29.33	4.96
Polenta	105.22	0.47	0.06	2.44	22.33	2.13
Quinoa with Sugar Snaps	123.24	3.29	0.38	4.45	20.17	2.56
Chicken Broth	125.74	3.54	0.50	4.20	19.42	2.56
Low Sodium (Chicken Broth)	125.93	3.42	0.57	4.71	19.81	2.56
Lentil Purée	89.11	1.03	0.23	6.04	13.53	5.27
Low Sodium	87.38	0.56	0.19	6.43	13.82	5.27
Curried Lentils	151.77	5.08	0.61	7.67	20.06	8.36
Low Sodium	148.89	4.31	0.54	8.32	20.54	8.36
Salads						
Tricolore Salade	42.21	3.64	0.48	0.92	2.23	1.20
Spinach and Mushroom Salad	92.55	5.64	0.76	4.93	8.62	3.50
Watercress Salad and Endive with Blue Cheese	55.88	4.19	1.30	2.52	2.91	1.83
Low Fat	36.39	0.08	0.02	1.44	8.24	2.33
Watercress and Pear Salad with Walnuts	73.98	5.94	0.70	1.51	4.65	1.21

THE ULTIMATE DIABETES COOKBOOK

CHOLESTEROL (mg)	CALCIUM (mg)	IRON (mg)	MAGNESIUM (mg)	PHOSPHORUS (mg)	POTASSIUM (mg)	SODIUM (mg)	WATER (g)
1.88	28.54	1.98	47.70	160.40	465.26	383.99	164.22
1.44	34.31	1.98	47.70	160.40	454.01	49.75	171.45
0	14.76	0.70	34.80	64.20	156.22	13.39	81.52
0	12.59	0.59	14.81	29.47	109.02	253.57	115.85
0.96	16.44	0.59	14.81	29.47	109.02	30.49	105.27
1.25	17.67	0.70	38.73	104.56	257.72	266.84	135.98
0.96	21.52	0.70	38.73	104.56	250.22	44.02	123.78
0.83	16.95	0.63	38.19	87.73	142.03	179.46	94.87
0.64	19.51	0.63	38.19	87.73	137.03	30.91	87.31
0	20.42	0.73	49.10	96.48	136.20	1.410	125.70
0	24.02	0.95	44.19	99.39	189.25	163.53	126.51
0	24.02	0.95	44.19	99.39	189.25	111.03	127.00
0	26.81	1.15	51.28	115.16	268.37	8.49	127.00
0	27.70	1.22	39.41	106.08	242.13	21.88	156.28
0	37.43	1.62	45.24	229.16	630.78	120.43	199.91
0	19.71	1.43	2.55	4.87	32.39	278.8	73.12
1.06	23.96	1.43	2.55	4.87	32.39	31.93	61.41
1.00	22.01	1.43	7.82	15.82	79.13	202.70	87.40
0.77	25.09	1.43	7.82	15.82	73.13	24.43	83.23
0	4.59	0.33	13.08	24.15	46.57	5.59	160.88
0	38.47	2.49	55.44	110.81	239.54	258.97	106.46
0	38.47	2.49	55.44	110.81	239.54	258.72	107.22
0.96	42.32	2.49	55.44	110.81	239.54	35.89	95.87
0.94	23.54	2.31	27.08	119.20	299.97	205.76	185.00
0.72	26.42	2.31	27.08	119.20	294.34	38.64	188.92
1.56	25.97	2.37	32.09	128.91	347.77	322.13	116.99
1.20	30.78	2.37	32.09	128.91	338.39	43.59	113.62
0	35.39	0.48	10.32	23.33	151.02	37.28	49.89
0	155.81	4.45	100.90	119.76	722.02	109.62	167.02
5.37	85.57	0.21	13.87	58.65	235.29	105.75	87.55
0	49.35	0.18	11.64	32.10	227.15	184.84	85.56
0	49.79	0.27	14.79	37.06	166.70	45.35	54.00

Nutrient Analysis of Recipes and Variations for One Serving

RECIPE	CALORIES (kcal)	TOTAL FAT (g)	SATURATED FAT (g)	PROTEIN (g)	CARBOHYDRATES (g)	DIETARY FIBER (g)
Arugula and Cucumber with Parmesan Dressing	46.05	3.08	0.99	1.93	3.33	0.66
Low Fat	31.46	0.87	0.48	2.26	4.29	0.66
Arugula and Fennel with Avocado Salad	86.95	5.68	0.83	1.85	9.24	2.80
Low Fat	56.76	2.81	0.37	1.48	7.85	1.86
Mushroom and Mesclun Salad	61.14	3.71	0.50	2.22	6.23	1.54
Chopped Parsley Salad	51.51	3.68	0.51	1.26	4.62	1.59
Marinated Tomato Salad	39.53	2.55	0.34	0.80	4.45	1.00
Tomato and Cucumber Salad	44.97	2.59	0.36	1.09	5.58	1.37
Sliced Cucumber Salad	32.47	1.86	0.27	0.69	3.58	0.98
Spicy Cucumber and Yogurt Salad	33.65	1.18	0.69	1.81	4.56	0.89
Israeli Salad	29.20	1.69	0.14	0.67	3.52	0.95
String Bean and Tomato Salad	80.63	5.32	0.53	1.83	8.42	2.71
Low Sodium	66.05	3.86	0.53	1.83	7.84	2.71
Green Beans and Red Onion Salad	91.37	6.69	1.46	3.30	6.24	2.17
Low Sodium	74.87	5.36	0.53	2.41	5.98	2.17
Red Pepper and Zucchini Salad	36.84	2.49	0.33	0.95	3.53	1.02
Asparagus Salad	74.75	5.14	0.61	3.21	6.27	2.02
Broccoli and Cauliflower Salad	69.72	5.52	0.74	2.10	4.70	2.49
Chunky Mediterranean Salad	45.65	3.02	1.42	1.77	3.63	1.15
Low Protein	23.70	1.25	0.18	0.59	3.29	1.15
Sesame Snow Pea Salad	63.83	2.33	0.25	3.19	8.63	2.95
Radish Salad	37.67	2.38	0.36	0.92	3.60	1.34
Low Fat	22.47	0.51	0.08	0.87	4.06	1.35
Curried Coleslaw	92.39	5.79	1.17	3.40	8.59	2.96
Low Fat	41.93	0.39	0.06	2.39	8.91	2.75
Celeriac Slaw	98.22	3.92	0.81	2.47	14.71	2.62
Low Fat	73.35	0.75	0.14	2.49	15.79	2.62
Kohlrabi and Jicama Slaw	75.82	3.68	0.26	2.11	10.36	5.28
Fennel Feta Salad	71.32	4.78	1.36	1.89	6.27	2.07
Low Sodium	44.28	2.47	0.31	0.94	5.67	2.04
Chickpea Leek Salad	124.62	4.73	0.47	3.19	18.92	4.42
Low Sodium	131.86	4.54	0.58	4.33	20.15	5.03
Oriental Couscous Salad	147.62	4.32	0.32	4.39	22.97	3.43
Low Sodium	141.10	4.32	0.32	4.06	21.59	3.29

THE ULTIMATE DIABETES COOKBOOK

CHOLESTEROL (mg)	CALCIUM (mg)	IRON (mg)	MAGNESIUM (mg)	PHOSPHORUS (mg)	POTASSIUM (mg)	SODIUM (mg)	WATER (g)
5.07	68.80	0.34	15.65	36.58	152.22	42.23	67.31
2.47	81.03	0.34	16.67	46.57	170.00	51.29	69.22
0	75.80	0.96	31.94	41.93	402.57	26.54	114.93
0	73.74	0.77	24.63	34.24	290.26	24.67	101.00
0	46.49	1.22	11.46	76.44	373.87	24.68	105.83
0	53.55	2.07	20.49	27.56	260.97	27.13	101.00
0	5.41	0.42	10.03	22.39	203.47	8.19	84.68
0	17.66	0.53	15.72	31.64	258.47	9.03	123.54
0	14.97	0.22	12.58	23.33	163.73	2.23	106.92
3.98	58.16	0.41	17.69	53.72	219.29	17.90	128.47
0	15.12	0.50	10.18	18.60	145.01	5.34	72.26
0	38.39	1.30	23.14	42.00	324.31	104.23	116.82
0	38.39	1.30	23.14	42.00	324.31	40.07	110.87
5.56	60.72	0.92	26.29	69.59	211.36	198.94	62.67
0	29.91	0.88	25.11	48.53	207.48	129.19	59.22
0	14.32	0.42	14.39	25.42	178.56	34.70	75.55
0	29.66	1.01	17.36	69.10	203.82	43.60	100.01
0	29.23	0.59	14.64	43.46	202.41	48.99	86.82
7.41	62.35	0.34	10.17	46.01	181.72	135.64	76.30
0	21.35	0.29	8.57	17.94	176.58	42.73	71.70
0	39.25	1.79	24.56	53.12	238.60	31.52	90.09
1.52	31.88	0.31	9.02	24.69	207.70	43.39	86.77
0.39	30.99	0.30	8.97	24.31	208.75	47.13	87.92
4.40	78.96	0.79	27.01	70.50	347.18	52.39	119.39
0.82	75.22	0.69	16.87	30.71	289.22	64.00	120.51
3.21	74.51	1.14	28.56	153.26	428.64	153.75	128.98
0.24	74.09	1.12	27.23	142.36	413.38	161.00	130.30
0	30.39	0.70	25.40	54.15	422.05	22.07	132.55
5.56	65.73	0.62	12.94	56.17	273.81	183.12	72.87
0	33.60	0.55	11.75	35.11	269.94	52.24	67.23
0	51.19	1.69	9.41	11.81	115.18	146.75	103.20
0	51.28	1.97	29.09	80.69	234.49	9.62	77.24
0	19.40	1.05	7.84	19.36	96.34	234.34	76.49
0	20.03	1.07	7.02	15.74	63.56	155.66	76.00

Nutrient Analysis of Recipes and Variations for One Serving

RECIPE	CALORIES (kcal)	TOTAL FAT (g)	SATURATED FAT (g)	PROTEIN (g)	CARBOHYDRATES (g)	DIETARY FIBER (g)
Moroccan Couscous, Chickpea, and Carrot Salad	203.35	3.30	0.35	7.08	38.69	6.49
Low Sodium	201.27	3.49	0.37	7.41	37.53	6.73
Tabouli	153.18	10.95	1.21	3.38	12.91	3.24
Low Fat	69.09	2.51	0.35	1.95	11.08	2.76
Grilled Vegetable and Mixed Rice Salad	85.05	2.55	0.36	1.83	14.29	1.55
Oriental Chicken Salad	151.86	6.08	0.90	18.29	5.72	2.47
Low Sodium	151.86	6.08	0.90	18.13	5.89	2.47
Low Protein/ Low Sodium	130.91	8.22	0.94	8.81	7.80	2.68
Low Protein	130.91	8.22	0.94	8.97	7.63	2.68
Shrimp and Cucumber Salad	203.78	6.12	1.37	30.15	5.87	1.00
Low Fat	177.17	2.66	0.52	30.22	7.22	1.00
Tomato Avocado Tuna Salad	136.82	6.14	0.93	13.34	8.89	2.45
Low Protein	129.63	7.06	1.05	7.97	11.44	3.26
Breakfast/Brunch						
Cheese Omelet	194.26	11.97	6.30	18.32	3.25	0
Low Fat (egg white)	150.13	6.67	4.67	19.05	3.38	0
Low Fat (egg substitute)	153.54	9.43	5.22	15.03	2.53	0
Western Omelet	226.83	14.44	5.47	17.84	5.37	1.03
Low Sodium	165.88	9.74	3.15	14.22	5.37	1.03
Low Fat (egg substitute)	186.12	11.90	4.39	14.55	4.66	1.03
Low Cholesterol	182.71	9.13	3.84	18.57	5.50	1.03
Egg White Frittata	113.32	4.73	0.64	12.24	5.69	1.46
Eggs Florentine	227.64	15.17	5.92	15.53	7.10	1.29
Huevos Rancheros	311.60	15.05	6.81	18.21	25.92	0.52
Low Cholesterol	220.80	7.24	3.68	12.44	25.71	0.52
Huevos al Nido	155.40	8.77	2.20	9.85	10.18	1.53
Low Cholesterol	94.60	3.47	0.57	7.07	9.97	1.53
Crustless Vegetable Quiche	91.86	4.11	1.49	8.38	5.68	0.87
Low Fat	78.53	2.95	0.66	8.38	5.68	0.87
Low Sodium	78.86	2.82	0.56	8.36	5.36	0.87
French Toast	223.95	7.04	2.81	9.83	35.05	6.69
Low Fat (egg substitute)	214.12	5.06	1.89	11.70	34.95	6.69
Low Fat (egg white)	195.72	3.68	1.60	10.23	35.02	6.69
Cottage Cheese Pancakes	161.43	3.86	2.37	9.24	22.14	1.50
Low Fat	151.89	2.90	1.68	9.24	21.91	1.50

THE ULTIMATE DIABETES COOKBOOK

CHOLESTEROL (mg)	CALCIUM (mg)	IRON (mg)	MAGNESIUM (mg)	PHOSPHORUS (mg)	POTASSIUM (mg)	SODIUM (mg)	WATER (g)
0	31.87	1.87	12.48	34.63	114.83	95.38	31.79
0	32.31	2.06	13.62	42.07	122.89	7.12	31.79
0	30.12	1.26	40.20	63.45	201.48	9.31	81.76
0	20.72	1.00	23.30	31.73	151.28	8.31	81.40
0	12.33	0.70	22.93	47.00	153.04	4.07	84.96
44.63	34.20	1.13	25.87	156.13	317.19	226.42	126.09
44.63	34.20	1.13	25.87	156.13	317.19	173.92	126.09
0	144.33	1.77	39.35	134.24	310.37	143.57	184.66
0	144.33	1.77	39.35	134.35	310.37	196.07	184.66
218.14	119.88	3.71	71.22	337.16	498.57	240.89	255.75
214.15	119.55	3.68	68.77	317.78	469.45	248.99	256.36
13.82	18.07	1.60	34.38	116.96	528.91	173.58	186.07
6.91	18.47	1.51	35.56	92.78	611.73	100.40	215.75
232.08	179.02	0.62	12.35	244.71	218.55	519.91	98.88
20.00	158.02	0.04	14.7	167.37	251.05	567.44	118.21
20.84	194.30	1.76	7.52	251.14	335.82	496.28	70.70
231.17	37.77	1.02	21.34	149.18	329.54	490.30	164.67
218.74	36.37	0.83	18.07	108.39	255.88	172.92	150.49
19.93	53.05	2.16	16.51	155.61	446.82	466.66	186.00
19.09	16.77	0.45	23.68	71.84	362.04	537.83	147.87
0	30.36	0.93	30.60	62.42	410.46	175.00	172.26
437.59	139.11	2.55	46.27	198.02	447.76	180.81	152.30
232.00	246.72	2.36	12.88	198.76	229.72	835.62	109.58
12.50	148.72	1.77	11.56	117.10	194.48	683.39	107.44
213.49	68.12	1.53	25.85	170.07	456.27	134.01	168.78
1.49	45.12	0.95	24.52	88.41	441.03	126.78	161.80
8.33	60.32	1.03	22.01	84.24	259.69	220.95	97.26
5.00	60.32	1.03	22.01	84.24	268.02	214.29	65.49
1.50	49.86	1.08	23.88	84.49	256.94	92.49	96.80
114.09	99.60	2.50	18.42	127.10	117.92	354.27	66.42
6.00	112.70	3.04	21.92	155.26	224.89	397.44	83.13
5.59	92.55	2.22	21.83	109.04	134.74	378.24	77.87
13.04	152.72	1.03	23.43	152.32	173.74	632.48	83.17
8.03	144.93	1.07	24.94	152.62	171.64	647.18	82.64

Nutrient Analysis of Recipes and Variations for One Serving

RECIPE	CALORIES (kcal)	TOTAL FAT (g)	SATURATED FAT (g)	PROTEIN (g)	CARBOHYDRATES (g)	DIETARY FIBER (g)
Blueberry Muffins	62.43	1.47	0.78	2.17	12.30	2.54
Low Sodium	62.50	1.47	0.78	2.17	12.40	2.54
Peach Shake	138.02	4.58	2.51	4.62	21.75	1.71
Low Fat	100.90	0.30	0.15	4.79	21.20	1.71
Desserts						
Brownie Bites	85.45	5.03	3.26	1.06	9.74	0.38
Flan	167.55	5.47	2.38	5.65	23.35	0
Low Fat	151.33	2.50	0.70	7.95	23.06	0
Chocolate Pudding	166.76	7.40	4.49	3.97	22.96	0.43
Low Fat	145.40	4.83	2.89	4.08	23.13	0.43
Chocolate Mousse Torte	152.71	8.39	4.67	2.70	17.22	1.00
Deysee	110.27	1.62	1.00	2.71	21.29	0.31
Low Fat	100.99	0.12	0.03	2.99	22.71	0.31
Ginger Bread Pudding	169.14	3.23	1.28	6.53	29.06	1.90
Low Fat	147.93	0.83	0.01	6.25	29.33	1.90
Chocolate Chip Cookies	92.58	4.34	2.85	1.09	12.88	0.40
Low Sodium	79.90	3.07	1.83	1.34	12.88	0.40
Low Cholesterol	93.02	4.59	1.37	1.12	12.89	0.40
Peanut Butter Cookies	78.61	4.09	1.45	2.12	9.48	0.41
Low Sodium	78.68	4.09	1.45	2.12	9.51	0.41
Oatmeal Currant Crispies	82.73	4.20	2.47	1.17	10.49	0.67
Ginger Cookies	45.28	2.23	1.61	0.50	5.78	0.08
Tuilles	52.78	3.29	1.93	0.80	5.05	0.10
Mini Pavlova	30.28	1.65	1.02	0.48	3.57	0.11
Maple-Glazed Bananas	134.02	2.77	1.75	0.75	28.58	3.01
Chocolate-Dipped Strawberries	20.91	1.44	0.81	0.29	2.20	0.35
Baked Apples	182.04	6.26	1.62	1.94	32.85	5.45
Apple Brown Betty	153.91	3.80	2.00	2.12	29.27	1.83
Peach and Blueberry Cobbler	145.39	4.35	2.58	1.89	25.71	2.16
Berries with Zabaglione	63.13	1.59	0.41	1.22	9.89	1.91
Raspberry Soufflé	94.08	0.13	0.01	3.70	17.72	1.39
Poached Pears	81.16	0.52	0	0.59	20.49	2.03
Fruit Salad	63.02	0.27	0.02	0.68	14.24	2.29

CHOLESTEROL (mg)	CALCIUM (mg)	IRON (mg)	MAGNESIUM (mg)	PHOSPHORUS (mg)	POTASSIUM (mg)	SODIUM (mg)	WATER (g)
3.49	49.42	0.84	35.61	83.28	101.57	135.01	25.04
3.49	44.54	0.83	35.63	105.34	147.40	80.58	25.07
17.50	135.95	0.13	6.73	10.48	371.12	64.70	182.27
2.45	156.63	0.18	20.21	134.21	374.47	65.90	186.95
30.21	4.46	0.29	7.55	19.87	26.39	6.62	4.82
116.94	94.47	0.31	2.91	43.51	160.08	70.89	101.19
54.84	117.77	0.85	12.90	137.30	249.96	111.67	120.72
14.18	126.21	0.45	19.52	118.86	190.11	64.75	72.16
4.75	129.87	0.44	17.61	125.37	202.05	67.36	74.74
74.14	9.10	0.21	2.31	59.73	89.78	42.87	18.94
5.97	60.23	0.56	10.93	62.45	103.84	22.22	67.79
0.94	60.90	0.54	5.42	18.81	32.64	26.40	64.14
37.35	96.96	1.15	24.51	65.43	243.40	177.78	79.93
0.94	95.47	1.02	18.11	10.47	224.01	177.54	76.08
17.71	5.66	0.49	7.04	16.60	33.53	56.11	3.24
15.17	5.66	0.49	7.04	16.60	33.53	34.54	4.26
0	4.66	0.46	7.16	12.92	35.08	64.72	3.57
4.44	12.79	0.33	10.37	27.20	52.70	42.78	3.65
4.44	11.30	0.33	10.37	33.94	66.70	5.36	3.65
10.54	6.55	0.38	8.31	28.10	35.95	66.44	27.42
6.00	5.01	0.25	4.15	4.51	30.25	36.99	2.69
8.29	2.59	0.11	2.21	5.85	12.16	38.64	4.81
6.04	3.78	0.02	1.14	4.17	16.08	7.60	10.05
7.50	6.79	0.39	1.48	0.28	321.98	0.91	76.35
1.70	3.85	0.16	3.62	9.78	35.46	0.69	11.89
5.00	11.38	0.76	17.97	38.31	28.57	18.93	134.23
7.50	38.52	1.17	8.28	10.65	163.50	78.08	109.17
11.46	52.11	0.61	6.42	70.51	130.25	173.92	76.82
53.16	17.93	0.48	9.34	36.75	148.53	3.31	83.38
0	6.70	0.16	7.45	7.23	162.42	55.49	48.57
0	12.31	0.04	2.38	2.67	134.86	1.14	116.17
0	9.27	0.24	8.20	15.09	170.31	3.34	92.61

Nutrient Analysis of Recipes and Variations for One Serving

INDEX

Italics indicate a recipe variation.

INDEX

INDEX

INDEX

Index

INDEX

Index

Index